# dispatches *from* blogistan

## a travel guide for the modern blogger

D1715270

suzanne stefanac

New
Riders

**Dispatches from Blogistan: A travel guide for the modern blogger**
Suzanne Stefanac

New Riders
1249 Eighth Street
Berkeley, CA 94710
510/524-2178
800/283-9444
510/524-2221 (fax)

Find us on the Web at: www.newriders.com
To report errors, please send a note to errata@peachpit.com

New Riders is an imprint of Peachpit, a division of Pearson Education

Copyright © 2007 by Suzanne Stefanac

Senior Executive Editor: Marjorie Baer
Production Editor: Susan Rimerman
Interior Design: Mimi Heft, Danielle Foster
Composition: Danielle Foster
Cover Design: Mimi Heft
Cover Production: Andreas Schueller

## Notice of Rights
All rights reserved. No part of this book may be reproduced or transmitted in any form by any means, electronic, mechanical, photocopying, recording, or otherwise, without the prior written permission of the publisher. For information on getting permission for reprints and excerpts, contact permissions@peachpit.com.

## Notice of Liability
The information in this book is distributed on an "As Is" basis without warranty. While every precaution has been taken in the preparation of the book, neither the author nor Peachpit shall have any liability to any person or entity with respect to any loss or damage caused or alleged to be caused directly or indirectly by the instructions contained in this book or by the computer software and hardware products described in it.

## Trademarks
Many of the designations used by manufacturers and sellers to distinguish their products are claimed as trademarks. Where those designations appear in this book, and Peachpit was aware of a trademark claim, the designations appear as requested by the owner of the trademark. All other product names and services identified throughout this book are used in editorial fashion only and for the benefit of such companies with no intention of infringement of the trademark. No such use, or the use of any trade name, is intended to convey endorsement or other affiliation with this book.

ISBN 0-321-39555-7

9 8 7 6 5 4 3 2 1

Printed and bound in the United States of America

# dedication

Dedicated to my mother Kathryn who has always cheered me on.

# acknowledgements

Many thanks to my wise editor, Marjorie Baer; to David D. Perlmutter for volunteering out of the blue to write the foreword; and to S. Foot for hosting the blog and tweaking the CSS to suit my quirky whims. And endless thanks to the many fine individuals who allowed me to pick their brains and who patiently read and commented on drafts.

# contents

foreword                                        v

1  blogs explode onto the scene                 1

2  a brief history of open discourse            11

3  blogs as linkfests                           35

4  blogs as diaries                             45

5  blogs as clubhouses                          59

6  blogs as newsrooms                           71

7  blogs as soapboxes                           91

8  packing your toolkit                         105

9  anatomy of a blog page                       135

10 writing that engages                         157

11 promoting your blog                          171

12 keeping it legal                             191

13 social networks on the rise                  217

A  glossary of terms                            229

B  glossary of acronyms                         239

   index                                        241

# foreword

"Why would anybody write a book about blogs?"

So asked a blogger on learning of my own project to write a book about political blogging in America today. His rationale was logical. There are solid reasons that the book form is not the right one with which to address the phenomenon of weblogging.

*Books are too slow.* Blogging is changing so fast that trying to document it in a book is like using a stylus and clay tablets to describe a horserace in progress. The long lead time for publishing books is daunting. My own book is taking two years. Surely everything I have to say will fail its freshness test.

*Blogging is in its infancy.* Its earliest forms, online at least, go back almost a decade, but as a mass participatory exercise, blogging is only a few years old. Isn't it foolhardy to predict the future of anything based on such early moments in its lifespan?

*Blogging is all about interaction.* Yes, there are monoblogs out there, blogs that consist solely of one individual discoursing without any comments or published feedback; but most blogs, and certainly the most successful, are communities of a kind, where people argue back and forth via posts and comments. The solo-authored book, on the other hand, is purely a conversation with oneself, regardless of responses we might get from friends, reviewers, and editors.

That said, there are valid reasons to write a book on blogs, and Suzanne Stefanac's *Dispatches from Blogistan: A travel guide for the modern blogger* is the best practical book on blogs I have read.

First, blogs are a phenomenon about which a lot of people know a little and a few people know a lot. Opinion surveys, such as those by the Pew Foundation and others, find tens of millions of people throughout the world blogging. At the same time, great numbers of Americans and others have no idea even what a blog is. There is a wide audience almost completely unfamiliar with the basics or intricacies of blogging at any level.

Next, the simplicity of starting up a blog and the ease with which one can create initial entries mask the real complexity of a sustained blogging effort. Each year millions of blogs are orphaned; their fathers and mothers give up on blogging, or move on to a different medium of online expression. The explanations for such a drop-off are many. The sheer workload of creating new entries every day, especially on political topics, exhausts those who are not so hardy or not so dedicated to their ideologies or causes. Furthermore, some of my students report, they don't blog because of the nastiness it invites into their computers, from spam to angry political opponents to sexual solicitors.

But I believe another reason people walk away from blogging is that they realize how much more they have to learn about creating a successful blog and don't know where or from whom they can obtain the secrets of the trade. Here, in *Dispatches from Blogistan*, Ms. Stefanac illuminates, point by point and step by step, nearly everything one could possibly want to know about the often undescribed and unelaborated details of becoming a blogger of influence. She defines every technical aspect of blogging, and explains the significance of everything from the "reltag microformat" to providing "proper infrastructure for posts" to the legal ramifications and case law on blogging. Further, she also offers a short course in writing, self-publicity, and creating interesting and enlightening topics for one's blog readers. As a university professor, I can't bring myself to declare that Ms. Stefanac has compacted four years of English composition, design studies, public relations training, and rhetorical instruction into her several hundred readable pages, but *Dispatches* does serve as both an accessible textbook for the classroom and an at-home self-educator.

*Dispatches* also marks a turning point in the development of blogging as a phenomenon. Blogging has lent itself to hyperbole. Just think about all the claims and counter-claims made about blogs:

*Everyone (from the Pope to every peasant in India) is going to blog.*

*Blogging will replace all other forms of media content creation.*

*Blogging is an expression of pure democracy.*

At the same time, other people argue:

*Participation in blogging is falling off, and many people are giving up on blogging.*

*Most people do not have the time, energy, interest, or ability to blog.*

*Blogging is chaotic anarchy, a cesspool of vicious ideologues and egomaniacs.*

A squad of scholars, journalists, and bloggers could probably marshal evidence in favor of all of those exaggerations, pro-bloggers and anti-bloggers and mainstream media eager to over-promote or kick the feet out from under any new media phenomenon. But I hope that we are now entering a phase of blogging and thinking about blogging in which we no longer treat it as something amazing, weird, or apocalyptic, but instead study it soberly and thoughtfully as an important vehicle, venue, platform, medium, and metaphor for a new age of fractured, niched mass communication. *Dispatches from Blogistan* maps out this confusing territory, seemingly so strange and quirky but increasingly becoming part of many people's lives.

*Dispatches* is also an important marker in that it affirms that blogging is not something completely new, that it is not such a revolution in thought and action that we can put away all previous knowledge about human interactivity. For my entire career teaching political communication, I have taught my students the one master lesson of persuasion: *Successful mass communication is that which best approximates successful personal communication.* The presidential address on television that most effectively persuades at-home viewers to support a particular policy is the one that elicits reactions in focus groups like, "I felt he was talking to me personally." The best business, military, educational, and political leaders are those who, either by nature or by study, or both, find ways to speak to large audiences yet touch them individually with words and imagery. The personal nature of blogs, then, is quite old. Ancient Romans, classical Mayans, and medieval Saxons would have understood the principle of personal bonding that nourishes the best blogging. Today, my students tell me, the blogs they read the most are those created by bloggers they like and trust the most.

Finally, *Dispatches* demystifies blogging, not by claiming that nothing learned in school can help one with something so new, but by pointing out that the rules of good writing, good public relations, good research, good design and style, and good intellectual creativity have not changed over the thousands of years of human civilization. This is also a point of which educators will approve. One well-respected, extremely successful political consultant comes into my classes and tells students—all of whom yearn to be respected, successful political consultants—"If you want to learn how to create great images for political ads, study the films of John Ford and Renaissance painting. If you want to create effective music for those ads, take courses in music theory and classical composition. If you want to write great copy for those ads, read *Moby Dick* and the classics of literature." I believe Ms. Stefanac is arguing the same here. To be a popular, respected, and successful blogger, or simply to design a more aesthetically and intellectually pleasing blog, there is indeed a large realm of new technical knowledge that one should learn. But there are also fundamentals of thinking, writing, and image-creating that are essential to one's blog project, and these stretch from Homer and Aristotle to the present day.

In all, *Dispatches from Blogistan* should be part of the library—virtual or physical—of anyone who blogs, cares about blogging, or is even mildly interested in learning about one of the most controversial and powerful phenomena of the modern media age. Blog without this book at your own risk, or perhaps even your peril.

—David D. Perlmutter, Summer 2006

**David D. Perlmutter** is a professor and associate dean for graduate studies and research in the William Allen White School of Journalism and Mass Communications at the University of Kansas. A documentary photographer, he is the author of three books and the editor of a fourth on war, politics, visual images, new media, and public opinion. He is writing a book on political blogs for Oxford University Press. Read his own blog at http://policybyblog.squarespace.com/.

# blogs explode onto the scene

There's no easy definition for the word *blog*. The Merriam-Webster dictionary, which named the neologism its Word of the Year in 2004, defines the term as an online personal journal that houses reflections, comments, and hyperlinks. It's a tidy definition, and true enough, but it doesn't really capture the fervor and breadth and flux of the phenomenon.

The numbers are boggling. The word blog wasn't coined until 1999, and yet by late summer 2006, blog search engine Technorati (technorati.com) was reporting nearly fifty million blogs worldwide, with an average of one new blog launching every second, and more than a million new posts being uploaded each day. Over the course of the previous three years, the number of blogs had doubled every six months, and it continues to grow at an almost exponential rate.

What's more, this growth isn't localized. English may have been the lingua franca of blogdom in the beginning, but today two-thirds of all blogs posts are written—in descending order by frequency—in Japanese, Chinese, Korean, Spanish, Italian, Russian, French, Portuguese, and German, followed by a good number of other languages.

> *One in every thirty Russian Internet users now has a blog. Although*
> *Russian bloggers make up less than three percent of worldwide*
> *bloggers, statistics show that we make up ten percent of all postings!*
> *Our numbers may not be so large, but we do like to write!*
>
> —**Sergey Kuznetsov**, Russian journalist, activist, entrepreneur
> (www.stoppanic.ru)

There've been those who mocked blogs from the beginning, planting rumors that blogging was dead before it had even begun to toddle. Perhaps nineteenth century British philosopher John Stuart Mill was right when he observed, "Every great movement must experience three stages: ridicule, discussion, adoption."

The numbers cited above prove that discussion and even adoption are rampant within blogdom, which gives rise to an inevitable question. What's driving all this blogging? Why are so many otherwise sane and busy people making the time to read and post to all these blogs?

# blogging as a natural progression

I'll be honest. For some time, I was among those indifferent to the platform. Philosophically, I liked that anyone who can open a web browser can now be a publisher. Technically, I recognized the enormous potential that lay in mapping and mining all those millions of links between blogs. And culturally, I liked the immediacy and brashness of blogging, the fact that news and ideas and jokes ripple across the surface of blogdom with little regard for borders, convention, or overlords.

But at the same time, like many other critics of blogs, I'd been somewhat put off by the repetition, posturing, and general mediocrity found on many blogs. I was willing to fight for the rights of bloggers to publish whatever they liked. I just didn't want to have to read it.

Or write it. My reticence to launch a blog was partly due to being a bit of a privacy nut. (I'm writing this little first-person confessional at the behest of my editor, who hasn't steered me wrong yet, but it still feels a little awkward.) And partly, my reticence grew out of being a longtime journalist. I already had publishing venues open to me—albeit ones mediated by pre-existing reader expectation, editorial whim, and finicky advertisers. Perhaps most importantly, as a reporter, I'd been trained to keep myself out of the story. Writing in the first person or from too personal a vantage point just felt wrong.

But as more and more friends and those whom I respected launched their own blogs, a new landscape began to open up for me. Not only was I learning more about individuals whom I thought I already knew, I found myself following their links to pages that intrigued, informed, and amused. Pages I'd never have found if trusted sources hadn't pointed me there. By the time I started subscribing to the newsfeeds of the blogs that suited me best, I was hooked.

As seems to have been the case for so many others, blogging turned out to be part of a natural progression. I've worn many hats over the years. My mother likes to joke that I can't keep a job, but the truth is that I've been lucky enough to follow, if not my bliss, then at least my inclinations. I've been a chemist, a rock critic, a third-world vagabond, a technology journalist since the early eighties, and a web strategist since the mid-nineties. Television seemed a natural next step and I found myself heading up interactive efforts for an hour-long nightly program that aired for a year on MSNBC. Around the same time, I was lucky enough to begin an eight-year stint mentoring television producers for the American Film Institute. During the late nineties, entrepreneurship was on the rise and so when I was invited to co-found an interactive television company with one of my oldest friends, I jumped at the chance. As is the case with most media these days, television's traditional one-way broadcasting paradigm is shifting to a participatory environment and I wanted to help.

When the opportunity to write this book first presented itself, I asked some of my friends and colleagues what they thought. Predictably, I suppose, those with little interest in blogging were mystified as to why I'd even consider it, while those who do blog not only encouraged me but agreed to participate as interviewees. Their wise words and bodies of experience ended up informing this book and inspiring my efforts through the long months of researching and writing. You can read these interviews on the Dispatches from Blogistan site (dispatchesfromblogistan.com).

# blogs enabling new conversations

One of the biggest challenges in writing a book like this is that the topic itself is in constant flux. Developers take advantage of the open source nature of the software and databases underlying blogging to continually offer new and updated tools. Bloggers are madly homesteading the resulting information landscape, constantly extending the boundaries and throwing down new roots. I tried to make it my job to elicit the deeper and more perennial truths fueling all this activity and to try and discover the vectors most likely to survive the chaos of these early beginnings.

In the process, a number of things became clear. Among them is the fact that blogs, by their nature, spawn communities. Bloggers regularly engage in lively cross-blog conversations, leaving comments and pointers on each other's blogs, all the while knitting the repartee together with literally billions of clickable links.

> *Blogs are not themselves community. They are individuals standing on corners and yelling. Comments are community. Comment on other people's blogs and spread your words and stories around the net.*
>
> —**Laura Lemay**, book author and blogger

On one level, this is an unprecedented dynamic. Never before in history have so many individuals been able to exchange ideas with so many others—regardless of geography, class, or affiliation. And yet, a quick review of the history of communications reveals a thread, a timeless human urge to engage in public discourse, to have a say in one's community, and to influence its evolution.

The urge has been quashed again and again by tyrants, popes, and almighty editors, but with the introduction of each new enabling technology—language itself, writing, printing, broadcasting, and now the Internet—more and more individuals have taken advantage of the new media to let their voices be heard and to engage in dialogues that extend beyond the clan, or even the nation. With the integration of each new form of media, we've watched as the privileges of the few have transformed into the rights of the many.

Today, the barrier to entry for engaging in public discourse has never been lower. Even the homeless are taking advantage of connected computers in libraries to launch well-organized blogs that update in real time, are available everywhere at once, and that invite dialogue. The spectrum of blogs is almost impossibly broad: quirky, curated linkfests, excruciatingly honest diaries; obsessive enthusiast catalogs; up-to-the-minute knowledge stores; unfiltered eyewitness news reports; and heated political commentary.

It was an interesting exercise reading various histories of communication while at the same time following ongoing discussions among bloggers. It became increasingly clear that bloggers hadn't invented this dynamic whole cloth, but rather were taking advantage of the latest in a long line of technological advances to exploit an innate and ancient urge, an urge to communicate with peers and to help shape our own communities.

# an open door policy pays off

Another truth that became apparent is the fact that while the urge may be ancient, it is the open nature of the infrastructure underlying blogging that has allowed the phenomenal rate of adoption.

Blogging builds on the architecture of the Internet itself. The visionaries responsible for designing the Internet were charged with building an open, networked communications infrastructure that could survive just about any kind of attack or disaster. They did this by designing the simplest system they could imagine, one that breaks information down into tiny chunks called packets, each of which obeys one primary instruction: find the shortest path to its destination.

> *Blogging tools have probably innovated faster than any tool suite in publishing history. This is all because there is never a second's lock-in. If you publish your material using proprietary technologies for reading and subscribing to your material, you're locked in. When you're locked into something, the risk that someone will exploit that lock-in is very high. It's too high for me.*

— **Cory Doctorow**, science fiction author and Boing Boing editor (craphound.com and boingboing.net)

Once all the packets arrive via their many routes—and amazingly, in almost every instance, they do all arrive—they neatly reassemble themselves into that email to the kids, the spreadsheet your boss just sent you, or the latest comment to appear on your blog.

This all happens trillions of times a day without anyone ever "owning" the Internet or policing the geeky protocols that choreograph all those packets. Quite simply, developers and web authors voluntarily adhere to the open guidelines because they work.

Blogging extends this open-standard, decentralized theme, relying on tools and services that cost little or nothing and that are stable, freely distributed, relatively easy to customize, and, given the nature of the Internet, nearly impossible to suppress.

Furthermore, this open approach means that blogs are seamlessly integrating with other new web-based services like wikis; photo, video, and music sharing sites; descriptive tag environments; and social bookmarking services. All of these new data repositories gain their value from content contributed by individuals like you and me. One striking aspect of these systems is that individuals are willing to not only create this content, but to make it public, because there are immediate and tangible rewards.

While researching and interviewing individuals with a stake in this new blogging world, it was heartening to see so many developers and bloggers adamant in their support of the open standards that have enabled all this creative effort.

> *Blogs aren't really literary endeavors. They're about an architecture of participation, about commons-based peer production, about long tails. Blogs are, by their semantic nature, mini-Internets. Aggregators. We throw things against the wall and see what sticks. We're basically watching as a new intellectual landscape takes shape.*

> —**Bruce Sterling**, science fiction novelist and futurist

# trust as the key to discovery

Sussing out ancient urges and celebrating open approaches is all well and good, you say, but what downsides did I discover? Well, the problem most often cited in connection with blogging can be summed up in one word: discovery. Finding the gems—the bloggers and the posts that satisfy your own unique interests and style—amidst all this glut is daunting.

A number of solutions for finding (and being found) are starting to emerge. New blog-specific search engines respond to real-time requests for information. Mechanisms for "tagging" individual posts with free-form descriptors are proving remarkably useful when searching for niche content. Services that allow visitors to vote yea or nay on individual links and to accrue reputations in the process are helping to create viable social maps of this emerging data universe.

These tools all serve as important first steps, but with literally a million new blog posts coming online each day, the task of discovery remains herculean. Solutions need to downplay the tendency to promote the same few blogs to the top of every list. They need to help us identify the mechanisms that will allow us to drill down and find the specific blogs and posts that best suit our needs.

> *Readers of today and tomorrow will need to learn new ways of judging*
> *authenticity, expertise, and reliability. Authority is something that*
> *will emerge gradually from a dialogue and a record of one's past*
> *statements, much the way Wikipedia slowly grows more authoritative.*
> *Credibility will no longer be handed down with credentials.*

—**Christian Crumlish**, author and activist blogger
  (x-pollen.com and thepowerofmany.com)

Perhaps most importantly, we need better collaborative tools that can help us gauge the value of individual links by generating a kind of topography of trust and earned reputation. Many first-rate thinkers are working on this problem and you'll find a number of their observations and stabs at early solutions later in the book.

What became clear as I delved deeper is that trust is the glue that will hold the blogosphere together. We live in a world where even our most venerable news organizations are losing credibility because of missteps like shoddy reporting, ignored stories, and biased perspectives. This climate of doubt makes it even harder for bloggers to gain the good will of their readers, but in the long run, the fact that bloggers work in the open, invite feedback, and publicly correct mistakes will work to the benefit of those presenting trustworthy information.

> *Mainstream and citizen journalism are merging, so no need for panic.*
> *Mainstreamers need to speak truth to power; citizens need to do more*
> *fact-checking.*

—**Craig Newmark**, founder of Craigslist
  (craigslist.com and cnewmark.com)

# and so, why not blog?

To launch a successful blog, you don't have to be an expert in anything. You don't have to be a practiced essayist. You don't need to be a technical wizard. You don't have to spend that much time. A study released by the Pew Internet & American Life Project in mid-July, 2006, reports that nearly

60 percent of those surveyed said they spend less than two hours a week tending their blogs.

Perhaps most importantly, you don't have to have exalted goals. The same study found that more than half the bloggers interviewed had launched their blogs with no expectation other than to express themselves creatively and to document personal experiences.

Wisely, only seven percent of those surveyed were in it for the money. The truth is that there isn't that much money in blogging yet. A few of the link-magnet blogs at the top of the ranking lists manage to make a living and a handful of niche blogs make nickels from hawking t-shirts, hosting targeted ads, and online tip jars, but few are likely to see significant revenues in any near term.

> *I never thought blogging would be valuable to me as a diary, but the slight uptick in formality from a journal—i.e., pictures, a little better writing, editing, etc.—makes it a great resource. I read through the archives and not only had I forgotten posts, but I forgot the whole project/subject matter of the post! The bad part is reliving your old jokes again.*
>
> — **Mr. Jalopy**, raconteur and connoisseur of fine things
> (hooptyrides.blogspot.com and jalopyjunktown.com)

In the end, it comes down to inclination. If, like millions of other bloggers out there, you decide that blogging is for you, give it a shot. The risk is low. All it takes is a certain fearlessness, a willingness to be open, and a sense of humor. If that ancient urge hits, you might as well surrender to it. There's no telling what you might learn about yourself and the world.

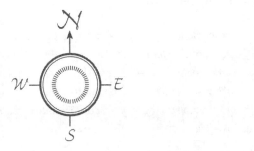

# a brief history of open discourse

2

The total number of blogs worldwide is doubling every six months. Tens of thousands of new blogs launch each day. What is it about blogging that inspires so many to embark on the rocky waters of self-publishing?

Certainly, the newest tools make it easy enough. And blogging can be cheap, often even free. Plus, there's the pop culture allure that comes with mainstream media's constant references to blogs and their makers. But is it possible that there is something deeper, more innate, at work here?

A quick survey of history reveals an intriguing thread. Across time and cultures, we can trace an intermittent urge toward self-expression and public discourse. We watch as individuals begin to take a stand, often in opposition to those in power, often buoyed by recent advances in technology. It is not unusual for these initial urges toward open discourse to be thwarted, succumbing to tyrants, barbarians, popes, petty despots, and perhaps most killing of all, apathy.

And yet, these nascent egalitarian flowerings leave change in their wake. Our own news is so full of terror and horror that it's sometimes hard to keep perspective. It can be instructive to remember that a mere one hundred and fifty years ago, the world's most powerful governments still sanctioned slavery. One hundred years ago, only New Zealand and Australia allowed women to vote. Fifty years ago, American citizens were legally denied basic human rights because of race.

Today's citizen journalists have some big shoes to fill. All of these advances were hard won. The populist urge was fueled time and again by individuals with vision and passion and, as we'll see in this chapter, the foresight to take advantage of technological innovations that broadened the means of distributing that vision. Blogs are still a new medium, but the history detailed below suggests that they tap into a basic human desire to communicate with our peers in a direct and uncensored manner.

# the earliest seeds of open discourse

As long as 28,000 years ago, humans seem to have been sharing news and information about hunting, phases of the moon, and spiritual beliefs by means of scratches on bone, sticks, and mammoth ivory. We know from texts and statuary that by 2600 BCE, scribe was a valid job description in Egypt. Over the next two millennia, we see culture after culture fashioning alphabets in order to record harvests, battles, and oral traditions.

When Ashurbanipal ascended Assyria's throne in 668 BCE, the warrior scholar assembled tens of thousands of cuneiform tablets, among them a

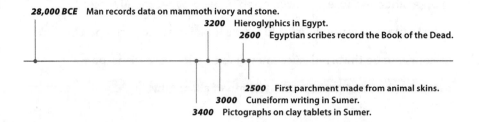

*28,000 BCE*  Man records data on mammoth ivory and stone.
*3200*  Hieroglyphics in Egypt.
*2600*  Egyptian scribes record the Book of the Dead.

*2500*  First parchment made from animal skins.
*3000*  Cuneiform writing in Sumer.
*3400*  Pictographs on clay tablets in Sumer.

copy of the flood myth *Gilgamesh* that bears a curse at least as chilling as any of today's copyright warnings, "May all these gods curse anyone who breaks, defaces, or removes this tablet with a curse which cannot be relieved, terrible and merciless as long as he lives, may they let his name, his seed be carried off from the land, and may they put his flesh in a dog's mouth."

In Greece, Homer had already codified the *Iliad* and *Odyssey*, methodically preserving their oral traditions by recording them on parchment. Hesiod, meanwhile, was taking a different tack. His *Words and Days* is remarkable for the time in that it describes everyday events in a casual, almost conversational style. "First of all, get a house, and a woman and an ox for the plough," he advises would-be farmers, "a slave woman and not a wife, to follow the oxen."

This urge to tell it like it was started to take hold, and by the time Socrates began asking his questions in the fifth century BCE, an entire generation roamed the *agoras*, exchanging ideas and reveling in a newfound sense of civil liberty.

The path had been rough. Throughout Greece, fierce tribal chiefs had crowned themselves kings. Their sons, whether fit or not, had been handed their thrones. The weakest were overthrown first by oligarchs and then tyrants. The faces of the privileged elite may have changed, but the lot of the common Greek had remained dire.

By Socrates' time, the Greek city states were in place and new leaders were appealing to an agitated populace, the *hoi polloi*. Under Pericles, Athenian hereditary titles and wealth gave way to a budding meritocracy in which opportunity and justice were meted out to all citizens equally. Of course, to be considered a citizen you had to be a free, land-owning male, a criterion that was to reassert itself across cultures for millennia.

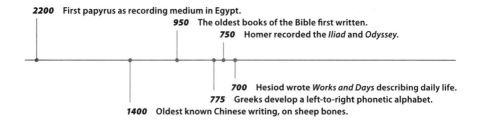

**2200** First papyrus as recording medium in Egypt.
**950** The oldest books of the Bible first written.
**750** Homer recorded the *Iliad* and *Odyssey*.

**700** Hesiod wrote *Works and Days* describing daily life.
**775** Greeks develop a left-to-right phonetic alphabet.
**1400** Oldest known Chinese writing, on sheep bones.

But still, this signaled a sea change in the way individuals might view themselves and their place in society.

Socrates was born at the dawn of this political experiment. Throughout his youth, the agora rang with open debates on Good and Evil, Duty and Rights, the Individual and the State. It was in this vital climate of rhetorical exchange that Socrates' philosophy of self-examination would mature. He may have eschewed the written word, complaining that texts simply repeat the same thoughts over and over, but his adamant belief in the free exchange of ideas rings as true today as it did 2600 years ago.

The Athenian experiment lasted less than a lifetime. By 399 BCE, the Thirty Tyrants had taken control, and they lost little time in condemning Socrates for impiety and the corruption of youth. Socrates' suicide by hemlock served as an all too terrible proof that the root of the Greek word for witness is *martyr*. Gradually, the agora fell silent and this brief flowering of open discourse withered.

> During the same period in China, Lao Tzu, Confucius, and Sun Tzu had recently recorded their truths for the ages. In Babylon, the Israelites were putting the final touches on the Torah, the first five books of the Old Testament. And in less than a century, the *Mahabharata* would recount the history of India and its gods. We can only imagine the cultural impact if these disparate cultures had been networked.

By the time Julius Caesar assumed power, the written word had become a powerful political tool. Caesar was quick to realize that the roads linking his far-flung provinces could facilitate more than just the movement of troops and merchants. In 59 BCE, he dictated that daily reports from Rome be posted throughout the empire for all to see.

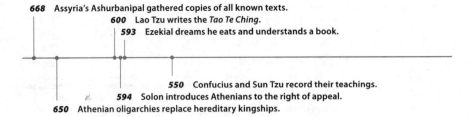

**668** Assyria's Ashurbanipal gathered copies of all known texts.
**600** Lao Tzu writes the *Tao Te Ching*.
**593** Ezekial dreams he eats and understands a book.

**550** Confucius and Sun Tzu record their teachings.
**594** Solon introduces Athenians to the right of appeal.
**650** Athenian oligarchies replace hereditary kingships.

Called *Acta Diurna*—literally, "news of the day"—these missives recorded on sheepskin and metal sheets not only listed official decrees and judicial rulings, they also broadcast the results of gladiatorial contests, announced notable marriages, births, and deaths, and recorded astrological omens, as well as recapping ever-popular celebrity trials and executions. These uniform daily reports could hardly be considered democratic in nature, but they did lend a sense of cohesion to the motley Empire. Respect for the written word wasn't universal, of course. In 48 CE, Caesar's successors sacked and burned the Alexandrian libraries, but the *Acta* did continue without a break until the year 200. By then the marauding hordes were moving in from the eastern steppes and not that interested in old news from Rome. But the legacy of the first daily news lives on.

> Some etymologists believe that the word journalist derives from these *Acta Diurna*, which you can test for yourself, by pronouncing the word "diurna" aloud with an aspirated "j" sound.

# the east takes up the mantle

Western history books tend to skip over the next few centuries, relegating them to murky Dark Ages, but the truth is that a refined culture flourished to the East. As early as the year 104, for instance, there are reports of writings on paper at the Chinese court of Ho'ti. It wasn't long before various stencil and rubbing techniques allowed the mass production of both religious and secular texts. So important had the reproduction of texts on paper become, that in 751, Arab traders kidnapped several Chinese paper makers in Samarkand, thereby introducing the art to their own culture.

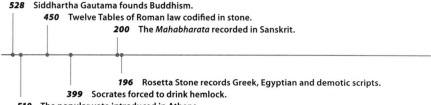

**528** Siddhartha Gautama founds Buddhism.
**450** Twelve Tables of Roman law codified in stone.
**200** The *Mahabharata* recorded in Sanskrit.

**196** Rosetta Stone records Greek, Egyptian and demotic scripts.
**399** Socrates forced to drink hemlock.
**510** The popular vote introduced in Athens.

The Islamic world was enjoying a golden age. Startling and revolutionary thinkers were altering the intellectual landscape of the entire Middle East. As early as 525, a Persian priest named Mazdak gained a large following advocating the abolition of private property, the redistribution of wealth, nonviolence, and vegetarianism. All men are born equal, Mazdak preached. It was a prescient message. Unfortunately, his impoverished followers forgot his admonitions against violence and began sacking the homes and harems of the upper classes, and Zoroastrian clerics were quick to put down the Mazdakian rebellion.

Only a few years later, Mohammed stepped into history. "Obtain knowledge," he wrote. "Its possessor can more easily distinguish right from wrong." The Prophet went so far as to preach, "The scholar's ink is holier than the martyr's blood." Within two hundred years of Mohammed's death, the kidnapped paper makers had passed on their trade. Libraries were suddenly common across Islam, and an entire industry devoted to publishing thrived. It didn't hurt that Arabic had become the common language of learning, allowing intellectuals from India to North Africa to Spain to formulate and share ideas.

> During the tenth century, the grand vizier of Persia, Abdul Kassem Ismael, was so enamored of reading that he traversed his vast realm with his entire personal library, the 117,000 manuscripts arranged in alphabetical order on a caravan of 400 camels. Today he could just pack a laptop!

In 1004, Caliph al-Mamun founded the House of Wisdom in Baghdad. Ordering the translation of Greek, Latin, Chinese, Byzantine, and ancient Egyptian texts into Arabic, he dictated that the vast library remain open to one and all. Not only that, the fourteenth-century historian Maqrizi wrote,

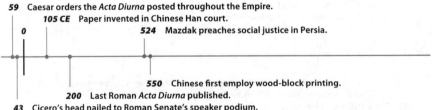

**59** Caesar orders the *Acta Diurna* posted throughout the Empire.
    **105 CE** Paper invented in Chinese Han court.
**0**               **524** Mazdak preaches social justice in Persia.

                      **550** Chinese first employ wood-block printing.
      **200** Last Roman *Acta Diurna* published.
**43** Cicero's head nailed to Roman Senate's speaker podium.

"Whosoever wanted was at liberty to copy any book he wished to copy." It was the first true intellectual commons, but no golden age lasts forever.

With the rise to power of the Turkish Seljuk Caliphate in 1057, the teachings of Abu Hamid al-Ghazali put a halt to this philosophical flowering. In writings like *The Incoherence of Philosophers*, al-Ghazali lashed out at reason and all its works, declaring them bankrupt. Only a direct intuition of God was worthy of contemplation, he dictated. Almost overnight, orthodoxy replaced free philosophical investigation and religious toleration throughout the Middle East. Publishers found themselves relegated to the sole task of reproducing religious texts.

# printing presses change the world

Some would argue that the first true printers were the sixth century Chinese monks who invented xylography, the art of woodblock printing. Indeed, by 868, a Buddhist monk, Wang Chieh, employed the method to print the entire *Diamond Sutra* on scrolls sixteen feet long by one foot wide. By 972, Buddhist monks were printing multiple copies of the *Tripitaka*, a 130,000 page text.

Still, woodblocks had their limitations. Laborious to carve, they were rarely used for anything but static texts. In the twelfth century, Pi Sheng, a Chinese cloth vendor, began molding individual porcelain characters that could be used to print custom messages on silk banners. Four hundred years before Gutenberg, this is technically the first known use of movable type. By 1313, a Chinese printer named Wang Chen was able to

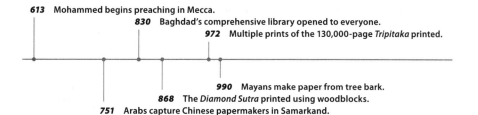

**613** Mohammed begins preaching in Mecca.
**830** Baghdad's comprehensive library opened to everyone.
**972** Multiple prints of the 130,000-page *Tripitaka* printed.

**990** Mayans make paper from tree bark.
**868** The *Diamond Sutra* printed using woodblocks.
**751** Arabs capture Chinese papermakers in Samarkand.

print a treatise on agriculture using more than 60,000 characters carved from hard wood.

> Shortly after, Korean artisans began casting type in bronze, and King Sejong had the foresight to commission the development of the *han'gul*, a simplified phonetic alphabet that would greatly facilitate printing. This willingness to adopt new technologies is mirrored in South Korea today, where more than 90 percent of the population has broadband access and at last count more than 15 million bloggers were posting regularly.

Throughout this period of innovation in the East, plagues, famines, and wars between petty fiefdoms had called a halt to the exchange of new ideas in the West. Only the clergy and a few odd nobles could read, and even fewer could write. British scribes had recorded *Beowulf* and the *Song of Roland* by hand at the turn of the first millennium, but most books were religious in nature, and the Catholic Church jealously protected the right of their monastic *scriptoria* to copy and illuminate texts. It took a single monk two years to copy a Bible, so it was little wonder that few texts existed outside the walls of monasteries and a few castles.

By Gutenberg's day, however, a new mercantile class was asserting itself, and an education was one of the markers sought to prove status. Additionally, trade guilds encouraged literacy among their members because it helped them enforce the rules that buttressed their local monopolies. Plus, money was replacing barter, and new banking communities were fast growing up. Increased trade and communications among urban centers further strengthened the resolve and resources of the middle class. The traditional hegemony of the clerics and nobles was about to come under attack.

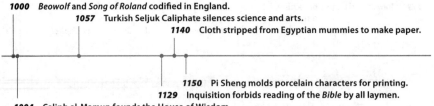

**1000** *Beowolf* and *Song of Roland* codified in England.
　　　**1057** Turkish Seljuk Caliphate silences science and arts.
　　　　　**1140** Cloth stripped from Egyptian mummies to make paper.

　　　　　**1150** Pi Sheng molds porcelain characters for printing.
　　　　　**1129** Inquisition forbids reading of the *Bible* by all laymen.
**1004** Caliph al-Mamun founds the House of Wisdom.

Johann Gensfleisch zum Gutenberg was a perfect son of his times. Born in 1397 to a wealthy merchant family in Mainz, Germany, he had the advantage of a fine education and excelled in his trade as a goldsmith. And yet, when he was 31, his family was forced to move to Strasbourg after fellow craftsmen revolted against the nobles ruling Mainz.

An entrepreneur at heart, Gutenberg busily cast trinkets to sell to the many religious pilgrims traversing Europe at the time, but he must have been keenly aware that there was a growing market for books among his peers. Returning to Mainz, he brought his metalworking skills to bear and soon began casting individual letters of type from an alloy of lead, tin, and antimony with such precision that he was able to hold together whole plates using parts he'd scavenged from a wine press. By 1451, he had a working hand press and a commission from the local cardinal to print copies of indulgences that could be sold to help finance the most recent Crusade.

> Indulgences were believed to be exemptions from punishment after death for sins committed while living. For centuries, clerics had raised a good deal of revenue selling hand-written bits of parchment or paper detailing exactly how many days reprieve from hell a sinner had purchased. While hardly on a par with today's options for personalized marketing campaigns, mass-produced indulgences with blanks the priests could fill in were a welcome innovation.

Flush with the success of this first printing commission, Gutenberg realized that he would need an investor if he were to grow his new venture. A Bible was the obvious next project, but a single page would require nearly 3000 pieces of type and, to print all those pages, he would need to employ a staff and build more than one press. You can imagine the pitch. At the time, a hand-copied Bible cost roughly a quarter million dollars in

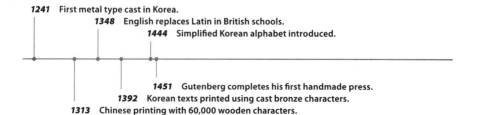

*1241*  First metal type cast in Korea.
        *1348*  English replaces Latin in British schools.
                *1444*  Simplified Korean alphabet introduced.

                *1451*  Gutenberg completes his first handmade press.
        *1392*  Korean texts printed using cast bronze characters.
*1313*  Chinese printing with 60,000 wooden characters.

today's currency. If a machine-printed book cost even one-quarter that amount, there was a tidy profit to be had. It wasn't long before Mainz financier Johann Fust loaned Gutenberg 800 guilders. A second loan for the same amount won Fust a partnership in the new printing business and Gutenberg began work on the Bible in earnest.

Sadly, things went the way of many new technology startups. Gutenberg defaulted on the loan and Fust took over the printing of the Bibles. Some believe that Fust met a fitting end a few years later at the hands of the Paris Inquisition. The same court had condemned Joan of Arc as a heretic only a few years earlier, and its judges were always on the lookout for any who might challenge their rule. Whether Fust was among their victims is open to debate, but it wasn't long before the Church began persecuting printers in earnest.

# the printed word sparks a reformation

The Church and royal houses across the Continent had much to fear in those days. By 1500, presses were operating in every major city in Europe and all those cloistered *scriptoria* full of monkish scribes were suddenly finding themselves victims of late-Medieval downsizing. Only fifty years after Gutenberg's first Bible, the expansion of printing mirrored today's explosive growth in blogging. More than a million printed *incunabula* (the word used to describe books at the time) were in circulation, among them more than 10,000 unique titles. And not all of them were religious tomes. Particularly in the south, Greek and Latin classics, secular histories, and a spectrum of contemporary texts were being sold in every

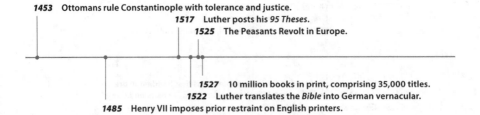

1453  Ottomans rule Constantinople with tolerance and justice.
1517  Luther posts his *95 Theses*.
1525  The Peasants Revolt in Europe.

1527  10 million books in print, comprising 35,000 titles.
1522  Luther translates the *Bible* into German vernacular.
1485  Henry VII imposes prior restraint on English printers.

market. The Church Fathers were up in arms. Many referred to printing as the "Schwarze Kunst," or Black Art and, in concert with many of the nobility across Europe, they were determined to rein it in. Savonarola's showy conflagrations may have been the best known book burnings of the time, but a fiery suppression of this new medium was in vogue across the land.

When Martin Luther posted his 95 Theses in 1517, it is unlikely that this local Catholic pastor anticipated the irreparable schism that would follow. The document was largely an appeal for a public dialog on the topic of indulgences. "Out of love for the truth and the desire to bring it to light," Luther began, he wished, "to defend the following statements and to dispute them in this place. Therefore, we request that those who are unable to debate us orally do so by letter."

> Today Luther might have started a blog, explaining that many local parishioners were no longer coming to him for confession, but rather traveling to nearby parishes where the priests were willing to sell indulgences. The ensuing debate about these "get out of Hell for a fee" cards might have taken place in a long series of blog entries and comments. Whether or not the Pope would have used the trackback feature to voice his own opinion on a papal blog is hard to call.

The Pope had no choice but to reply. The Church's hegemony had never been in more danger. The Peasant's Revolt, half a million strong, was still eight years away but unrest was in the air. A priest questioning an established Church practice such as indulgences was not something a wise Pope could afford to ignore. Particularly when the practice in question was one that generated such useful revenues.

The Pope's icy response only served to steel Luther's resolve. In 1522, he published the first vernacular translation of the Bible, and between 1518

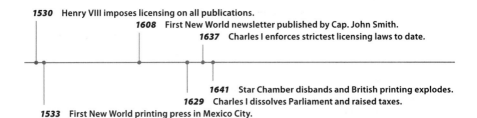

**1530** Henry VIII imposes licensing on all publications.
**1608** First New World newsletter published by Cap. John Smith.
**1637** Charles I enforces strictest licensing laws to date.

**1641** Star Chamber disbands and British printing explodes.
**1629** Charles I dissolves Parliament and raised taxes.
**1533** First New World printing press in Mexico City.

and 1525, one-third of all printed materials dispersed across Europe were authored by Luther. The Reformation was well underway.

# meanwhile, england is not so merry

Desperate for a hero in his holy battle against Protestantism, in 1521 Pope Leo named England's Henry VIII "Defender of the Faith" for his bold and sometimes brutal opposition to the writings of Luther. By 1530, Henry could see that books threatened more than just the clergy, whom he by now found pesky anyway, and so he imposed a broad licensing system that required all publishers to seek royal permission before printing. To enforce this "prior restraint" of the press, Henry called on the Star Chamber, a secret court with jurisdiction over political opponents, religious dissenters and now, those who would dare to publish without the increasingly rare royal imprimatur. By 1533, when Henry was himself excommunicated for putting his desire for an heir above the tenets of the Church, he had effectively squelched British publishing.

And so things remained for the next hundred years. Printing presses were fueling revolts all across Europe, but in England the Star Chamber was still quashing all unsanctioned texts. A brief flurry of gossip sheets called "news books" catered to mass tastes, but in 1637 a new licensing decree imposed even harsher penalties—in some cases capital punishment—on renegade printers.

William Prynne may, perhaps, be considered lucky. Despite the fact that his pamphlet denouncing actresses, *Histrio Mastix*, was licensed,

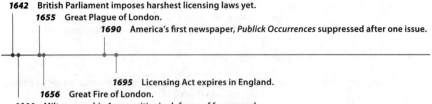

1642 British Parliament imposes harshest licensing laws yet.
1655 Great Plague of London.
1690 America's first newspaper, *Publick Occurrences* suppressed after one issue.

1695 Licensing Act expires in England.
1656 Great Fire of London.
1644 Milton pens his *Areopagitica* in defense of free speech.

the Chamber declared the Puritan lawyer guilty of sedition. This was no doubt because the book was a thinly veiled attack on Charles I's French Catholic Queen. As in all similar cases, truth was not a defense. Prynne's ears were cropped. Convicted again in 1637, the Chamber fined Prynne 5000 pounds, ordered the removal of the stumps of his ears, and branded his cheeks with the initials "SL," which stood for "seditious libeller." Those who take today's free speech guarantees lightly might do well to remember Prynne's plight.

This time, however, repression backfired. The ideological wars that had been plaguing the rest of Europe for decades finally exploded across England. A civil war between the Royalists and Parliamentarians broke out with both sides hoping to woo the populace. In 1641, the Long Parliament made a great show of abolishing the much-feared Star Chamber, but it seems to have been unprepared for the torrent of publications that flooded the market. By 1642, licensing laws were back in effect, but reining in free thought turned out to be harder than ever before.

# free speech finds a home in america

Among the most notable of the publications to appear in opposition to official censorship was John Milton's *Areopagitica, a Speech for the Liberty of Unlicensed Printing*. In this seminal tract of 1644, the articulate future author of *Paradise Lost* wrote, "Let [Truth] and Falsehood grapple; who ever knew Truth put to the worse in a free and open encounter?" This concept, that in an unfettered marketplace of ideas, truth will win out,

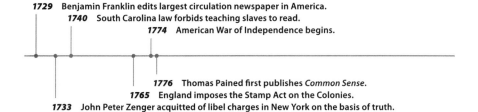

*1729*  Benjamin Franklin edits largest circulation newspaper in America.
*1740*  South Carolina law forbids teaching slaves to read.
*1774*  American War of Independence begins.

*1776*  Thomas Pained first publishes *Common Sense*.
*1765*  England imposes the Stamp Act on the Colonies.
*1733*  John Peter Zenger acquitted of libel charges in New York on the basis of truth.

became known as the "self-righting principle" and lies at the heart of all subsequent debates about the value of free expression.

> Today, many defenders of blogs and wikis call this principle "the wisdom of crowds," after a book by James Surowiecki. The book's subtitle expands on the idea: "Why the many are smarter than the few, and how collective wisdom shapes business, economies, societies and nations."

The *Areopagitica* triggered an enormous contemporary debate, with an ever greater number of citizens clamoring for the right to free speech, but it was another fifty years before the British allowed the Licensing Act to lapse. The fact that England chose to continue imposing licensing laws on its colonies was to prove a fateful decision.

On both sides of the Atlantic, pamphleteers argued and cajoled. Among the most influential turned out to be a writer who considered himself a lifelong failure. In his native England, Thomas Paine been thrown out of school, was expelled as an apprentice in his own father's corsetry business, had gone to sea but hated it, and was twice fired as a tax collector. Finally, at age 33, Paine fatefully met Benjamin Franklin in a London coffeehouse. The American journalist found Paine "ingenious" and encouraged him to emigrate to Philadelphia.

Penniless, Paine landed on American soil in 1774, not long after the Boston Tea Party and just before the American Revolution's first shots were fired in nearby Lexington and Concord. The Colonies were in turmoil. A rebellious intelligentsia, led by the likes of Thomas Jefferson, James Madison, and Paine's own sponsor, Franklin, modeled themselves after the Enlightenment ideal and were actively agitating for independence from British rule. A great many rank-and-file colonists, meanwhile,

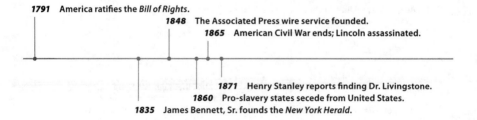

*1791* America ratifies the *Bill of Rights*.
*1848* The Associated Press wire service founded.
*1865* American Civil War ends; Lincoln assassinated.

*1871* Henry Stanley reports finding Dr. Livingstone.
*1860* Pro-slavery states secede from United States.
*1835* James Bennett, Sr. founds the *New York Herald*.

found the idea of a rebellion—particularly one that promised to be long, expensive, and bloody—a less than savory option.

Not that any colonists liked the idea of "taxation without representation," of course. The Stamp Act of 1765 proved particularly odious. It required that all published materials in the Colonies—newspapers, legal documents, almanacs, even playing cards—carry a fairly pricey stamp. Denied any say in Parliament, the Colonists resented the tax and viewed it as an arbitrary attempt to impose the kinds of constraints on publishing that had by now been long abolished on English soil.

As newly named editor of *Pennsylvania Magazine*, Paine began by writing antislavery tracts, a lifelong cause, but it wasn't until he penned the pamphlet *Common Sense* that he struck a chord with rank-and-file Colonists.

"Perhaps the sentiments contained on the following pages," *Common Sense* begins, "are not yet sufficiently fashionable to procure them general favor; a long habit of not thinking a thing wrong, gives it a superficial appearance of being right, and raises at first a formidable outcry in defence of custom." Plainspoken and rational, Paine appealed as no others had to the farmers and tradesmen who had so far resisted the call to revolution. By the end of 1776, more than half a million copies of *Common Sense* were in circulation and his words were on the lips of new Patriots everywhere.

> Given that the population of the Colonies was only about three
> million at the time, Paine's blog ranking would have been impressive.

After American independence had been won, Franklin is said to have written to Paine, "Where liberty is, that is my country." Paine's reply, "Where liberty is not, that is mine." And so Paine returned to Europe. In 1791, he penned his *Declaration of the Rights of Man* in support of the French Revolution. In it, he argued passionately for the overturn of arbitrary

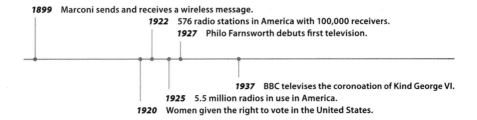

**1899** Marconi sends and receives a wireless message.
**1922** 576 radio stations in America with 100,000 receivers.
**1927** Philo Farnsworth debuts first television.

**1937** BBC televises the coronoation of Kind George VI.
**1925** 5.5 million radios in use in America.
**1920** Women given the right to vote in the United States.

government, illiteracy, unemployment, and war, citing these as the causes of Europe's long discontent. The French at first hailed Paine's treatise, celebrating him as a great articulator of their complaints and aspirations, but not long after its publication, Robespierre had him jailed for refusing the endorse the beheading of Louis XVI. "Kill the king," Paine had written, "but spare the man."

Even jail couldn't stop Paine's pen. From his cell, he published his most incendiary work yet, *The Age of Reason*. In it, he held to a belief in God, but not in religion. "I detest the Bible," he wrote, "as I detest everything that is cruel." It turns out this sentiment didn't sit well with many of Paine's former allies across the sea. When he returned to America after his release from prison in 1802, he met with no hero's welcome. Citizens of the land who had fought to guarantee the right to worship (or not) as they chose were incensed. Paine died a pauper in New York City at the age of 72. His obituary in the New York Citizen read, "He had lived long, did some good and much harm." Too bad there was no comments field. A few souls, at least, might have differed.

# newspapers take center stage

The nineteenth century saw the rise of massive popular newspapers. The form wasn't exactly new. There had been Caesar's *Acta Diurnal*, after all. The *Mixed News*, published in China in 713, is often cited as the first true newspaper. And Europe always seemed to have had a few gossip journals floating about. But by the mid-1800s, journalism on both sides of the Atlantic found itself responding to two powerful forces: (1) new technologies that greatly expanded the reach of individual publishers and

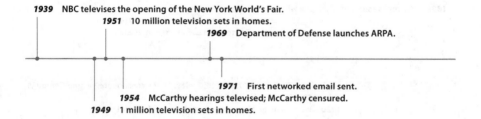

*1939*  NBC televises the opening of the New York World's Fair.
    *1951*  10 million television sets in homes.
        *1969*  Department of Defense launches ARPA.

        *1971*  First networked email sent.
    *1954*  McCarthy hearings televised; McCarthy censured.
*1949*  1 million television sets in homes.

(2) readers' demand for serialized stories that were at once titillating and uplifting. The history behind the famous meeting between Henry Stanley and Dr. David Livingstone provides an illuminating window onto how these forces conspired to shape modern journalism.

The story begins in 1835, when James Bennett, Sr., working from a dank cellar on Wall Street, founded the *New York Herald* as one of the new daily "penny papers," arguably the first modern newspapers. Populist in nature, the *Herald* boasted a circulation of 15,000 within the first year, due in no small part to unabashed, sensationalist news coverage and a vituperative editorial stance that entertained and offended one and all with its equal-opportunity bashing of politicians. Bennett lost no time in capitalizing on his paper's popularity. Tapping a newfound wellspring of advertising dollars, he soon turned his publishing enterprise into a staggering fortune.

Not content with mere fortune, Bennett was determined to leave his mark on the new world of journalism. Recognizing innovation as the key, he began employing European correspondents, a pioneering addition to any American newspaper staff at the time. In 1848, he was among the founders of a daring new wire service venture, known today as the Associated Press. At about the same time, he began integrating new steam-driven presses that could not only print thousands of copies per hour, they allowed his papers to be the first to boast illustrations. By the time photography was viable, Bennett was poised.

The American Civil War provided a picture-perfect opportunity for showcasing the ability of the newest presses to include grainy black-and-white images, and Bennett lost no time in hiring just about anyone with a camera. Soon, harrowing images accompanied every battle story.

Recognizing the advantage of telegraphy in the timely reporting of far-flung stories, he employed more than sixty war correspondents, training

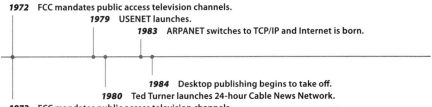

*1972* FCC mandates public access television channels.
               *1979* USENET launches.
                             *1983* ARPANET switches to TCP/IP and Internet is born.

                             *1984* Desktop publishing begins to take off.
                   *1980* Ted Turner launches 24-hour Cable News Network.
*1972* FCC mandates public access television channels.

each to write their stories with summary leads at the top just in case the telegraph signal dropped partway through transmission. All this allowed for quick and dirty coverage of what turned out to be a long, dirty, and for Bennett, Sr., ever more profitable war.

# bennett jr. takes up the reins

While Bennett, Sr. was busy integrating new technologies and training amateurs as writers and photographers (sound familiar?), his son, James Garner Bennett, Jr., attended school in France and hobnobbed with the Newport, Rhode Island elite, nurturing what turned out to be a lifelong devotion to yachting. He had just won the first trans-oceanic boat race in 1867, in fact, when news of his father's death suddenly thrust him into the publisher's role.

An ostentatious figure who was forced a decade later to flee America after drunkenly urinating into the fireplace at a New Year's gala at his fiancée's parents' palatial home, Bennett, Jr. proved himself just as daring a businessman as his father. Among his first acts after taking over the helm of the *Herald* was to hire the young renegade journalist Henry Stanley to head up an expedition into the uncharted wilds of Africa in search of the renowned and, by then, long-missing Dr. David Livingstone. Bennett knew that whether or not Stanley located Livingstone, a series of articles detailing the expedition would sell papers, lots of papers.

Dr. Livingstone was a Scottish missionary who had caused a sensation twelve years earlier with the publication of his book, *Missionary Travels and Researches in South Africa*. Detailing his experiences as the first European to travel deeply into the Kalahari, the book was an instant best-seller, and

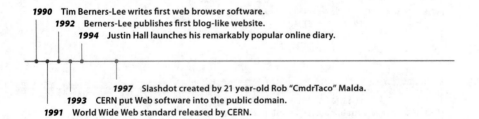

1990   Tim Berners-Lee writes first web browser software.
  1992   Berners-Lee publishes first blog-like website.
    1994   Justin Hall launches his remarkably popular online diary.

         1997   Slashdot created by 21 year-old Rob "CmdrTaco" Malda.
  1993   CERN put Web software into the public domain.
1991   World Wide Web standard released by CERN.

Livingstone found himself a darling of the Victorian lecture circuit. With each return from the Dark Continent, his retellings of lion maulings and mutinies among his porters further entrenched his fame. By the time he returned with the news that he'd named "the mist that roars" Victoria Falls after his queen, he was among the best known names on either side of the Atlantic and an unbeatable money-maker for the many publishers writing about him.

But after his many years of walking deeper and deeper into the heart of Africa, Livingstone wasn't completely comfortable with his fame or, as it turned out, with polite society. He resigned from the London Missionary Society, which had first sent him to Africa—he'd managed only one conversion and that one only temporary after all—and in 1858, Livingstone accepted a challenge from the Royal Geographical Society to locate the headwaters of the Nile.

He was never to return, but his widely read letters home increasingly focused on the horrors of the slave trade. Readers were horrified by his vivid descriptions of slave caravans made up of thousands of men, women, and children, all forced to walk hundreds of miles in neck yokes and leg irons, carrying loads of ivory and other items often too heavy to bear. Those who fell behind were killed on the spot, the trail of the caravans marked by the vultures and hyenas who fed in their wake. "To overdraw its [the slave trade's] evils is a simple impossibility," he wrote. "The strangest disease I have seen in this country seems really to be brokenheartedness, and it attacks free men who have been captured and made slaves."

In response to Livingstone's writings, British readers pressured Parliament to demand that the Sultan of Zanzibar ban the slave markets that were central to the trade. For the time being, at least, Britain was only marginally successful. Meanwhile, abolitionists in the United States found Livingstone's letters to be particularly powerful tools in

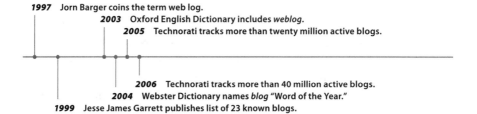

**1997** Jorn Barger coins the term web log.

**2003** Oxford English Dictionary includes *weblog*.

**2005** Technorati tracks more than twenty million active blogs.

**2006** Technorati tracks more than 40 million active blogs.

**2004** Webster Dictionary names *blog* "Word of the Year."

**1999** Jesse James Garrett publishes list of 23 known blogs.

their own campaigns against slavery, and he was celebrated as a hero throughout the Northern states.

But then the missives stopped.

Some who had been among Livingstone's last expedition claimed that he had been killed, but the public didn't believe it. After nearly five years with no word, James Bennett, Jr. decided to send in his expedition. To head up what seemed to many at the time to be little more than a publicity stunt, Bennett chose Henry Morton Stanley.

Stanley was a cunning choice. A Welshman of uncertain background masquerading as an American, he had served in the armies of both the North and South during the Civil War before embarking on a career as a journalist. His widely syndicated accounts of the American West were florid and captivating with tales of Wild Bill Hickok, General George Custer, and any number of Native American chiefs. His editors seem to have been tolerant of the fact that he often made up or at least embellished his stories. He was, after all, a deft and fearless writer, traits that Bennett recognized would serve them both well on an African adventure.

It was two years before Stanley found the trail Livingstone in the village of Ujiji on the eastern shore of Lake Tanganyika and uttered the now famous greeting, "Dr. Livingstone, I presume." Despite Stanley's plea that he return with him to Europe, Livingstone chose to remain and die in Africa. It is a fitting tribute that a month after his body was buried in Westminster Abbey in 1873, England's threat of a naval blockade of Zanzibar finally ended that island's slave market once and for all.

By this time, Bennett was ruling his publishing empire from self-imposed exile aboard his yacht, the *Lysistrata*, from which he communicated via telegraph, perhaps making him the first true telecommuter. In 1880, he partnered with gold baron John W. Mackay to lay two transatlantic telegraph cables, successfully undermining Jay Gould's then-existing cable monopoly.

In 1899, Bennett commissioned the 25-year-old Italian Guglielmo Marconi to install his barely tested wireless telegraph (AKA radio) on a bluff at Sandy Hook, New Jersey in order to scoop other papers covering the America Cup yacht races. The much-touted experiment was so successful that Marconi's new invention was soon required on all commercial ships and is generally credited with the rescue of the Titanic's 705 survivors.

But Bennett's long-distance administration proved to be the paper's undoing, and upon his death in 1922, the *New York Herald* found itself in an early media merger with its bitterest rival, the *New York Tribune*. A seminal chapter in modern print journalism was giving way to a new slew of enabling technologies.

# radio and television enter the fray

By the year of Bennett's death, radio was an established communications medium. The BBC had just launched and there were 567 commercial radio stations operating in the United States with more than 100,000 radio receivers in homes and offices. Foreshadowing the explosive growth of blogging, within three years there were 5.5 million radio receivers in use. This burgeoning popularity, along with a lucrative broadcast advertising model, struck fear in the hearts of newspaper publishers everywhere. From 1922 until 1939, in what news reports of the time dubbed the "Press-Radio War," the Associated Press severely restricted the use of its reports by radio stations, even those owned by newspapers!

Like newspapers, the bulk of the radio broadcasts were one-to-many operations that provided little opportunity for individuals to be heard. In the United States, however, Amateur Radio Licenses had been issued since 1912 and a vital subculture of radio aficionados was building its own equipment from scavenged parts and beaming its unique messages across increasingly crowded airwaves.

The first television debuted in 1927 when its 21-year-old inventor Philo Taylor Farnsworth sent a single line of electrons across a screen. Asked by an investor when they could hope to see some dollars, Farnsworth transmitted the image of a dollar sign. In 1937, the BBC telecast the coronation of King George VI, and two years later NBC televised the opening of the New York World's Fair. TV screens were a mere 5 inches by 12 inches.

By 1941, NBC and upstart CBS were airing newcasts to a few thousand homes. Newscasters had to sit under scalding hot lights and wear black lipstick and green makeup. In 1943, the FCC forced NBC to divest one of its networks and ABC entered the fray. By 1949, there were a million television sets sold; by 1951, there were 10 million sets, and a whole new schools of news and entertainment were born.

Television viewers found themselves spellbound throughout America's civil rights' struggles and the 188-hour House Un-American Activities Committee spectacle. By the 1960s, the turmoil that grew up in the wake of the Vietnam War, the first war to be fully televised, spawned a multi-headed guerilla media movement. Zeroxed 'zines, video collectives, and pirate radio stations clamored for attention.

The idea that individuals should be allowed to air their own programming was born in 1968, when Fred Friendly, a television advisor to the Ford Foundation, and New York City's mayor John Lindsay recommended that cable companies set aside two channels for citizen-created media. By 1972, the FCC required all cable systems to provide three free-access channels, one each for education, local government, and general public use. Debates raged. Those in favor of public access argued that the airwaves belonged to the public and that media monopolies should not be the only voices heard. Detractors pointed to the more daring content—both political and sexual—being aired on the new public access channels and demanded that the cable operators screen the programming for content. In 1996, the U.S. Supreme Court ruled that because cable operators act on behalf of the federal government in providing public access, they are bound by the First Amendment and may not censor the public. Despite the fact that public access television is mandated both in the United States and in many other countries, the number of unique voices heard is still small and in the wake of continuing deregulation, the future of public access television is in question.

# the internet levels the field

During the 1970s, few were aware that deep inside the U.S. Department of Defense labs, a new platform for communications was emerging. Built to "protect classified information in multi-access, resource-sharing computer systems," ARPANET was like a virus that quickly outgrew its petri dish. By the time Ted Turner launched his 24-hour Cable News Network (CNN) in 1980, there were more than 200 hosts on ARPANET and Tim Berners-Lee had just published a paper outlining his Enquire program, a precursor to the World Wide Web. Three years later, Time magazine would name the computer "Man of the Year." Two years after that, desktop publishing software turned millions of wordy nerds into instant publishing mavens.

Today, the British Library is arguably the world's largest physical library and it contains 150 million items. Brewster Kahle's Internet Archive houses more than 40 billion web pages, most of them written by folks like you and me. This urge to publish, this desire for public discourse, runs throughout our history. We've watched as kings, popes, and media moguls have all attempted to squelch the public voices that rise up again and again. We've witnessed the social impact of informed, lively dialogue and the transparency that comes with open discussions. Whether or not the millions of blogs and related social networks growing up online today will bear fruits as worthy is yet to be seen, but it seems to be an experiment that is worth our time and effort, and perhaps, even our hearts.

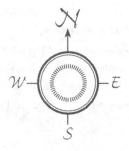

# blogs as linkfests  3

The word "blog" is relatively new, but the concept of web pages that contain pointers to other web pages is as old as the World Wide Web itself. Originally, the phrase "web log" was applied to geeky, behind-the-scenes files that recorded a website's activity—number of visitors, page views, navigation paths, downloaded files, and the like. By the time Jorn Barger published the phrase as a single word on his Robot Wisdom website in 1997, many agreed with him that "weblog" meant "a webpage where a weblogger 'logs' all the other webpages she finds interesting." It would be another year before Peter Merholz further shortened the word to "blog" on his peterme.com site, but by this time, there was a thriving subculture of individuals busily curating the ever-expanding online universe and providing its readers with annotated pointers to web pages of interest. As the number of websites overall continues to grow, these websites that act as filters, as compendia of curated links, are proving increasingly useful.

# hypertext before the web

Arguably, Sir Tim Berners-Lee authored the first blog. During the early 1990s, while a researcher at the CERN particle physics lab in Switzerland, Berners-Lee began thinking about how he and other researchers might author, manage, and display interlinked documents. He found himself building on ideas first promoted by Vannevar Bush, Douglas Engelbart, and Ted Nelson.

**HOT LINKS:**
**LINKFESTS**
............................................

**Snapshot of Berners-Lee's website in 1992**
http://www.w3.org/History/19921103-hypertext/hypertext/WWW/News/9201.html

**Robot Wisdom**
http://www.robotwisdom.com

**Slashdot**
http://slashdot.org

Bush (no relation to the Bush political family) was an American engineer known best for having overseen the Manhattan Project and the launch of the National Science Foundation, but it was an idea that Bush had been noodling since the 1930s that inspired Berners-Lee, as well as Engelbart and Nelson before him. Bush had imagined a *memex* machine—"a devise in which an individual stores all his books, records, and communications, and which is mechanized so that it may be consulted with exceeding speed and flexibility." In 1945, Bush published an article, "As We May Think," in the *Atlantic Monthly* laying out his proposal.

Engelbart was still an electrical engineering student when the article appeared, and he found it melded well with his own emerging philosophy of information science. A true visionary, Engelbart understood that interactions between humans and computers would need to be both sophisticated and intuitive if the new contraptions were to prove truly useful. Putting his philosophy into action, Engelbart subsequently invented the computer mouse, oversaw the development of the first bit-mapped computer screens, promoted the idea of multiple windows on those screens, and generally laid the groundwork for all the graphical user interfaces (GUIs) that followed. In addition, as early as the 1960s, despite the fact that there was no Internet to accommodate his vision, he began developing guidelines for the collaborative display and use of hypertext, although this was yet another term still to be invented.

Ted Nelson gets the credit for coining the term *hypertext*. In 1963, Nelson used the word to describe his own proposed system for interlinking networked documents. (He used the term interchangeably with another of his neologisms, *intertwingling*.) Nelson's resulting Xanadu project never really got off the ground, partly, perhaps, because it dictated a fairly complex environment that traced the pedigree of every link and allowed for robust management of versions and rights; but his championship of the concept had wide-ranging influence.

# the world wide web is born

Berners-Lee was the next to take up the mantle of hypertext. He seems born to the task. His British parents, both mathematicians, had met while developing the Ferranti Mark I, the first commercially available computer, so it's hardly surprising that while studying physics at Oxford in the early 1970s, Berners-Lee managed to build a microprocessor-based computer from scrounged electronics and an old television.

Once out of school, he wrote typesetting software for newly intelligent printers, as well as a multitasking operating system, but it was the still murky concept of hypertext that had captured his imagination. In 1980, while a contractor at CERN, he proposed a program he called Enquire, a hyperlinked read-write environment that would facilitate the sharing of research among colleagues. The system would have allowed individuals to not only author and read pages, but to edit and annotate each other's pages. It was a grand vision, but the larger network infrastructure necessary to realize it still wasn't in place.

By 1991, however, TCP (Transport Control Protocol) data packets and the DNS (Domain Name Server) system for mapping hostnames were in place. In short order, Berners-Lee published protocols for HTTP (HyperText Transfer Protocol), HTML (HyperText Markup Language) and URLs (Universal Resource Locators). Using the Application Builder native to the just-released NeXT computer, he built the first graphical, point-and-click browser, which he dubbed *WorldWideWeb*.

It's worth noting that Berners-Lee's first browser included a WYSIWYG (what you see is what you get) editor that allowed anyone with access to a page to edit it. The web browsers that gained a foothold, however, like NCSA's Mosaic and the text-only Lynx for Unix, did not enable editing or annotating. As a result, over the course of the next decade, web pages existed almost exclusively as read-only documents. The collaborative publishing vision shared by Berners-Lee, Bush, Engelhart, and Nelson was on hold.

# linkfests serve as filters

The most popular website during the Web's earliest days was Berners-Lee's own, largely because he provided links to each new web server as it came online. Although the newer browsers rendered these pages as read-only environments, email and BBSs (electronic bulletin board services) buzzed with commentary, criticisms, and heated debates about the new sites. So, while it wasn't technically a blog, Berners-Lee's website did exhibit two characteristics common to today's blogs: It served as a resource for web pointers from a trusted editor, and it served as a spur to dialog and collaboration.

A few years later, Slashdot had become the website geeks visited for their daily link fix. The name comes from a clever domain name gambit—the URL is pronounced "h-t-t-p-colon-slash-slash-slashdot-dot-org." Regular visitors sometimes type the name of the website as "/." Launched in 1997 by programmer Rob "CmdrTaco" Malda, the site still skews fairly heavily toward tech talk, but links to more worldly topics are increasingly common and often generate the greatest number of comments and links from other websites. A mention on the Slashdot site can still wreak havoc on an (un)lucky recipient's server, with the ensuing traffic sending it into a *404-Page Not Found* tailspin. Indeed, sites that become unavailable in the wake of a mention's traffic are said to have been *slashdotted*.

Whether or not Slashdot is properly considered a blog is a debate that erupts among the faithful every few months. The website does place newest content at the top and it does cull from other blogs (as well as just about every other type of website out there). And it does allow comments.

But, blog purists argue, Slashdot does not reflect the tastes and whims of an individual or stable crew of identifiable editors. It is not a vehicle for taste or agenda. Rather, Slashdot is the granddaddy of a school of web filter sites that some are calling *meme trackers*. We'll look at a number of these sites, including Slashdot, Digg, Reddit, TailRank, Metafilter, and Memeorandum, in Chapter 13, "Social Networks on the Rise." At heart, all of these sites allow readers to submit stories for top-page consideration, and then individual stories are promoted or demoted on the basis of votes by general readers or a rotating suite of dubbed participants. Consequently, rather than being the identifiable voice of one individual or a few discrete voices, these sites serve as maps of public interest. Or, at least, the interests of those bothering to read through submissions and place their votes.

# a sampler of blogs that primarily provide links

Choosing a handful of examples to illustrate the many varieties of blogs that specialize in providing their readers with links to other web pages is a challenge. Not only are there thousands to choose from, many would fit just as well in the sample listings that accompany the other chapters in this section. So it is with this caveat that I offer a few sites that regularly entertain and inspire.

**Boing Boing** (boingboing.net) While some argue that Slashdot can't properly be defined as a blog, few would label Boing Boing as anything else, even though, like Slashdot, the links showcased on the immensely popular site are primarily chosen from among reader submissions. The difference is that the stories highlighted on Boing Boing's pages are chosen by five editors, each of whom has become quite familiar to regular readers over the course of the blog's existence. Other bloggers link to Boing Boing's quirky posts more frequently than they do to any other blog, granting the site top ranking on just about every top blog list. In addition, the site boasts another metric of success: financial viability. The sheer number of daily visitors allows the site to sell lucrative ads through its partner, Federated Media. Cory Doctorow is one of Boing Boing's editors and you'll find excerpts from an interview with him at the end of this chapter. The entire interview can be read on dispatchesfromblogistan.com.

**Ursi's Blog** (ursispaltenstein.ch/blog) Those seeking pointers to odd and beautiful images are certain to find something to suit their fancy among the many links appearing daily on Ursi Spaltenstein's site. The Swiss blogger regularly showcases the works of photographers, animators, video artists, architects, pop culture archivists, and more. Her commentary appears in both German and English and betrays a genuine personal fascination with the beauties she chooses to highlight.

**Information Aesthetics** (infosthetics.com) Those attempting to make sense of the vast seas of data washing over us often find that visualizations of the findings are an invaluable tool in gaining a better understanding of our world and its vectors. Andrew Vande Moere, a lecturer in design computing and cognition at the University of Sydney in Australia edits Information Aesthetics, a stunning compendium of links to the best in today's data visualization techniques. Topics include architecture, art, clothing, infographics, and more. This may sound a bit dry, but just a quick stroll through present and past links proves that a picture is worth a great deal more than any suite of mere numbers.

**Ogle Earth** (ogleearth.com) Google Earth (earth.google.com) provides remarkable high-resolution images of just about every region on earth. Collated from satellite imagery, aerial photography and 3D reconstructions, the sheer number of options for zooming in on locales can be daunting. Stefan Geens of Cambridge, U.K. edits Ogle Earth, a compendium of links to the best of the many "mash up" sites taking advantage of the free and open nature of Google Earth data. Artists, researchers, and activists use the information to illustrate facts as diverse as how continents lined up during the Cretaceous Period to providing satellite images that prove human rights violations in Zimbabwe. Ogle Earth is an excellent one-stop shop for staying abreast of the best of these map-related efforts.

**WFMU's Beware of the Blog** (blog.wfmu.org) Online radio stations are increasingly popular, but few attract the attention or accolades of WFMU, "the freeform radio station of the nation." Both a traditional FM radio station and an online phenomenon, WFMU is located in Jersey City, NJ. The listener-funded station has been named best radio station in the country by *Rolling Stone* four years in a row. The accompanying blog's content is as eclectic as the music programming, providing pointers to websites, news stories, videos, and downloadable music. Not so incidentally, the blog provides easy links to current programming and the station's formidable archives.

# interview with cory doctorow

Cory Doctorow is a powerhouse. Besides being an award-winning science fiction author, he is one of five editors at Boing Boing. In addition, from 2002 until early 2006, Cory was the Director of European Affairs for the Electronic Frontier Foundation, working closely with the United Nations, standards bodies, governments, and more to address issues of international copyright and rights to privacy and free speech. (Cory was still with the EFF when this interview took place.) He still serves on the boards of many groups working to advance both new technologies and the cultures growing up around them. You can try and keep up with Cory by reading his personal blog, Craphound. You can read the entire interview from which these quotes were excerpted on the Dispatches from Blogistan website.

## on boing boing's beginnings

Mark and Carla (Sinclair) and Gareth (Branwyn) were publishing *Boing Boing,* and it was a very popular print magazine. But then the distributor went under. Mark and Carla were in the same building where they were plotting *Wired* magazine over near South Park (in San Francisco). They started working together and eventually all ended up working at *Wired.*

When Blogger came out, one of Mark's jobs as a tech journalist was to try stuff out and see how it worked. His experiment to test Blogger was to see what would happen if Boing Boing were a blog. At first, he wrote the blog for a relatively small audience. It was a nice hobby for him. His breakout moment was when it was leaked that Dean Kamen had produced the Ginger, which was this unknown project. The buzz was that Steve Jobs and a bunch of other really smart people said it would change the world.

Mark was an engineer, as well as a journalist, and so he knew a little about how to find this sort of stuff out, and so he went to the U.S. Patent and

Trademark Office and found the patent application that had been filed on Ginger. He wrote on Boing Boing that Ginger was probably a scooter. (Ginger turned out to be the Segway scooter.) The story got picked up by a lot of places, and CNN showed the blog on the air that night. I think he'd been getting a few dozen hits a day up until then, and suddenly he got 7000. It was like, holy shit!

## on gauging "fair use"

The purpose of fair use is to provide an escape valve to an author's monopoly over the copying, performance, display, and subsequent creations based on his or her works. That monopoly is intended to serve as an incentive for the creation of more work. So generally speaking, fair use is all the uses that you might make without an author's permission that either (a) don't provide a disincentive—if you do this authors will create less, or (b) have some socially beneficial purpose, like parody or criticism.

Boing Boing is essentially a page full of quotes. We write up a little bit about a page or service that's interesting and then we quote enough to tell you exactly what you need to know about it before you click on the link. This is what Bruce Sterling calls "attention conservation."

We have two potential infringements. One is a display infringement—making a derivative work and displaying it—the derivative work in this case being our commentary on it. And the other infringement is the copying itself. We host a duplicate or a derived duplicate from someone else's media asset.

I believe that these are fair on two levels. First, I believe that these are fair for the most part because this is, if not criticism, then at least commentary. Commentary is generally considered socially beneficial and so allowed. But this is not an area of settled law, which is why we're taking out insurance.

## on why online publishing makes sense

I think this makes sense for most creators, in fact so many creators that the ones that this doesn't apply to, there's a kind of rounding error. It's basically statistically invisible. The biggest threat for most creators isn't piracy, it's obscurity. Putting something on a website won't make it popular, but keeping it off a website makes it pretty much impossible to make it popular.

I see this now with short science fiction in spades. Science fiction is pretty much the last genre where people read short stories in any real numbers, and mystery to a lesser extent. There are several major awards given out for short science fiction. The problem is that the way science fiction works, is you sell a story to a magazine, it comes out for four weeks and then it's gone forever. So it's hard to get popular through organic word of mouth, like "You should read this story, it's brilliant." It just doesn't happen, because you might hear that, but you can't find the story.

The received wisdom was that you shouldn't put your stuff online because people aren't as interested in buying reprint rights to material that's been online. But if you look at the awards ballots for short fiction and science fiction for the past couple of years, it is totally dominated by fiction that was first published online. And, fiction that has a lot of word of mouth and fiction that wins awards gets bought for reprints, even if it's online. So now, I think that any short fiction writer who doesn't at least put their content online after the magazines are off the shelves is nuts.

# on the open source nature of social network software

Blogging has really been about the ability of the blogger to take their data and jump from one platform to the next. What that's done is it's made the blogging tool makers be on their toes. Userland dominated the field, and then Blogger kicked the shit out of them. And then Movable Type kicked the shit out of Blogger. And then Blogger surged and people moved from Movable Type back to Blogger and so on and so forth.

This is really cool. What this has meant is that blogging tools have probably innovated faster than any tool suite in publishing history. This is all because there is never a second's lock-in.

There's a big differences between open source software in general and software used in connection with blogging. A perfectly valid criticism leveled at open source software in general is that it's hard to use. It's largely written by and for geeks. There are great exceptions to that. Like Firefox. But it's, in the main, true. Anyone who's ever tried to configure Apache knows this.

Now, blogging tools—the suite of open blogging tools—are intended for use by people who are not particularly technologically savvy. I think that's amazing. So you don't really have an excuse to not use a tool suite that's open and free—free as in speech—that will let you always pull your content back out.

## on blogging and democracy

I do think that blogging is strongly correlated with democratic fundamentals. Obviously, the freedom of the press belongs to those who own one. Now everyone owns a press. All links are one link away. Even if your podcast only has 12 listeners, if one of them is in a country that's 10,000 miles away from you, that's a 10,000 mile reach for your podcast! That's something that was reserved for only very rich entities who could afford sales offices overseas.

One of the things about the long tail that's very exciting, is the idea that we can make, consume, and shape media that's reflective of our interests instead of being slotted into some interest by some rights holder or some publisher.

The problem with that model is that it produces a kind of tyranny of the majority. It may be true that 80 percent of the people are interested in, you know, Hershey bars, but we don't run democracies on the tyranny of the majority. We run democracies to explicitly protect minority opinions.

After all, popular speech never needs defending.

# blogs as diaries

Diaries used to be kept under lock and key, but today—thanks to blogging—millions of personal journals are on public exhibition. Certainly a subset of bloggers choose to hide their chronicles from the eyes of all but a chosen few, but for the most part, online diarists happily upload the minutiae of their lives, inviting the world to not only observe, but to comment and link to their revelatory posts.

Sure, some of these diaries are dreck, full of self-indulgent whinging and roostering, but who's to say that the latest egotistical romp hasn't provided psychic ballast for its maker or given solace to some reader? The sheer number of blog readers essentially guarantees that while you may not get the fifteen minutes of uber-fame Andy Warhol promised, persistence and a smidgeon of style should yield any blogger at least fifteen regular readers.

At their best, diaries teach us about ourselves, each other, and the world. They teach us about our own boundaries as well as the comfort zones of those around us. Today's online journals incorporate text, audio, photos, and video logs—often instantaneously via cell phone or other handheld devices, providing both present and future observers with a phenomenal level of detail about daily life in the early twenty-first century.

# the earliest public journals

The word diary comes from the Latin *diarium*, meaning "daily allowance," and as we read in Chapter 2, Julius Caesar made the news of the day known via daily missives called the *Acta Diurna*. Minor officials copied the style, recording their own *diurnas*, or journals. These weren't exactly diaries, but they were often written in a conversational style and, in the course of detailing a harvest or bragging about a warlord slain, teach us much about daily life in late Roman times.

As the first millennium rolled around, members of the Japanese imperial court began recording some of the first true diaries—journals documenting daily life. Many were written by ladies of the court and some contained details intimate enough that they came to be called "pillow books." Murasaki Shikibu, a lady-in-waiting to the empress, turned her diary entries into what is often cited as the first modern novel, *The Tale of Genji*. You can read a translation of her diaries online (see "Hot Links: Blogs as Diaries").

By the seventeenth century, Japanese literature had begun to spawn lively and insightful travel diaries. Among these, the journals of Matsuo Basho stand out. A samurai turned itinerant poet, he spent most of his life walking, and his concise, lyrical observations about the many regions through which he traveled offer a remarkably detailed window onto life in Japan during the period. Basho is credited with refining *haikai*, a form of poetry that differed from the subsequent *haiku* in that it prized a light, almost comedic touch. Plus, it required a second author to compose two seven-syllable lines to follow the now traditional *haiku* lines made up of five, seven, and five syllables. The call-and-response dynamic of *haikai* echoes the comments and trackbacks common on today's blogs, but it is in his travel diaries that Basho's writings come closest to today's blog entries.

# leonardo da vinci sets the standard

A century earlier in Italy, Leonardo da Vinci's introduction to his now-famous notebooks could have described the game plan of many a contemporary blogger: "This is to be a collection without order, drawn from many papers, which I have copied here, hoping to arrange them later each in its place, according to the subjects of which they treat."

Over the course of his lifetime, his journal entries number in the tens of thousands with more than 5,000 sketches, many of them illustrating prototypes that often took centuries to be realized—among them, helicopters, parachutes, tanks, and even a tire jack.

> If tag clouds had been in place during the Renaissance, da Vinci's would have been impressive. Descriptors like architecture, mechanics, painting, and human anatomy would have taken the foreground with dozens of other topics filling in the field.

Today, we can peruse da Vinci's pages by visiting the British Museum's fine website (see "Hot Links"). As inhabitants of the twenty-first century, we find his notebooks to be fascinating both as historical documents and as windows onto his unique genius, but da Vinci did not intend his pages for the public eye. Like many diarists before and after, da Vinci recorded his thoughts and dreams for himself, not for others. In fact, he wrote most of the entries employing a curious "mirror writing" style that involved using his left hand and writing from right to left. Scholars believe he did this to essentially encrypt his entries, attempting to thwart uninvited eyes.

We are lucky to have da Vinci's notebooks as a model. Modern diarists would do well to take a cue from his pages. Each entry is carefully conceived, concise, honest, and challenging.

# british diarists document their times

A century after da Vinci closed his last notebook, John Beadle, an Essex minister, published an advice manual for those wishing to keep a diary. His 1656 catalog of the types of journals popular in the day suggests that the pastime was beginning to be shared by a fair number of his more schooled countrymen. "We have our state *diurnals*," he begins, "relating to national affairs. Some wary husbands have kept a diary of daily disbursements. Travellers a Journall of all that they have seen and hath befallen them. A Christian that would be more exact hath more need and may reap much more good by a journal such as this."

Four years after Beadle published his manual, Samuel Pepys (pronounced "peeps"), a member of the British Parliament, began penning a private diary. When he began the diary on January 1, 1660, England was on the brink of Civil War. Oliver Cromwell was dead and the Rump Parliament was arguing about whether to invite Charles II to return from exile. By May, Pepys was among a party sent to fetch the King from France. The diaries he kept over the course of the next nine years are full of political machinations and intrigue, but what appeals to most readers today is the disarming openness with which he details his private life. We read as his infatuation with women and wine wars with his natural steadfastness and sense of duty. We follow him on his daily rounds of meetings, pubs, and grand ballrooms. We quake at his portrayal of the Great Plague of 1665 and the Great Fire of London in 1666. We are charmed that he ends so many entries with a simple, "And so to bed."

Like da Vinci, Pepys originally recorded his musings for his own pleasure and edification, but his entries are now in the public domain. The entries turn out to be so blog-like that on January 1, 2003, a Londoner by the name of Phil Gyford began publishing Pepys's diary as a blog, one day at a time (see "Hot Links"). Gyford's intent is to continue posting entries over the course of the next nine years. It's a remarkable endeavor. Not only are entries being tagged with handy descriptors like "art and literature," "food and drink," "travel and vehicles," "government," and "religion," a bevy of academics and citizen scholars are madly annotating the entries, knitting them into the existing historical record.

Many fans of Pepys's diaries are also reading the journals of his contemporary John Evelyn, a prolific author who published works on architecture, politics, theology, horticulture, and even cooking. Born to a family made wealthy by the sale of gunpowder, Evelyn traveled in the same social and professional circles as Pepys, and the two exchanged a great deal of correspondence. Students of the period are finding great grist in their letters, as well as in Evelyn's own diaries, hosted online by Tufts Digital Library (see "Hot Links"). Evelyn's writing style is a bit less inviting than Pepys's, but his lifelong motto would serve any blogger well: *Omnia explorate; meliora retinete.* (Explore everything; keep the best.)

# diaries transcend class and culture

Until the twentieth century, diaries were largely a pastime of the privileged classes. As the middle and even lower classes became better educated, however, diaries gained a foothold throughout society. One rather remarkable example was written by a young girl in the rough mining town of Butte, Montana. On January 13, 1901, she wrote, "I, of womankind and nineteen years, will now begin to set down as full and frank a Portrayal as I am able of myself, Mary MacLane, for whom the world contains not a parallel. I am convinced of this, for I am odd. I am broad-minded. I am a genius."

A Chicago publishing house agreed that there was genius in her musings and published *The Story of Mary MacLane* to great acclaim in 1902. Any teenager will identify with her anomie: "Every Friday I wash up the bathroom. Usually I like to do this. I like the feeling of the water squeezing through my fingers, and always it leaves my nails beautifully neat. But the obviousness of those six tooth-brushes signifying me and the five other members of this family and the aimless emptiness of my existence here— Friday after Friday—makes my soul weary and my heart sick." Bloggers of any age may identify with the struggle her writings describe: "It is my inner life shown in its nakedness. I am trying my utmost to show every-thing—to reveal every petty vanity and weakness, every phase of feeling, every desire. It is a remarkably hard thing to do." If you read her journals online, the language is a bit more archaic than most of what you'll find on, say, a LiveJournal site, but one of the charms of MacLane's narration is that the sentiments ring as true today as they did at the dawn of the last century (see "Hot Links").

By the mid-twentieth century, diaries were common among even the poorest strata of society, but few individuals struck a chord as deep as Carolina Maria de Jesus. A mother of three living in a cardboard shack in a desolate *favela*, or slum, in São Paulo, Brazil, she supported her brood by collecting and selling waste paper. She'd had only two years of schooling, but in 1955 she began recording details of her life in the *favela* on salvaged bits of paper. A reporter writing about the slums discovered her writings and the resulting book, *Quarto de Despejo (Child of the Dark)*, electrified readers, becoming a best seller in North and South America, as well as in Europe (see "Hot Links"). The success of her diary not only allowed Maria de Jesus to rise up out of abject poverty, it triggered international concern and aid for those still struggling in the *favelas*.

Again and again throughout history, we watch as diaries strike a chord that few other forms of literature are able to match. Among the many authors who have plumbed their depths and illuminated our own are Henry David Thoreau, Virginia Woolf, Anaïs Nin, Buckminster Fuller, Anne Frank, Frida Kahlo, and Jim Carroll. The blog form most often dis-missed as frivolous is the personal journal, but in the hands of an author who is honest and fearless, the diary has shown itself to be a noble form.

# blog diaries take center stage

The first online diary to capture mass attention was the brainchild of Justin Hall. He was a freshman at Swarthmore College when he launched "Justin's Links from the Underground" in 1994. The Web was still shiny and new enough that Hall's generous and quirky links to other websites were enough to win him a faithful following, but the intrepid proto-blogger didn't stop there. With increasing audacity and a seductive, vernacular style, Hall began a process of personal unveiling. The details were explicit and sometimes titillating, sometimes heartbreaking. Whether writing about his latest romantic escapade or his father's suicide, Hall seemed to speak directly to the reader. Before long he had a sizable following and was being invited to write for venerable print magazines like *Wired* and *Rolling Stone*.

Among Hall's fans, there was a growing subset who wanted to follow his lead and launch their own digital tell-alls, but today's blogging software didn't exist yet. So, in the summer of 1996, Hall set off on a road tour that would prove as personal and homespun as his web pages. Basically, if a fan sent him a bus ticket and an offer to let him sleep on the sofa, Hall would show up, laptop in tow, and proceed to teach HTML basics to anyone who was interested.

By 2003, *The New York Times Magazine* would dub him "the founding father of personal blogging," but after more than a decade of constant exposure, in early 2005, Hall decided to put the diary aside. He's moved on and is now a graduate student at University of Southern California studying video game design. The thousands of diary pages are still online for those willing to excavate (see "Hot Links").

# blog diary sampler

There are literally millions of blogs that, in one way or another, qualify as diaries. Selecting a handful to illustrate the potential is difficult. To find your own suite of favorites, follow links from blogs you already find entertaining or illuminating, do searches on your favorite topics, ask friends what they are reading. I submit the following blogs as examples of a few that I find consistently worth a few moments' time.

**Beyond the Beyond** (blog.wired.com/sterling) Fans of Bruce Sterling's novels may have followed his fiction blog on the Infinite Matrix website (see "Hot Links"), but in the summer of 2003 he moved over to *Wired* magazine's family of blogs, and Beyond the Beyond was born. While not a classic diary, his prolific entries do catalog his personal obsessions— Bollywood, exotic pop music, dead media watch, web semantics, photos of manhole covers, and weird art. The blog also provides a forum for astute observations about global politics, design theory, and the evolution of RFIDs (radio frequency identification chips, pronounced *"arphids"*), among many other heady topics. Sterling graciously granted an interview for this book. You can read excerpts from it at the end of this chapter; read the entire interview on dispatchesfromblogistan.com.

**Beyond Northern Iraq** (stuarthughes.blogspot.com) BBC producer Stuart Hughes lost his right leg in 2003 when an anti-personnel landmine exploded while he was on assignment in Iraq. Undeterred, Hughes continues to travel the world, reporting for the BBC on a wide array of topics. Beyond Northern Iraq is his personal blog. Besides providing behind-the-scenes reportage, photos, podcasts, and video, Hughes uses the blog to champion those who campaign against landmines, as well as individuals who have overcome disabilities. Hughes' own success in running foot races is inspiring.

**Belle de Jour** (belledejour-uk.blogspot.com) Any blog with the subline "Diary of a London Call Girl" is bound to find a few readers. The fact that the anonymous author of the blog writes copy that is savvy and titillating enough to earn two subsequent book contracts and a column in the *Sunday Telegraph* means that the blog continues to intrigue and gain new readers. Some hypothesize that the author isn't a hooker at all, but rather a professional writer. The controversy only serves to enhance the blog's popularity.

**Living with Legends: Hotel Chelsea Blog** (www.hotelchelseablog.com) Some diary blogs transcend mere human personality. Although Hotel Chelsea resident Ed Hamilton is the primary author of the blog, it is the legendary hotel itself that is celebrated thoughout the many entries. Over the decades, the New York City icon has housed an array of famous and, as the years passed, infamous writers, artists, and musicians. Today it is one step up from a fleabag but filled with more stories than ever, as the charming posts easily attest.

**Echoplex Park** (schlomolog.blogspot.com) Schlomo Rabinowitz, self-styled "enabler to the stars," hosts a videoblog that explores the author's visual take on topics as diverse as love, death, irony, and Deuteronomy. Besides conceiving, shooting, editing, and contextualizing the blog's video segments, Rabinowitz edits the Evilutionary Virtual Log (evilvlog.com), a multimedia group blog, and oversees Node101 :: Bay Area (bayarea.node101.org), a resource site for other video bloggers. He's also a founder of Vloggercon (vloggercon.blogspot.com), an annual meatspace conference.

**PostSecret** (postsecret.blogspot.com) Finally, there is PostSecret, one of the most popular tell-all blogs around. The authors are myriad and all anonymous. According to the website, "Each secret can be a regret, hope, funny experience, unseen kindness, fantasy, belief, fear, betrayal, erotic desire, feeling, confession, or childhood humiliation. Reveal anything—as long as it is true and you have never shared it with anyone before." It's a voyeur's delight.

## HOT LINKS: BLOGS AS DIARIES

**The Diary of Murasaki Shikibu**
http://digital.library.upenn.edu/women/omori/court/murasaki.html

**Leonardo da Vinci's Journals–British Library**
http://www.bl.uk/onlinegallery/ttp/ttpbooks.htmlg

**The Diary of Samuel Pepys**
http://www.pepysdiary.com/

**John Evelyn, Diary and Correspondence**
http://nils.lib.tufts.edu/cgi-bin/ptext?doc=Perseus%3Atext%3A2000.01.0022&query=head%3D%235

**The Story of Mary MacLane**
http://www.marymaclane.com/mary/works/books/story.html

**Justin Hall's Archive**
http://www.links.net/re/

**Infinite Matrix Sterling Archive**
http://www.infinitematrix.net/archive/archive.html#sterling

# interview with bruce sterling

Bruce Sterling is a man of many hats. A science fiction author with dozens of stories and books and critical articles to his credit. An editor responsible for launching the cyberpunk movement. An ecological activist. A design critic. A futurist extraordinaire. He's currently living in Eastern Europe working on his latest novel. You can read the entire interview from which these quotes were excerpted on the Dispatches from Blogistan website.

## on enthusiasm

One of the potential problems with blogging is that it's populated by eager individuals, many of whom have really cool ideas, but what they don't always have is the willingness to do the grunt work necessary to pick through their ideas to find the really good ones. Writing is hard work. Back when copier machines were new and everyone decided to publish a 'zine, lots of people managed to put out one really good issue. Hardly anyone managed to put out three or four. If they did print more than one, the enthusiasm almost always waned. The Internet is littered with abandoned blogs.

## on attention economics

I sometimes use the phrase "attention economics" when talking about how we are constantly bombarded with text, images, sounds, and video. This interferes with our ability to pay attention or to even know what to pay attention to. We end up feeling like we're wasting time. What we end up wanting are more efficient avenues for gathering and exchanging information. If bloggers want people to pay attention to what they're doing, they ought to think like standup comics—you always want to leave the audience wanting more.

## on reputation economics

Another phrase I find myself using is "reputation economics." The thing about the Internet is that everyone is now a critic. Anyone can review a book on Amazon. They may never have reviewed anything before. They may be terrible at reviewing, but some of these newly minted critics are very, very good at playing the ratings game. They intuitively know how to boost or deflate the reputation of an author. Add to this the fact that bloggers continually hype one another and link to one another. They are essentially inventing each others' reputations. In the end, what you find is that these reputation economies reward those who understand the rules of engagement, but they don't necessarily advance the goals of the group as a whole.

# on democratization

I think it's naive to say that blogs and wikis represent an increased democratization of culture. The blog system we have now is largely populated with ferociously eager, self-appointed blowhards. This is not to say that I don't find this stuff entertaining, but in point of fact, blog content is not the product of voting. Like the fourth estate itself, it isn't democratic.

# on citizen journalism

The thing about citizen journalism is that it depends on where you live and how much trouble you want to make for yourself. If nobody thinks you're dangerous, you probably aren't doing anything that has any chance of changing the world. The pen may be mightier than the sword, but if you actually ended up going mano a mano with some guy wielding a sword and all you had was a fountain pen, you might find yourself out of luck.

# on privacy

I have real problems with the word *privacy*. It meant something at one point. For one thing, it meant being left alone. But now, there are so many types of intrusions, the whole term will have to be renegotiated. There are just too many ways in which we violate one another. So it's less about intrusions by the NSA or other official surveillance groups and more about the many ways in which we violate one another. Anyone who even reads an unflattering Wikipedia article about someone else could be said to be violating the other person's privacy. It's so easy to throw things like sex scandals out via the Net. The barrier to entry is so low.

I worry about this participatory panopticon more than I do private detectives or government spooks following you around. We just don't have the terminology in place to describe that. To what port do you go to get your reputation back if someone has messed with it? What's happening is that everybody is now a tiny piece of one colossal Big Brother.

## on emergent semantics

I've primarily been a novelist. I'm generally more interested in things that don't exist yet, rather than those that do. Things that are still taking shape. The problem with this is that there isn't always a proper terminology for talking about emergent reality. We say things like "Web 2.0" or "folksonomy," and all those supposedly in the know nod knowingly, but the truth is that we don't know quite what these things are yet.

This fuzziness is okay because we really don't want to freeze the language too early. If you do, you're in danger of freezing an emergent technology into the shape of today's understanding of that language. Our nostalgia for the words themselves interferes with our ability to understand the new technology and whatever advantages it may hold for us.

## on folksonomies

A folksonomy is nearly useless for searching out specific, accurate information, but that's beside the point. Folksonomy is working because people are finding their own value in it. They don't tag a photo or a blog post because they think it will benefit society. They tag because it makes it simpler for them to find it again in the future. And really, they tag because it's so damn easy. They don't need to memorize an entire Latin taxonomy or search through some hierarchical listing for an exact term. It's spontaneous. They type in the first word or words that come to mind. What's great about this is that it works. Mobs are mapping the online universe of information one tag at a time. The map isn't perfect. But it's dirt cheap and there's plenty of room for scholarly finessing as we go along.

Who knows, maybe the whole thing will implode as the number of tags explodes, but it's a great experiment and one that's working better than anyone expected.

# on wikipedia

Lots of people object to Wikipedia as a resource. They have lots of valid questions about the authority of its entries and I'm sympathetic, but in the end, I'm willing to bet that every damn one of these critics secretly turns to Wikipedia when doing research. The entries aren't always that well written, but the data is constantly improving, which is not something you can say about traditional encyclopedias. I go in and fix little Wikipedia stuff all the time. It never takes more than five or ten minutes. If you know there's something wrong with an entry, it's useless to go on about how wrong it is. Fix it.

# on blogjects

I've been thinking a lot about semi-autonomous objects that have a presence on the Web and that generate records of their interactions with people and with other objects. You can search on them. You can track them. We're working toward a future in which you can design them virtually and then have them made by fabricators. What would be great would be if products were tagged before they were even made. That way, you could not only track the manufacture, distribution, and use, but when it's junk, you'd know to have it recycled and you'd know whether or not it actually was recycled. The whole system could be much more sustainable than today's model.

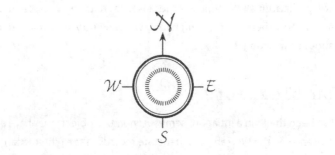

# blogs as clubhouses 5

Obsessions can be lonely. Finding like-minded souls who share and fuel our passions has always been a challenge. Today, however, fellow obsessives are finding each other via enthusiast blogs that document, catalog, and celebrate their pet topics. Far-flung communities of interest are growing up all across blogdom. What distinguishes the best of these blogs and allows the authors to assume a place of influence within their affinity groups?

If you'll indulge one of my own obsessions—etymology, the study of the roots of words—I think we might be able to elicit the answer from a surprising source: the critics of these enthusiast blogs.

Some dismiss the authors of these blogs as "dilettantes." This sounds like a negative label until one looks far enough back in time. The word comes from the Latin *delectare,* which means "delight." Other critics label the enthusiasts "amateurs." While this term has devolved to mean "dabblers with little hope of tangible reward," it originally comes from the Latin *amator,* "one who loves." Still others look askance at the communities growing up around blog-powered obsessions, dubbing them "cults." The root here is the Latin *cultus,* which is also the root of our word "cultivate," meaning "to tend, or take care."

Nestled within these supposed objections, we find the secret to the success of many of these blogs. They are authored by individuals with an honest love of their topics and who take delight in cultivating both their topic areas and their audiences. So, whether your passion is nerdy word mongering, street fashions, flamethrowers, extraterrestrial artifacts, or like Mr. Jalopy, whose interview appears at the end of this chapter, the internal combustion engine, a well-focused blog stands an excellent chance of attracting the attention of others who share the obsession. Thanks to search engines and compulsive interlinking among aficionados, vital communities are growing up and thriving in just about every niche imaginable.

# quick tips for enthusiast bloggers

Chapter 9, "Anatomy of a Blog Page," and Chapter 11, "Promoting Your Blog," provide detailed techniques for optimizing and promoting your blogs, no matter what the topic, but here's a quick summary of the points most salient to those exploring niche topics.

**Do it for love, not money or fame.** You may actually end up making a bit of cash from sales, embedded ads, or employment opportunities related to your topic, but if your heart isn't in it and the content is forced, your efforts are likely to fall flat and fail to attract a steady audience.

**Adjust the focus of your blog to aid discovery.** Your blog title, design, headlines, categories, and, of course, the body of your entries should all tie into the topic. Remember that for search purposes, if your topic is too broadly defined, the area will already be dominated by giants. Too narrow and it will have little chance of growing a sustainable fan base.

**Post regularly and to the point.** Aficionados are hungry for fixes and will generally return to blogs that satisfy their interests most often. While eclectic can be fine for some types of blogs, enthusiast blogs are most successful when they stick to topic. Don't let too much time pass between posts or readers may get out of the habit of visiting your site, but at the same time, don't fall into the trap of posting drivel just to see another entry online. To maintain the loyalty of your readers, the content needs to be either useful or entertaining. An ideal post, of course, is both.

**Engage your audience.** Write in a style that is conversational, that never talks down to anyone, and that is generous in its acknowledgement of the contributions of others. Respond promptly and without prickliness to reader comments. Even if you choose not to enable comments, you can make your readers feel welcome and richer for the experience of visiting your site.

**Stick with it.** We all get bored or frustrated, and most bloggers have faced days when it just seemed easier to either shut down a blog or pretend it is no longer online. Truly successful bloggers are those who weather these moments and build faithful readerships over time.

# the most important tip: personality

All of the tips listed above will help to win fans, but the enthusiast blogs earning the most plaudits are those that not only highlight the authors' obsessions, but that also serve as showcases for their personalities. Each of the blogs listed in the sampler below benefits from the honest display of strong tastes and well-crafted opinions. Mac Tonnies and Guy Kawasaki have the advantage of being professional writers, but Mr. Jalopy is an example of a blogger who honed his presentation in an online environment.

Mr. Jalopy may publish under a pseudonym, but readers of his two blogs, Hoopty Rides (http://hooptyrides.blogspot.com) and Jalopy Junktown (http://jalopyjunktown.com), can't help feeling that they're getting to know the author. The text is tidy, lively, and bristles with personality. The photos are crisp, quirky, and compelling.

Hoopty Rides launched in late summer 2004 and focuses largely on the joys of all things automobile. Model A's, drag racers, muscle cars, and Mercedes are among the vehicles lovingly showcased. The refurbishing of Mr. Jalopy's own fleet provides grist for many a fine post, as do his pointers to odd and beautiful automobiles elsewhere online. Mixed among these vehicular paeans, Mr. Jalopy found himself beginning to catalog the fruits of another of his obsessions—weekly rounds of local garage sales—and so, in the spring of 2006, Jalopy Junktown was born. What knits the content of the two blogs together is the unique sense of style that Mr. Jalopy consistently brings to his pages.

Whether detailing the construction of one of his own projects, like the iPod embedded in a salvaged, waist-high, wooden console (it can even digitize vinyl records!) or providing images of a Hot Rod Reunion, the presentation somehow manages to be enthusiastic without seeming naive. Excerpts from an interview with Mr. Jalopy appear at the end of this chapter (the entire interview can be read on dispatchesfromblogistan.com), but here are a few selections from his blogs that illustrate the style that has garnered him a fair amount of fame, if not, alas, fortune. Obviously, these excerpts represent only one style, but they do illustrate the power of personality when publishing enthusiast blogs.

## from mr. jalopy's blogs

"A day at the Hot Rod Reunion is enough to make you consider selling all your worldly possessions and moving into a shotgun shack in outer San Berdoo. A one room, clapboard side house with a black-and-white TV, a round top refrigerator filled with biscuits, jam and Budweiser, a sagging sofa, a pedestal fan, a wood grain formica dinette with a single chair, jelly jar drinking glasses and NHRA membership. Because, if you had a top fuel, front engine rail in your garage, what else would matter?"

"Please take a moment to consider this striking and remarkably sturdy gas can. Note the bold stamped X and ripples on the side to add strength to the structure. Even GAS is not a paint stencil, but an integral embossed element. The seams are welded with beautiful, perfect TIG welds. A more graceful handle I can not imagine. A gas can for connoisseurs."

"I am fascinated by machines that operate without electricity. Powered by individual effort, steam, fuel or gunpowder, there is just something satisfyingly low tech about a machine that operates without the tether of an electrical cord. Clearly, I am of a generation raised with Foxfire books. Naturally, since I collect nearly everything without concern for size or utility, I have slide rules, Curtas, a telephone that operates with a hand crank, a counting machine and this staggeringly beautiful, and back-breakingly heavy, stencil maker. One would think that worldwide demand for stencils has not changed appreciably in the last 50 years, but when was the last time you saw such a machine?"

"As a little kid I was obsessed with model rockets and still have an entire shelf devoted to rocket kits, launch pads, engines and partially melted parachutes. I am powerless over garage sale Estes rockets and I keep promising myself I will take a day off from the hustle bustle and drive out to 90th and G to have an amateur NASA day. Just the rockets, my dogs, an ice chest, binoculars and a coffee can for the collection, examination and release of scorpions. Beef jerky, singed eyebrows and an old car with a slow oil leak. Sweet rich abundance that is life."

"It is difficult for me to overstate the importance of the Apple II. I still remember the smell of unwrapping my Apple II. The disk boot command (PR#6) is burned into my brain with greater clarity than my social security number. As if it was in my hands right now, I know the exact weight and shape of a Hayes Microcoupler. My GBBS bulletin board had all the K-K00l M0dz. And even though I was only 14, my friends and peers were rocket scientists, lawyers and college professors."

# blogs as clubhouse sampler

Visiting some enthusiast blogs feels like dropping in on a venerable salon. Others feel more like the corner saloon. Either way, it is the sense that one has been invited into a special club that gives them their allure.

**Mother Tongue Annoyances** (www.mtannoyances.com) My favorite word-centric blog is Tim Warner's Mother Tongue Annoyances. Warner is dead serious about his linguistic pet peeves, but his light tone and obvious love of language make following his meanderings through modern English usage a pleasure. It doesn't hurt that the design of the blog is classic and easy on the eye.

**Posthuman Blues** (posthumanblues.blogspot.com) Mac Tonnies may be physically based in Kansas City, Missouri, but his heart and mind live among the stars. A science fiction author and extraterrestrial theorist, Tonnies mixes erudition, speculation, and humor in his discussions about space travel, cryogenics, climatology, video games, neo-punk comics, and more.

**The Sartorialist** (thesartorialist.blogspot.com) Fashion captures the imagination of many individuals, but few have an eye as refined as Scott Schuman's and even fewer bother to take their inspiration from the street. Schuman roams Manhattan streets with his camera at the ready, capturing trends and unique styles across all walks of life. His pithy commentary complements the photos and provides a running thread that keeps style mavens coming back for more.

**Signum sine tinnitu** (blog.guykawasaki.com) Guy Kawasaki first made a splash in tech circles as the Macintosh computer's first official evangelist. Subsequently, he penned a column for *Forbes* and several books (*Selling the Dream, Rules for Revolutionaries*, and *The Art of the Start*, among them) and today, he posts regularly to his blog, Signum sine tinnitu. The Latin title translates to "signal without noise." It's an apt title as Kawasaki attempts to demystify his personal obsessions—entrepreneurship, marketing, and the vagaries of venture capital.

**The Klezmer Shack** (www.klezmershack.com) Ari Davidow maintains a blog that caters to both practitioners and fans of klezmer music, as well as "world music from a Jewish slant." Klezmer is a tradition of secular Jewish music that has enjoyed a recent revival. The blog highlights bands, events, radio shows, and record labels, as well as providing a form of classified ads. You can even buy a Klezmer Shack t-shirt.

**Flame Effects** (flame-effects.blogspot.com) Mikey Sklar dropped out of the engineering game and moved to Truth and Consequences, New Mexico. These days, he spends his time "making totally non-commercial electronics." Well, and maintaining his Flame Effects blog. The blog's subline sums up his intent: "A crude attempt to document fire art in one location." Sklar showcases startling photos of works of art that incorporate fire and provides links to a bevy of fellow arty pyromaniacs.

# interview with mr. jalopy

Mr. Jalopy is quite protective of his anonymity but proved wonderfully forthcoming in this interview. Besides checking out his two blogs, Hooptyrides and Jalopy Junktown, fans of his writings will want to check out his many articles for Make magazine (makezine.com), a do-it-yourselfer's bible. Mr. Jalopy was invited to write for the magazine as a consequence of some of his early blog posts.

## on launching a first blog

I launched Hooptyrides in August 2004 after goofing around with a photo-sharing site for a couple months. Hooptyrides is largely about noble, though modest, automobiles. Initially, I pictured a project log but reverse chronological order is perhaps the worst possible way to track a project.

The greatest net benefit turned out to be having a place to point that describes me, my writing style, and my projects. It has been very helpful in making the leap to being a semi-professional writer. It is the new clips file.

## on launching a second blog

Over many years of garage saling, I have made a variety of attempts at cataloging what I get at garage sales using everything from photo sites to Filemaker databases but I would always lose interest after a couple weeks. For Jalopy Junktown to become a journal of garage saling, I wanted to keep the entries short and quick with the hope that it would be updated more often than Hooptyrides. And it is more than just a garage sale journal, as it also points to spectacular items that I come across at auctions and on the Internet. With a broader range, Junktown was almost immediately as popular as Hooptyrides. And it climbed in Google searches much quicker. Probably due, in large part, to being linked from Hooptyrides. If my goal was to make money, I wonder if ten blogs that link to one another with a RSS roll-up 'directory' wouldn't fare much better in searches.

## on print vs. blog writing

Writing for print is excruciatingly difficult. It is a fixed length, needs to be concise, clear, clean, and, hopefully, not embarrassing. There is a big responsibility to be accurate with the facts in print media. If for no other reason, it is difficult to revise once the magazine is on the newsstand. When I am writing for Hooptyrides, I am writing for my buddies. Fast and loose, peppered with dirty words and outrageous statements.

## on making money

There is one big difference between selling stuff on eBay and selling it on my blogs. Stuff sells on eBay and it doesn't sell on my blogs.

To sell items, it is all about Google. You need to understand how Google works. And that is a big subject. If you have no "google cred," then your site will never get search hits except for very, very specific, obscure, and unpopular topics. If you have moderate "google cred," you will get search hits for more common topics. I would say Hooptyrides has moderate google cred as I have been linked from high-volume, high-cred sites like Boing Boing, Jalopnik, Gizmodo (gizmodo.com), and autoblog (autoblog.com).

If I were to sell a Nikon D70 camera, I would never get a search hit because there are many sites that mention (and sell) the D70. Now, if I were to sell something more obscure, I would get a fair share of search traffic and Hooptyrides would appear on the first page. I used to get 5 Google hits a day. Now I get 300 Google hits. Search for "learn to weld" or "1987 Mercedes 300TD" and I will be on the first page. But I could post about Coca-Cola for a month and still wouldn't show up on the first thousand search hits.

I have a simple AdSense ad on Hooptyrides that generates a pittance of money. But, free pennies are still more than no money. Amazon Associates generates more money, is more transparent, and is a little awkward to use.

## on blogging tools

Blogger (blogger.com) is pretty good. It needs some more bells and whistles. Not having categories is a real pain in the neck. If I realized how important that was, I would have made sure to pick a platform that supports categories. Blogs have a severe, inherent navigational issue. Kerouac supposedly wrote by feeding a giant roll of paper into a typewriter. No pages, just a giant roll. Blogs are like that. You keep adding on to the end of the roll of paper. But, as a reader, you are starting at, effectively, the end of the novel and working your way forward! That is a disaster. Categories really help with that.

To deal with it, I have added a sidebar with some links to previous key posts, projects, and my fleet of junk cars. But that was pain in the ass to create. I am not very web savvy, so I had to poke around other sites, view the source, and steal the code to make it work.

Blog software is going to see a life cycle like early eBay. In the early days, eBay was difficult to use and that restricted their user base. There was no Paypal, no shipping calculator, not even image hosting! Blogging is easy, but monetizing it is not. And even though most people (myself included) will never get rich from blogging, lots of people will want to add rich content like movie trailers, song clips, publicity photos, and even compelling TV commercials. And all that stuff can lead to a sale.

I am shocked at how slowly blog software has evolved. Blogs look better than they did 2 years ago, but it has been a function of smart people piecing together a bunch of disparate components. It is staggering that Yahoo, Amazon, and Google have not put together a killer blog app. Google owns Blogger, so why is there not a template that integrates AdSense out of the box? Clearly, developing blog software is more complicated than I think or this would already be done.

## on writing under a pseudonym

I am un-Google-able. I have no interest in a daily high school reunion in my inbox.

## on turning comments off

If I turned on commenting, I am afraid people might get the wrong impression and comment. The lack of civility online drives me insane and I would rather not welcome it. My email is listed. Other blogs have taken pot shots at me. That's plenty of feedback.

## on the future

I am going to launch a store. As far as the actual blog, I really hope Blogger adds categories. I would do more projects if that happened.

## on favorite blogs

Finkbuilt (finkbuilt.com) shares a lot in common with Hooptyrides. Steve Lodefink is also an advocate of projects for project's sake. He keeps busy and tells a good story.

Coop does step-by-step "paint blogging" on positiveapeindex (positiveapeindex.blogspot.com). He tracks paintings from sketch to the gallery wall. Even though I am not an artist, I find it fascinating to watch experts deliver the goods. I wish there were more blogs that took the time to share like Coop does. Besides the paint blogging, Coop is a friend of mine with similar passions, from hot rods to old timey restaurants. Plus, he is arguably more obsessive than I am.

Things Magazine (thingsmagazine.net) is just superb. If forced to categorize, I would say it is about the design of grand minutiae. Everything from WWII bunkers to auto upholstery, they bundle links with ideas. The writing is crisp and effortless. I am interested in everything and they link to everything. Works out well.

And of course, Boing Boing (boingboing.net). It is really five blogs in one, as each of the editors has a very distinct voice. I find their barely contained sense of awe to be inspiring. Besides being a great link farm to goofy Japanese toys and weird sex stuff, Boing Boing reminds me daily that if we don't act we are going to flush our digital rights down the toilet.

Jalopnik (jalopnik.com) is my favorite automotive related site. The editor is about my age and we share lots of automotive interests from the glory of the El Camino to why race car paint schemes matter.

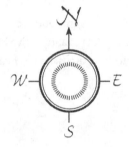

# blogs as newsrooms

Newspapers are in trouble. At a May 2006 Berkshire Hathaway shareholder meeting, company chairman and financial seer Warren Buffett declared, "Certain newspaper executives are going out and investing in other newspapers. I don't see it. It's hard to make money buying a business that's in permanent decline. If anything, the decline is accelerating."

Television news is witnessing its own decline. The Project for Excellence in Journalism (stateofthenewsmedia.org) reports that while American network news programs remain profitable, evening news ratings have fallen 59 percent since their peak three decades ago, and the average age for evening news audience members is nearly 60 years old.

Where are younger folks getting their news? Online. And it's not just the kids. The Pew Internet & American Life Project (pewinternet.org) reports that more than 50 million Americans choose to get their news online each day.

Enter citizen journalists. This new breed of reporter takes advantage of the broad distribution of the Web to distribute news stories that traditional media ignore, misrepresent, or have no access to—eyewitness reports during Hurricane Katrina or daily journals uploaded by citizens in war-torn areas, for instance. Additionally, unlike print and broadcast journalism, which allow for very little feedback or open discussion, citizen journalists generally encourage others to comment on their reports; add and dispute facts; share viewpoints; and point to other related stories.

Critics of citizen journalism often question the credibility of bloggers' reports. "How can we know when news reports on citizen blogs are accurate and fair?" they ask. It's an honest query but begs a larger question. How can we ever be sure that a news story is accurate and fair, whatever the medium?

Journalism as a profession has evolved over the course of several centuries, and at its best, has come to be associated with the idea of free speech. The early architects of democracy realized that a populace needs access to relevant facts and ideas if it is to make informed electoral decisions, and that a free press—one without fear of government control or reprisal—is integral to this process.

Repeated governmental abuses over those centuries have inspired many nations to enact formal guarantees for the free expression of ideas by their citizens. But once those assurances are in place, it has been up to the journalists and editors themselves to fashion news that adheres to codes of ethics and editorial guidelines that fulfill this promise of reporting that is fair, accountable, and transparent in its sources and intent.

Ideally, citizen journalist bloggers inherit both the privileges and the responsibilities of their professional forebears. Given the falling fortunes of mainstream media, they also inherit a growing distrust on the part of the citizenry. The frequency with which news media have been forced to report malfeasances within their own ranks is part of the problem. The shadow cast by dishonored journalists like Jayson Blair, Stephen Glass, and Janet Cooke darkens not only the efforts of fellow professional journalists, but of citizen journalists, as well.

And these few bad seeds within professional ranks are not the only problem facing mainstream news outlets. Driven by a perennial quest for ratings, most beat a few high-profile stories to death, only to abandon them when newer, more lurid trials, Washington insider scandals, or sports drug exposés promise to plump lagging numbers. This homogenization of the news, combined with the demise or sale of most local newspapers and broadcast television and radio stations to megacorporations, means that many communities are left without regional news reporting. Little wonder the public is less engaged.

The best of the traditional news outlets are working hard to regain the trust of their audiences, and one of the ways they're doing this is by extending a hand to the better citizen journalist efforts. Besides incorporating blog materials, and sometimes even hiring bloggers who show the greatest promise, blogs and bloggers are increasingly featured as news stories themselves.

Which brings us to the responsibility half of the equation. If citizen journalism is going to mature and gain the trust and support of large audiences, its most visible practitioners are going to have to adopt the same ethical guidelines as professional journalists. They will need to check their facts, report without bias, and disclose any conflicts of interest. Perhaps most importantly, they need to decide whether they are going to objectively report on the news or whether they are going to engage in editorial commentary and advocacy stances (covered in the next chapter, "Blogs as Soapboxes").

The history of journalism is rife with terror, conflict, and lapses, but the overall vector is still promising. Those who choose to blog under the banner of citizen journalism are following in the steps of giants. With open minds, generous spirits, and keen editing, they stand a chance of making their own mark on history.

# the dawn of journalism

News reports didn't start out unbiased. In Chapter 2, we saw that the content of early news periodicals like the Roman *Acta Diurna* and *Mixed News* in China were dictated by those in power. There was little expectation that these official missives would reflect any views other than those held by the ruling parties.

Emperors, kings, and popes had little trouble controlling the news until the introduction of the printing press in the mid-fifteenth century. At first, severe penalties for publishing without royal or papal *imprimaturs* kept most of the early "newsbooks" in check, and the few who dared publish without permission did so anonymously.

Still, despite the restrictions, a demand for more and better news started to grow up as an educated middle class took hold. By 1566, citizens of Venice were hungry enough for updates on the war with Turkey that they were willing to pay one copper *gazeta* for a one-page news sheet. The official name of the periodical was *Notizie Scritte,* but readers preferred calling it by the name of the coin used to purchase it, a habit that caught on across Europe.

For the most part, however, until the mid-seventeenth century, royal and papal censorship continued to constrain news reporting all across Europe.

# england experiences upheavals

When England abolished the dread Star Chamber in 1641, the nation witnessed a brief flowering of news periodicals. Many were conceived in the vibrant coffee houses of the day where patrons avidly argued religion and politics.

In particular, British royalists and parliamentarians vied in print, ridiculing and attempting to expose the wrongs and weaknesses of the other. One of the leading voices on the parliamentarian side was John Dillingham's *The Parliament Scout*, which is often cited as the first investigative journal. Dillingham wrote that the Scout "suggested something new in journalism—the necessity of making an effort to search out and discover the news." A similar publication was *The Spie*, which promised readers that its purpose was "discovering the usual cheats in the great game of the Kingdome. For that we would have to go undercover."

Many more periodicals went undercover or disappeared altogether when the Commonwealth was declared in 1649. Almost immediately, a series of new licensing laws silenced the squall of voices.

Among the few permitted periodicals was the *Oxford Gazette*, the first regularly published English newspaper. The paper began in 1665 while the royal court sat at Oxford during a London plague. When the court returned to London, the publication dutifully followed, changing its name to the *London Gazette*; it is still published today.

The first British daily newspaper was *The Daily Courant*, founded in 1702 by Elizabeth Malet. The last of the Licensing Acts had just lapsed and a broad spectrum of news sheets and pamphlets had once again begun circulating. In the initial issue of the *Courant*, Malet wrote that she had established the paper to "spare the public at least half the impertinences which the ordinary papers contain."

During the thirty years that *The Daily Courant* survived, the Enlightenment bloomed across Europe and the American colonies. Authors like Voltaire, Jean-Jacques Rousseau, David Hume, and Isaac Newton ignited an intellectual revolution, a revolution that redefined the dynamic between the individual and the state. For the first time, citizens began demanding broad freedoms, calling them inalienable rights. Chief among these rights was the free expression of ideas.

But social institutions are often slow to change. Although a fair number of periodicals appeared in England during this period, few lasted more than a few issues. Draconian licensing laws were no longer in place, but various other suppression tactics did come into play. In a few instances, government officials unhappy with a publication's editorial stance went so far as to purchase the papers with public funds, relaunching them with content friendlier to those in power.

> Samuel Johnson's description of eighteenth-century journalism echoes some of the current criticisms about both mainstream news and blogging. He wrote that the news periodicals of the day "afford sufficient information to elate vanity, and stiffen obstinacy, but too little to enlarge the mind."

# american journalism ignites a revolution

On American shores, newspaper publishing got off to a rocky start with the launch of Benjamin Harris's *Publick Occurences both Foreign and Domestick* in 1690. British officials shut it down after one issue, partly because Harris had neglected to petition for a license and partly because the paper had daringly reported that the French king was having an affair with his son's wife.

New York City's first newspaper, the *New York Gazette*, launched in 1725 and shamelessly pandered to the will of the colonial governor William Cosby. A second paper, *The New York Weekly Journal*, challenged the governor and made publishing history. Begun in 1733 by John Peter Zenger, the paper published the writings of several anonymous authors, one of whom wrote of Governor Cosby, " . . . if such an over grown Criminal, or an impudent Monster in Iniquity, cannot immediately be come at by ordinary Justice, let him yet receive the lash of satire, let the glaring truth of his ill administration . . . render his actions odious to all minds."

Cosby does seem to have been an odious official. A royal appointee, his first act upon arrival in the colonies was to demand an extortionist salary, and when the New York State Supreme Court denied him, he removed the Chief Justice and replaced him with a lackey. It comes as little surprise that the governor had Zenger arrested for "inflaming Minds with Contempt of His Majesty."

Zenger sat in a jail cell for eight months before his trial for seditious treason came before a jury, but his incarceration did little to stop the *Journal*'s contrary commentary since his wife, Anna, continued editing, writing, and publishing the paper during his absence. In addition, the case inspired increasingly supportive editorials up and down the Atlantic coast.

At the heart of the debate was the fact that, at the time, truth was not a defense against libel. In fact, when Zenger was finally tried in 1735, the judge instructed the jury that any criticism of the government constituted libel. Luckily for Zenger and legal precedent in America, an inspired lawyer named Andrew Hamilton came to the publisher's defense. Hamilton's arguments for free expression were so compelling that the jury ignored the judge's instructions and found Zenger not guilty. By the time the verdict was announced, colonial sympathies were largely in support of a free press.

This helps to explain the vehemence of the colonial reaction to the Stamp Act. While not, strictly speaking, a licensing act that censored news, the Stamp Act of 1765 did impose a pricey tax stamp on all legal documents, newspapers, pamphlets, and playing cards. The intent of the law was to cover the costs of keeping British troops in the colonies. Not only was this the first direct tax imposed on the American colonies, it meant that a great number of colonists would not be able to afford the news periodicals of the day. Protests included the tarring and feathering of a few tax collectors, as well as hanging one or two in effigy. Finding tax collectors willing to continue with the job proved so difficult that Britain repealed the law the following year, but the harm had been done.

# free press as a rallying cry

In the midst of the fury surrounding the law, a Stamp Act Congress made up of representatives from nine colonies, several of them publishers, had assembled to catalog their complaints. The resulting Declaration of Rights and Grievances did more than inform King George of the colonists' complaints; copies of the document were instrumental in seeding the American Revolution.

For the most part, American newspapers of the day were overtly partisan and existed largely as vehicles for impassioned political rants. In the prelude to the war for independence, authors like Benjamin Franklin and Thomas Paine parried with their counterparts at British loyalist publications. After the war, it was the Federalists and anti-Federalists who duked it out in print.

# the bill of rights is born

Few arguments in the new nation were as heated as the one revolving around explicit guarantees for a free press. The topic was so volatile that it threatened ratification of the Constitution by the thirteen colonies and was left out of the original document.

Alexander Hamilton (no relation to Andrew Hamilton above) was a founder of the Federalist Party and among those opposed to incorporating a Bill of Rights. He believed that such a document was not only unnecessary but dangerous. The rights were already implicit in the Constitution, he argued, and cataloguing a subset of rights could put other implicit rights in jeopardy.

James Madison at first agreed with Hamilton, but arguments by individuals like Thomas Jefferson finally convinced him to pen the first draft of a Bill of Rights. In 1791, after much internecine argument among the former colonies, the first ten amendments to the American Constitution were ratified and the right to free expression became explicit.

Madison's initial, reluctant support of the Bill of Rights switched to full-bore advocacy in the wake of the Sedition Act signed into law by Federalist President John Adams in 1798. The Sedition Act declared that "any false, scandalous and malicious writing . . . against the Government of the United States" would be subject to a fine or imprisonment. More than a dozen indictments against prominent publishers and even one opposition party Congressman followed in quick order.

Because the Supreme Court at the time supported the Federalists, Madison and Jefferson realized that a constitutional appeal would be of no use and so set their sites on unseating the Federalists in the election of 1800. Jefferson won the presidency and the Sedition Act expired without a challenge. In the wake of the Act, Madison declared that the role of journalists as watchdogs of government made them a "bulwark of liberty."

# newspapers bloom across america

As the nineteenth century dawned, government censorship still constrained publishing across most of the Continent. England's long history of state suppression of publishing was lifting, but the newspapers of the day largely served as propaganda organs for the Whig and Tory parties. In America, the situation had grown a bit more chaotic.

Alexis de Tocqueville, a French political theorist, toured the new nation and in 1830 published *Democracy in America*, in which he wrote about the many and varied newspapers then publishing throughout the colonies. "It is a simple and easy matter to start a paper," Tocqueville observed. "A few subscribers are enough to cover expenses and so the number of periodical or semi-periodical productions in the United States surpasses all belief. The most enlightened Americans attribute the slightness of the power of the press to this incredible dispersion; it is an axiom of political science that the only way to neutralize the effect of newspapers is to multiply their numbers."

> Tocqueville's description of the political pamphlets of the time could easily be applied to today's blogosphere: "In America, the parties do not publish books to refute each other, but pamphlets which circulate at an incredible rate, last a day, and die. By and large the literature of a democracy will never exhibit the order, regularity, skill, and art characteristic of aristocratic literature; formal qualities will be neglected or actually despised. The style will often be strange, incorrect, overburdened, and loose, and almost always strong and bold. Writers will be more anxious to work quickly than to perfect details. Short works will be commoner than long books, wit than erudition, imagination than depth. There will be a rude and untutored vigor of thought with great variety and singular fecundity. Authors will strive to astonish more than to please, and to stir passions rather than to charm taste."

# consolidation of the news follows

In the end, chaos often distills into order—and a lessening of diversity. By the mid-nineteenth century, news that used to travel by carrier pigeon and Pony Express began being transported by railroads, steamships, and the telegraph, and local newspapers began banding together to form shared news-gathering services while the larger papers formed wire services, guaranteeing almost instantaneous access to news reports. Further contributing to the consolidation, new printing presses that could produce thousands of copies per hour were replacing hand-cranked presses, driving many small printers out of business.

Between 1870 and 1890, the population of the United States doubled, while that of many cities more than tripled. Editorial staffs at newspapers and magazines catering to this hungry public grew more specialized. The roles of reporters, editors, and publishers were becoming more distinct.

It was a splendid era for large newspapers. Fortunes were made and fame could be granted at the whim of an editor. In Chapter 2, the rise of the Bennett empire provided one window on the times. During the same period, William Randolph Hearst, Horace Greeley, and Joseph Pulitzer were busily founding their own news empires. All purported to be dedicated to defending the public against both government and corporate abuses, but it isn't without cause that their papers became known as the "yellow press." Hearst's jingoistic rantings about the sinking of the warship Maine are often credited with starting the Spanish-American War, for instance.

This is not to say that all reporting and all news organizations were equally slanted. While the *New York Times* was not without its shameless stories, it had been founded on the principle of balanced reporting. When Tammany Hall's William Marcy "Boss" Tweed offered George Jones, the *Times* publisher, a five million dollar bribe in 1873, the newspaper not only turned down the money, it printed the full details of the story. Boss Tweed was unseated and subscription numbers for the *Times* soared. The other major dailies couldn't help but take notice. A journalistic conscience was dawning.

# investigative reporting gains a foothold

During the 1890s, a new school of reporters—among them, Lincoln Steffens, Ida Tarbell, and Upton Sinclair—began exposing corruption at all levels of government and business. For the most part, these authors were published in smaller periodicals, but the public responded, demanding change, and the impact of investigative journalism became increasingly apparent.

News reporting on both sides of the Atlantic became more deferential during the period surrounding World War I. Among the critics of this more subdued era was Walter Lippman, who castigated *The New York Times*, which had declared the Russian Revolution "nothing short of a disaster." This was wishful thinking on the part of the editors, said Lippman, who wrote that the coverage not only cheated the public of real information, it "was about as useful as that of an astrologer or alchemist." He recommended that any journalist "remain clear and free of his irrational, his unexamined, his unacknowledged prejudgments in observing, understanding and presenting the news."

# journalistic ethics take hold

During the 1920s, universities began tackling journalism as a realm of study. Textbooks appeared that explored concepts of accuracy, fairness, conflict of interest, transparency, and the protection of privacy. For the first time, objective reporting became an imperative within professional journalistic circles.

Additionally, newspapers were no longer the only source for news. Filmed newsreels began appearing in movie theaters and radio was becoming increasingly popular. The first radio station, KDKA, launched in Pittsburgh in 1920. By 1922, there were 576 radio stations broadcasting across the United States. By 1925, there were more than five million receivers in homes.

A major difference between print publishing and broadcasting in the United States is that broadcast radio and network television are subject to government licensing and, in some cases, censorship. The original rationale for licensing was based on the scarce number of frequencies available for broadcasting. Winning and retaining a license requires adhering to sometimes vague guidelines ostensibly aimed at supporting the "public good." New technologies mitigate the scarcity argument, and indeed, satellite radio and cable television are not bound by the same strictures, but violations of the Federal Broadcast Indecency Statute by those still bound can lead to large fines and revocation of license.

Through the Great Depression of the 1930s and World War II during the 1940s, news media continued a process of consolidation, with ever fewer outlets controlling more and more news. This gave rise to a new suite of media critics, among them A.J. Liebling, who penned the now famous line, "Freedom of the press is for those who own one."

It wasn't until the Red Scare of the 1950s that television assumed prominence among news audiences. Anti-Communist rhetoric was fast convincing many citizens that national security required censure of any who dared voice alternate views. Many journalists followed in lockstep, particularly after the House UnAmerican Affairs Committee began issuing its subpoenas, but a few brave souls, like Ed Murrow of CBS, refused to be intimidated. Murrow used his airtime to appeal to the public's higher principles. His thorough and well-reasoned reports were instrumental in the downfall of Senator Joe McCarthy and in tempering American sentiment.

At odds with his bosses over his editorial stance, Murrow found much still lacking in modern journalism. In a speech before the Radio and Television News Directors Association in 1958, he said, "During the daily peak viewing periods, television in the main insulates us from the realities of the world in which we live. If this state of affairs continues, we may alter an advertising slogan to read: Look Now. Pay Later."

# modern news takes shape

By the 1960s, the youth of America, along with a growing number of older sympathizers, were adamantly opposed to the racial divides at home and the Vietnam War abroad. The unrest was fueled by an explosion of photocopied posters, pamphlets, and periodicals, as well as unlicensed, low-power radio transmissions. The *I.F. Stone Weekly,* distinguished by the rigor and fearlessness of its eponymous founder, served as a bellwether for many early "citizen journalist" periodicals, among them the *Berkeley Barb, Ramparts,* the *Seed* in Chicago, the *East Village Other* and *The Village Voice* in New York, and the *Los Angeles Free Press. Rolling Stone* made its mark on popular culture by managing to publish investigative pieces while still attracting mainstream advertisers.

The Watergate scandals and the release of the Pentagon Papers during the 1970s, along with the Iran-Contra affair during the 1980s, deepened a distrust of government while giving rise to a few mainstream media stars, chief among them the *Washington Post*'s Carl Bernstein and Bob Woodward. The *New York Times,* determined not to let a competing paper dominate future stories, responded by creating a formal team of investigative reporters. CBS television launched *60 Minutes*, which quickly rose to the top of network news rankings.

The 1980s witnessed a further consolidation within media, with four press associations—Associated Press, United Press International, Reuters, and Agence France-Press—providing more than 90 percent of all international news. By the 1990s, a handful of newspaper groups owned most daily newspapers in the United States. All were struggling as advertising revenues declined, with further mergers and coalitions blurring the lines between print and broadcast media.

Adding to traditional media's woes was the emergence of the Internet. By 1997, when the *Dallas Morning News* decided to break its story about Timothy McVeigh's confession to the Oklahoma City bombing on its website rather than waiting for the morning paper, the Web had become a formidable platform for distribution of news.

# blogs gain momentum

With the introduction of simple-to-use blogging software in 1998, the barn doors opened wide. By the time the Katrina hurricane hit, major news outlets were taking advantage of cell phone images and reports from citizens on the ground. Bloggers were instrumental in generating the first public lists of survivors. And perhaps most importantly, citizen bloggers have continued to document the realities of life in post-storm New Orleans long after traditional media had moved on.

Citizen journalism still has some rough edges—indeed, it will probably always have some rough edges—but it is increasingly clear that there is no way to map today's media landscape without acknowledging its growing presence. Citizen journalist blogs belong to a long tradition of news reporting that harbors responsibilities, privileges, and hard-won rights. What's more, they foster a level of engagement on the part of citizens that may bode well for democracy.

Hopefully, this chapter has helped to provide a bit of context for bloggers who choose to serve as reporters. As the next chapter will illustrate, the oft-cited line between reporting and editorializing can be a difficult one to negotiate, but acknowledging the difference will help any blogger to present information that is truthful, useful, and that won't come back to bite them. Readers worried about this latter point may want to take a bit of extra time with Chapter 12, "Keeping It Legal."

# citizen journalist resources

Many fine online resources designed originally for professional journalists are available to citizen journalists and will help to guide researching and reporting news stories.

**PowerReporting** (powerreporting.com) Pulitzer Prize winner Bill Dedman maintains the Power Reporting website, a compendium of resources for investigative reporters. Whether your beat is arts, disasters, governments, religion, or the weather, this site provides useful pointers to web-based information.

**Journalist's Toolbox** (americanpressinstitute.org/pages/toolbox) The American Press Institute provides a constantly shifting suite of links to resources related to the news of the day.

**Poynteronline Resource Center** (poynter.org/resource_center) Poynter's links to other journalism websites, tip sheets, and various training options make this page well worth bookmarking.

**I Want Media** (iwantmedia.com/resources/index.html) Patrick Phillips, a freelance journalist and adjunct professor at NYU, offers useful links, statistics, and surveys, as well as pointers to numerous other journalist resource websites.

**SPJ Freedom of Information** (spj.org.foi.asp) The Society of Professional Journalists provides an excellent overview of the U.S. Freedom of Information Act and offers tips on requesting documents from the government.

# ethics primer for bloggers

There is no single, agreed-upon code of journalistic ethics. Professional organizations and individual news outlets each formulate their own guidelines. Still, there are certain key ethical points that help journalists present accurate and unbiased information that wins them the trust of their audiences. Below is a attempt to draw on the best of these codes, eliciting guidelines that suit the needs of today's citizen journalists.

## be fair

- ▶ Acknowledge any personal bias or influence.
- ▶ Clearly distinguish opinion from fact.
- ▶ Research all facts thoroughly and honestly.
- ▶ Question the motives of sources.
- ▶ Never mislead or misrepresent.
- ▶ Never plagiarize.

## be accountable

▶ Identify and link to sources whenever possible.

▶ Invite feedback and respond to it.

▶ Admit and correct mistakes promptly and publicly.

▶ Be courageous when holding those in power accountable.

▶ Avoid any real or perceived conflict of interest; if unavoidable, disclose all gifts, fees, payments, and the like.

## minimize harm

▶ Avoid pandering and sensationalism.

▶ Acknowledge that private individuals have a greater right to an expectation of privacy than public officials or those who court power, influence, or media attention.

▶ Practice discretion when writing about those who may be adversely affected by blog coverage, particularly if they are children, grieving victims of crimes, innocent bystanders, or suspects.

▶ Recognize common standards of decency.

## interview with farai chideya

Farai Chideya is a one-woman media empire. You may have seen her moderating the Democratic Presidential Debate in 2004, or as a commentator for CNN, MTV, Fox, MSNBC, BET, Oxygen, CBS, or ABC. She was a regular on Bill Maher's *Politically Incorrect* television program. Her writings include many articles for print periodicals, as well as three books: *Don't Believe the Hype: Fighting Cultural Misinformation About African Americans* (Plume Penguin, 1995), *The Color of Our Future* (William Morrow, 1999), and *Trust: Reaching the 100 Million Missing Voters* (Soft Skull, 2004). These days, she is a host/correspondent for *News and Notes with Ed Gordon* on NPR radio. Plus, she sometimes finds the time to post to one of her blogs—*Pop and Politics*, a blog that grew into a multimedia journalism education nonprofit (popandpolitics.com); *My Minifesto*, commentary on revolutionizing the economics of digital content; and her personal blog (faraichideya.com). Many thanks to Farai for taking the time to do the interview. Excerpts appear below; the full text can be found online (dispatchesfromblogistan.com).

## on trust and truth

Most trust within blogging is based on both emotional and empirical factors. Human beings aren't great at separating the two. Over time, as a journalist, I've begun to use more of an empirical method of seeking truth through the intersection of the experiences of people who've participated in or witnessed critical moments in history. I've been lucky enough to interview the President, fly on Air Force One, talk to Bono and Snoop and Brad Pitt, visit homeless veterans on the street, and talk to people who were imprisoned during apartheid.

I still don't know THE truth, but then again, I think that thinking you know THE truth is often an ego trap. Everybody's stories and life experiences guide you towards an understanding of complex issues. Most of what we understand is a hypothesis about how the world works. In some ways, you are on a quest for information that could never end. But that does not mean you should not act. Inaction is action.

## on gauging sources

I like to gather information from a variety of different, and sometimes opposing, sources. For example, my father's family is from Zimbabwe. To keep up on the news, I read news from inside Zimbabwe, from the U.S. and UK, and from China (which is heavily investing in this and other African nations). The Internet makes it possible for me to read official Chinese news releases in English, instantly. What I do with all that information is sort it through the filter of self-interest: What stakes do the journalists, their organizations, and their home nations have in the story? How might that have biased or at least shaped their reporting? Ultimately, you can look for "reliable sources" on or offline—and some are certainly more reliable than others—but you should also get multiple sources of information and make up your own mind.

## on traditional media and blogging

Mainstream or big media should be freaking out right now, and from what I sense, it is. Increasingly, newspapers, TV, and radio stations are creating their own blogs or contracting with independent bloggers. I think in some cases it works well and, in some cases, news organizations aren't ready for the higher level of opinion and critique that comes with the blogosphere.

## on journalistic ethics

Citizen journalists should be aware of journalism basics—the difference between reporting and opinion, libel law, etc. It's not that citizen journalists will be held to the same standards as "mainstream" journalists, but that coming up with a set of ethical rules you follow will make you better. If you repeat gossip as fact, however, you could actually get yourself in legal trouble, as well as be discredited among your peers.

## on rich media

In five years, every news organization will be multimedia. You already see the *New York Times* commissioning original short video pieces which stream on its web property; and ABC has a highly read political blog, "The Note." NPR, for whom I work, does a ton of work online. And The Onion, which was once distributed almost exclusively online, now has newspaper kiosks. In five years, there will be less and less meaning to being "print," or "online," or "audio" or "video." Anyone who can be multimedia will be multimedia.

## on blogs and democracy

Well, let's put it this way: nearly half of Americans are illiterate or have sub-optimal literacy. So you take the problems a lot of people have with the written language, and then you transfer that to a system which is still navigationally text-based, and you can see how that impacts how "democratic" any online culture is at this point. I love blogs and the Internet and social networking systems, but they are still limited to an educational, if not financial, elite. I believe those barriers are becoming lower, but they're still there and will be for some time.

# on intellectual property

I just had someone post pictures I took in New Orleans after Katrina without asking me or without seeking permission. This pisses me off. But the reality is, it's very hard to absolutely prevent people from copying your online works. I am trying to get the situation sorted, but it's very easy to copy and paste.

I am a big fan of Lawrence Lessig's Creative Commons licenses. If the person who posted my photos had just asked, I probably would have licensed the photos under a no-commercial-reproduction license to the nonprofit. I think the Creative Commons licenses will help reshape the intellectual property landscape, but even then—and certainly until then—the best policy is to follow basic courtesy, as well as legal protocol.

# on tagging

User-created tags are just fabulous. The only downside—and this isn't much of one—is that tags reflect the community of taggers. If new people with new interests enter the system, they may have to create their own lingo. For example, if you are interested in hip-hop, you might tag the same posting, variously, as "hip hop," "rap," "bay area beats," or "hyphy." It's up to users to decipher the common language among their tags.

# on privacy

Privacy today is mainly an illusion. There are many ways of dealing with that (besides the standard denial). You can live an utterly boring life and fly beneath the radar because your life is barely worth tracking. You can make yourself naked to those who observe you, much as some celebrities grant exclusives to tabloids. Or you can live fearlessly, and do what you please, all the while knowing that, for example, the federal Terrorist Screening Center maintains a list of 200,000 people suspected of terrorism, plus 150,000 additional partial names or IDs (according to a March 14, 2006, report by the Associated Press). They've so far made fewer than 60 arrests, but meanwhile, our credit card purchases, library books, and financial records could end up being sifted for evidence that we belong on this burgeoning list.

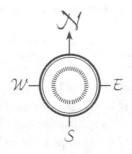

# blogs as soapboxes

When members of the mainstream media file reports about blogs, they most often focus on authors who voice opinions and who engage in debates about issues of public concern. This might suggest that pundit and advocacy blogs are the dominant form within blogdom, but it turns out that this isn't true. A Pew Internet blog survey released in July 2006 found that only sixteen percent of all American bloggers write about "issues of public life" or "general news and current events," with the greatest number of bloggers writing simply about "my life."

This doesn't lessen the impact of these advocacy blogs, of course. Whether writing about local or national politics, the environment, human rights, consumer issues, or corporate accountability, the best of these blogs are beginning to influence public perception and policy.

As with each of the broad categories of blogs mentioned in previous chapters, those devoted to advocacy causes do not always fall neatly within a single slot. It's not unusual for blogs that are primarily compendiums of links to exhibit strong points of view with individual critiques serving as mini-editorials. Diarists who primarily write about their own lives sometimes feel compelled to take a stand on a topic of public interest. Enthusiast bloggers may write passionately about some political issue that has the potential to affect their area of expertise.

This overlap is to be expected and generally serves both the bloggers and their communities well. Topical issues are explored, heroes celebrated, and villains exposed, but there is one category of blog that doesn't mix as well with opinion and advocacy—citizen journalist blogs. As chronicled in the previous chapter, the history of journalism is rife with examples of newspapers launched as bully pulpits for their owners or patrons. Even today, some print and broadcast media make little secret of their political or social agendas. But over time, the best of the news outlets have adopted codes of ethics that allow their reporters to present news coverage that is fair, accountable, and objective—coverage that gives the public enough information to draw its own conclusions, but that does not bear the weight of an agenda.

This is not to say that opinion writing is held in less esteem or is ignored by media professionals. Indeed, most newspapers proudly highlight their opinion pages, and television and radio shows feature columnists who boldly take public stands. But just as these outlets have evolved a clear demarcation between advertising and editorial (obvious differences in typeface and voice, for instance), the most professional of the lot make a clear distinction between objective reporting of news events and advocacy vehicles designed to sway the public.

# punditry is integral to our perception of news

The history of punditry is as old as news itself. The word "pundit" derives from the Hindu *pandit*, meaning a respected scholar. Anyone can voice an opinion, but some views carry more weight than others. Throughout history, individuals have occupied positions that influence public sentiment through persuasion and a sense of perceived authority. No doubt some of the troubadours who carried news from medieval town to town sometimes colored their stories to fit their own perceptions of events—and in rhyme, no less! Today's news professionals generally make a conscious decision about whether they will be reporters presenting events of the day with as little personal bias as possible, or news commentators who openly advocate a stance. Still, even in the most exalted circles, the line occasionally blurs.

One famous example occurred in 1968 after eminently respected CBS news anchor Walter Cronkite visited Vietnam during the Tet offensive. In an unprecedented and clearly labeled editorial, the newscaster called for an end to the war, saying, "It is increasingly clear to this reporter that the only rational way out will be to negotiate." Bill Moyers, who was one of President Johnson's press aides at the time, reports that after the segment aired, Johnson turned off the TV and said, "If I've lost Cronkite, I've lost America."

With the introduction of the Internet, the world of news became even more complicated. Newspapers and network evening news were no longer our sole resources for learning about world events. Access to a global network of constantly updated news greatly broadened the scope of what we consider news. Adding to the bounty, blogs allowed ordinary citizens to add their own voices to the fray.

Blogs as a platform for commentary really came into their own in the wake of the 9/11 terror attacks. Readers flocked to eyewitness reports like those of New Yorker Cameron Barrett (camworld.com) and impassioned conservative writings like those of Glenn Reynolds on his Instapundit (instapundit.com) blog. By May 2002, Markos Moulitsas Zuniga had founded the liberal blog Daily Kos (dailykos.com), and the tensions between the left and right were being played out daily on blogs.

Once again, journalist Farai Chideya offers perspective: "Big-media news is often a popularity contest among the people who deliver it, and an emotional bellwether for people who consume it. That's one reason that during 9/11, news got more personal and more humanistic rather than more analytical. As human beings we respond to emotion. And to the extent that citizen journalists (bloggers and more) can reach our emotions, they will have power to sway us—warranted or unwarranted. You can see this in some of the followings for left and right political bloggers. Those followings are based not just on information, but on how people 'vibe' with the tone and voice and emotional pitch of the blogger."

The U.S. elections of 2004 proved that blogs could be useful campaign tools. The success of Howard Dean's blog-based Meet Ups and donation drives sent campaign managers everywhere scurrying to get online. Today, there is scarcely a candidate running who doesn't either post to his or her own blog or encourage the efforts of supporters. Lawmakers the world round have learned that they ignore the voices of these bloggers at their own risk. After all, fallout from blog commentary managed to undo the careers of a number of public figures—news anchor Dan Rather, Democratic Senator Tom Daschle, and Republican Senate Majority Leader Trent Lott, among them.

Today, many people seek news commentary and advocacy reporting in surprising quarters. An astonishing number get their daily news fix from "fake news shows" like Comedy Central's Daily Show with Jon Stewart and the Colbert Report. Replete with video clips of actual news events and interviews with newsmakers, these programs use barbed satire to convey overt left-of-center political stances. Online, readers are flocking to popular blogs like the conservative Instapundit and progressive Daily Kos. Still others are subscribing to newsfeeds from a rich array of advocacy sources that allow them to stay abreast of local and niche topics.

In the best-case scenarios, citizens are learning to sort through this rich body of information, making independent decisions based on information culled from the glut. In the worst-case scenarios, individuals choose only sources that reinforce their predispositions, entrenching polarization and narrowing the debates.

# hewing to responsible guidelines

The influence wielded by the best of these blogs is inspiring almost as much discussion about the platform itself as it is about the topics being advocated. Readers may remember Denise Caruso's "Digital Commerce" column in the *New York Times*, but it is her work with her own Hybrid Vigor Institute (hybridvigor.org) and the Pew Charitable Trusts that lend heft to her thoughts about ethical guidelines in online environments. (You can read the entire interview with Caruso on dispatchesfromblogistan.com.)

"The most important thing," observes Caruso, "is for [bloggers] to identify themselves. I don't care necessarily if they have any formal cred on the subject they're blogging, but I do want to know who they are, and what skin they have in the game. It can be as simple as a mission statement, no matter how brief. I also look for whether they declare how they support the blog financially. You can see one revenue stream if there are ads on the site, but if they take money from other places I'd like to know it. It's just straight-up transparency."

Caruso believes that in the best circumstances, these writings can have beneficial results. If bloggers are "hewing to responsible guidelines," she continues, "it's all good. This means there are more informed people who take action and who inspire others to take action. More voices of minorities and the disenfranchised. More potential to spread the tenets and the benefits of free speech all around the world. More accountability. More opportunity for true representative democracy to reassert itself here and elsewhere."

"The danger is that people won't hew to responsible guidelines," Caruso warns. "Then people will take action based on disinformation or will be too overwhelmed by all the information and end up taking even less action than they do now. Also there are real dangers in narrowcasting only to the audience who agrees with you. This can actually lead to an even more factionalized society; i.e., 'ideology on demand.'"

# advocacy on a global scale

These dangers are real, but so are the benefits. Organizers of causes spanning the ideological spectrum are finding blogs a viable method of not only getting a message out, but of effecting change.

Among Cory Doctorow's other accomplishments (see Chapter 3), he was European affairs coordinator for the online-rights advocacy group Electronic Frontier Foundation. During that period, he found blogging to be a valuable tool in influencing decision-making on a global scale. "We would go to the World Intellectual Property Organization and transcribe impressionistically what delegates were saying during treaty negotiations," Doctorow observes. "We would blog, say, twice a day. Transcripts [of the WIPO meetings] are normally published six months after the event and after being sanitized by the Secretariat and by each speaker, who omit anything they don't agree with. The number of people interested in following the inner workings of a WIPO treaty is small but larger than the number of people who can be in the room. And some of these people are capable of exerting influence from a distance. When someone reads what we've written and contacts someone in government who has authority over the person negotiating the treaty, and that person gets a phone call on their lunch break and changes their tune in the afternoon, that's a really, really powerful tool for democratization."

Sergey Kuznetsov is another blogger contributing to the global impact of blogging. Kuznetsov is a professional journalist and activist who has the distinction of being the earliest professional journalist in Russia to publish on the Internet. He was also among the first to adopt LiveJournal as a blogging platform. In the United States, LiveJournal is largely populated by young bloggers, many of them girls. In Russia, however, the same service became a seminal platform for that country's seasoned writers and thinkers. The tension between the two types of bloggers has resulted in some unhappy developments. (Again, the full interview with Kuznetsov is available on dispatchesfromblogistan.com.)

"The first generation of Russian bloggers were our net-o-crats," Kuznetsov reports. "I think it was no accident that our Russian Internet VIPs were important writers and academicians. It reflects the high status of literature within the Russian intelligentsia. There is an old Russian saying, 'A poet in Russia is more than just a poet,' and it's still true. For poets, LiveJournal was an easy way to publish their poems and to get positive feedback from their readers."

Gradually, the prolific Russian blogger community began publishing on a broad array of topics, with many bloggers relying on LiveJournal. All was well until 2005 when service was purchased by the U.S.-based blog software company Six Apart and a series of incidents rocked the community.

The most infamous incident occurred in early 2005 when a Russian LiveJournal blogger posting under the name vchk uploaded an image of an old Soviet propaganda poster that had originally read, "Kill a German," but which he had altered to read, "Kill NATO." LiveJournal's Abuse Team suspended vchk's account, calling it an incitement to violence. The Russian community was shocked to find itself censored by an American company. Many Russian bloggers began posting the same image in a show of support and they, too, found themselves suspended. The Abuse Team members didn't speak much Russian and ended up suspending at least one member who was posting in support of the suspensions. The result was that many Russian bloggers abandoned the platform, choosing to publish using other blogging tools.

But Russian blogging remains lively. Kuznetsov continues, "The last year and a half has been a time of activism and political activity for Russian bloggers. Many civil movements use blogs as a platform for appealing to their potential supporters. This is normal when television is government controlled and oppositional newspapers are not very influential. The events of the last six months suggest the Russian blogosphere will be a battlefield on 2008 election eve. Blogs are an effective tool for building civil society in Russia. In fact, they are much, much better than newspapers and mass-media for this task."

# advocacy blogs are here to stay

The numbers alone suggest that pundits and dedicated advocates of all stripes are finding blogs to be a platform worth the investment in time and effort. Whether presenting their cases via text, photographs, video segments, or audio podcasts, these kibitzers, watchdogs, and rabble-rousers are influencing opinion—and in some cases at least, policy.

Some bloggers, like Instapundit's Reynolds and the Daily Kos's Moulitsas are regularly consulted and interviewed by mainstream news outlets. Within smaller spheres, individuals all around the world are making a difference in their communities by presenting arguments that are well-researched and presented fairly. Some worry about the potential for demagoguery within blog ranks, and this is always a danger, but never before have so many been able to let their opinions be heard by both their peers and those in positions of power. Better tools for filtering and gauging reputation are coming onboard every day. Individual bloggers are getting more proficient at presenting their cases in a manner that inspires confidence and action.

As Craig Newmark of craigslist.com puts it, "We're figuring out how to get masses involved without mob rule."

# sampler of advocacy blogs

Among the millions of blogs, those that dare to take a stand on topics of social interest are gaining both fans and influence. The range of topics is broad, from local party politics to issues of global proportions. The well-known pundit blogs garner the lion's share of attention, but a growing number of thoughtful advocacy efforts are each making a difference within their own topic areas.

**World Changing** (worldchanging.com) The founders of the World Changing blog, Jamais Cascio (interviewed below) and Alex Steffen, began with a simple premise. They believe that the tools, models, and ideas necessary for building a better environmental future lie all around us; they just need to be brought to the attention of a larger public. Their stated bias is toward solutions that incorporate democratic principles, human rights, and civic freedoms. Al Gore wrote the forward to their book of the same name.

**Bag News Notes** (bagnewsnotes.typepad.com) Michael Shaw is a clinical psychologist who takes a unique approach to presenting commentary about current events. On Bag News Notes, one of the many Huffington Post-associated blogs, he provides astute analyses of images found in the news, pointing out stereotypes and encouraging readers to become better at discerning agendas and misrepresentations in our increasingly visual communications environments.

**Committee on Conscience** (ushmm.org/conscience/podcasts) The Committee on Conscience, which guides the genocide-prevention efforts of the U.S. Holocaust Memorial Museum, presents a podcast series titled Voices on Genocide Prevention. The mandate of the group is to "alert the national conscience, influence policy makers, and stimulate worldwide action to confront and work to halt acts of genocide or related crimes against humanity." Led by staff director Jerry Fowler, the audio interviews are both heartbreaking and hopeful.

**The Arabist** (arabist.net) Published by Cairo journalist Issandr E. Amrani, The Arabist covers a spectrum of topics—politics, culture, economics, media, religion, and more—presenting information of interest to both citizens of the Arab world as well as the world at large. The blog's contributors feature a number of points of view, but all subscribe to the site's mission: "Debunking ill-informed, culturalist or alarmist works about the region."

**Voices of New Orleans** (chinmusicpress.com/books/doyouknow/voices) New Orleans-based Chin Music Press took its name from Mark Twain's description of the way in which a preacher spoke. Applying that same passion and quirkiness, the press launched the Voices of New Orleans blog in the wake of Hurricane Katrina. Drawing on a number of local authors, the blog provides a very human window onto that still-wracked city and its courageous rebuilding efforts.

**Campaigns Wikia** (campaigns.wikia.com/wiki/Campaigns_Wikia) Begun by Jimmy Wales, founder of the oft-cited Wikipedia, Campaigns Wikia targets activists of every political persuasion. While, strictly speaking, more a wiki than a blog, the project shows great promise of providing citizens with a viable platform for sharing political views. In Wales' own words: "Whoever you are and whatever you believe, you can share with me my sincere desire that the process starts to be about substance and thought, rather than style and image."

# interview with jamais cascio

Jamais Cascio is an Internet veteran who recognized the potential for online activism early. In 2003, he co-founded World Changing (worldchanging.com), an influential blog dedicated to environmental activism, with an emphasis on identifying workable solutions. More recently, he launched the Open the Future (openthefuture.com) blog, dedicated to many of the same interests but with a slightly more personal perspective. His experiences promoting activist causes both on- and offline provide valuable pointers.

## on online activism

Activism is the real-world application of the concept that combinations of people can be as powerful as accumulations of wealth. The Internet has made it possible for combinations of people to arise more swiftly and more expansively than ever before; blogging adds to this a layer of individual expression that does not detract from the power of the whole. The strength of activism derives directly from its web of participation, and blogging heightens this strength by making active participation easier and more visible than ever before.

This combination of ease and visibility is a disadvantage, too. We are inclined to give our attention to spectacle, and the voices of the strident and the angry and the ridiculous can, all too often, drown out the voices of the passionate and the engaged and the humane. Those whose power is threatened by the rise of web activism take advantage of these spectacles, painting them as the true voices of online activity, and claiming that all bloggers are strident and angry and ridiculous.

Blogging is notoriously ephemeral, as well. It's easy to start a blog, but it's even easier to abandon one. Writing with both passion and frequency requires far more energy than most people realize; moreover, web audiences can be fickle. Internet-enabled mass activism can disintegrate as easily as it emerges.

## on hyperlinks and truth

The key reason why blogs have such potential to reveal fragments of the truth is the embedded hyperlink. With blogs, the reader no longer has to rely on the author's voice or status to make a determination of right or wrong, or has to seek out sources that confirm or deny an author's statements. The author can—and should—put links directly in her or his assertions that back up claims, making it possible for the reader to understand where an argument comes from. Authors who don't use links to back up their arguments, or link only to other subjective sources, do their readers *and themselves* a disservice.

The best way to foster critical thinking, then, is to teach readers to follow the sources.

## on blogging and traditional journalism

The only journalists (by which I mean the writers of traditional news media) who should be nervous about the rise of citizen media are those journalists whose work can't stand scrutiny. Good journalists should be ecstatic about this development, and not just because of the fact-checking aspects. Hint to writers encountering blog backlash for the first time: the three most powerful words in the English language in this kind of situation are "I was wrong." You'll be amazed at how quickly opinion will shift about you when you own up to your mistakes.

Blogs can serve as distant early warning networks for journalists, alerting them to stories that they might otherwise miss. I don't mean that journalists should simply regurgitate what they've read online—as is far too common, especially in the "talking points" political journalism world—but they should learn to keep an eye out for stories that, with further investigation, need to be told.

The flip side of this, however, is that journalists should be willing to cite their sources, including blogs. When I see a news report that only credits "stories on the Internet," I see a reporter that can't be trusted.

## on the future of news

In five years, everyone (or many early adopters, at least) will have heads-up displays running all day with personalized "CNN crawls" running along the bottom edge of our peripheral vision—probably pulling headlines from the 2011 version of RSS feeds—with filters of some sort flagging headlines that are worth paying more attention to. The stories behind those headlines will be written by citizen journalists, paid journalists, and machine journalists mashing-up multiple sources to tell a complete story.

Television news will be filled with reports of auto accidents supposedly resulting from people watching their heads-up displays instead of watching the road.

## on product development

I believe that we're in the early days of a new information/communication world. Where the "perpetual beta" structure falls short, in my view, is that it's *mostly* unidirectional—platforms and services roll out new versions and features, but only pay grudging attention to the responses of users.

We need to stop thinking of this as alpha/beta release, and start thinking of it as co-evolution or iterated design. Users should be thought of as stakeholders and participants in the design process, and I expect to see radical approaches to product design that rely heavily on Digg or Slashdot-style collaboration. Imagine the "wisdom of the crowds" philosophy adapted to the design field. It probably wouldn't work all that well in every case, but it would result in enough surprising successes that it would eventually become part of the designer's toolkit.

## on new definitions of privacy

Privacy isn't just about keeping stuff secret, it's about maintaining control over information about yourself that others could use to hurt you physically, financially, or emotionally. If we believe that the ongoing growth of technologies of transparency is unstoppable, then our options are limited. We could:

▶ Try to slow the growth, fighting tooth-and-nail over every encroachment;

▶ Push for mutual transparency, so that everyone is more or less equally vulnerable, and therefore less likely to abuse your formerly private information (essentially a Mutual Assured Destruction model for privacy);

▶ Push for social changes that reduce the threat arising from disclosure of personal information.

A combination of all three is most likely to succeed, with sharp controls over financial information, MAD tactics for physical information (e.g., location), and social changes to reduce the threat that would come from things like the disclosure of video rental habits.

Most likely to happen is an all-out effort to fight privacy reductions, one that eventually fails.

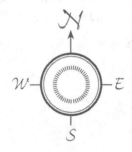

# packing your toolkit

The phenomenal popularity of blogging is often chalked up to egotism, voyeurism, or even idealism, but the truth is that none of these traits is new. What's new is the ease with which we can now exercise those egos and ideals. We open a web browser to a blog authoring page, compose an entry, post it with a quick click of the Submit button, and voilà, we're publishers on an international scale.

It sounds simple, and it is. Or at least it can be. Choosing your software tools from among the many dozens available can be frustrating. At the time of this writing, the Yahoo Directory links to 85 options for blog authoring software. Veteran blogger Robin Good lists 167 search sites to which you may submit your blog. And Emily Robbins lists 26 blog ping services (see "Searching Blogs" later in this chapter for an explanation of blog pings).

HOT LINKS:
BLOG TOOL LISTINGS
..............................

**Yahoo Directory**
http://dir.yahoo.com

**Search Submission**
http://www.
masternewmedia.org/
rss/top55

**Blog Ping Services**
http://www.
emilyrobbins.
com/how-to-blog/
?s=blog+ping+services

And if sheer numbers of options weren't daunting enough, the open-source nature of most of the software guarantees a constantly roiling sea of options contributed by savvier users. The better blog-related tools are evolving at a breakneck pace as their authors leapfrog one another, adding requested features while accommodating a dizzying array of free, third-party templates and plug-ins. Some blog tools go so far as to boldly acknowledge their "beta" status, a term historically used to mean that software is still in development and so, "user beware." Add to all this mayhem the argot growing up around blogging. *Pings*, *permalinks*, *trackback*, *blogrolls*, *moblogs*, and *splogs* are just a few of the neologisms peppering the discussions.

But not to despair. Despite all this profusion and flux, there are some basic guidelines that will help you narrow the field and find solutions that will grow with you. In this chapter, we'll look at the features that distinguish the best of today's blog authoring options and offer recommendations based on the solutions available at the time of writing. Along the way, you will hopefully pick up enough basic knowledge to help you make future decisions as new tools and services enter the fray. This is the longest chapter in the book. It was tempting to break it into smaller chunks, but in the end, it's important to choose tools that work well together and that suit your overall needs and interests. It's best to think of them as all part of one blog environment—an environment that is mutating as you read this. It's an exciting time to be a blog publisher. Hope the following tips and pointers help, and don't forget to have some fun.

# blog tools come of age

Blogs are a fairly new phenomenon, but the concepts underlying online self-publishing and public commentary are not. In 1992, Tim Berners-Lee, godfather of the World Wide Web (see Chapter 3, "Blogs as Linkfests"), first published *What's New*, a webpage that tracked early websites as they came online. At the time, Berners-Lee still envisioned a Web populated with pages that anyone could as easily edit as read, but websites were already devolving into a largely read-only environment. Still, updates to his *What's New* page generated a great deal of dialogue in email and on BBSs (electronic bulletin boards).

The new websites were mostly hand-coded by their creators using HTML (HyperText Markup Language), which Berners-Lee had developed while a researcher at the European particle physics lab at CERN. Most of these early pages were built by academics or individuals in government research. By 1994, a few ordinary humans were beginning to try their hand at HTML. Among these was college student Justin Hall. Hall's phenomenally popular online diary (see Chapter 4, "Blogs as Diaries") had attracted so many fans wanting to emulate his public saga that he began traveling the land, teaching anyone who would put him up to code their own pages. HTML wasn't that hard, Hall preached, but many remained intimidated, and some who had launched early electronic homesteads abandoned their pages when managing an entire website became more complicated and time-consuming than they'd hoped. A slew of commercial web authoring applications hit the market (Adobe SiteMill and PageMill, SoftQuad HoTMetaL, Claris Homepage, Microsoft FrontPage, Macromedia Dreamweaver, and Adobe GoLive, for instance), but the skills necessary to creating web pages that are graceful, easy to navigate, and that behave themselves across operating systems was still restricted to the few.

1999 turned out to be a watershed year for aspiring web publishers, particularly those emulating Hall's online diary and Berners-Lee's lists of annotated links, by then known as *weblogs*. The year started quietly. In January 1999, Jesse James Garrett published a list of the 23 then-known weblogs on his Infosift (jjg.net/retired/infosift) website, and by spring,

Peter Merholz had shortened weblog to *blog* on his site (peterme.com), but the total number of bloggers was still modest.

With summer, the first publicly available blog tools launched. The first was the brainchild of Andrew Smales, a Toronto programmer who released Pitas (pitas.com), the tagline of which still boasts, "The fresh, healthy, delicious home of free, easy to update, weblogs, newslogs, all that junk." Soon after, San Franciscans Evan Williams and Meg Hourihan released Blogger (blogger.com), a free, easy-to-use blog authoring environment that became so popular that in 2003 Google snapped it up.

An avalanche of blog authoring tools soon followed. Many were originally built to suit the specific needs of the software's creator, but thanks to open standards and a culture in which developers solicited input from pioneering and visionary users, the tools and services evolved quickly, adapting to the needs and interests of a larger and more general audience.

# authoring blogs: blog software features

Today, blog authoring software streamlines the creation of blog pages and comes complete with a bevy of blog-specific options. Not every package has every feature, and not all bloggers need all the features. Choosing the right tool for your needs is important, because although switching blog solutions is much easier today than it was even a year ago, it's still a tedious process, and you could lose loyal readers along the way. It pays to arm yourself with a checklist of the features you feel you can't live without and then match it against available authoring solutions. Among the most popular features are the following:

**web interface** All of the most popular blog authoring solutions enable authors to compose and post their blog entries from within a web browser window, allowing bloggers to administer their blogs using any computer connected to the Internet.

**reverse chronology** Almost all blogs post newest entries at the top of the main blog page, with date- and time-stamps clearly marking when they were posted. Earlier entries automatically move from the blog's front page to chronological and/or categorical archives.

**permalinks** Blog software generally assigns a unique URL to each blog entry, making it simple for your readers to link to individual posts once they scroll off the main page. Ideally, you should be able to tweak the resulting URLs so that they are descriptive and in plain language, without database gibberish such as ampersands and question marks.

**trackback** Built-in mechanisms simplify the process of notifying other bloggers that discussions about topics on their blogs are continuing on your own.

**comments** Ideally, blog software should allow you to choose whether to open reader comments to everyone, only to those who register, or only to designated readers.

**comment spam** To mitigate inevitable comment spam, blog software should allow you to moderate comments—holding them in a queue for review before going live, for instance. None of your readers should have to see comments that are nothing but links to gambling or drug sales sites.

**pings** We can search blogs in real-time because each time we post, most blog software sends tiny digital messages called "pings" to servers used by blog search engines. This allows the blog search engines to index your new content almost as soon as it's posted. Ideally, you should be able to customize the list of sites pinged.

**wysiwyg editor** As you type your blog post into the browser window in just about any blog authoring software, you may add bits of HTML code to the body of your text to do things like create links to other web pages or to make a few words bold or italic. Many of the blog software solutions are beginning to add WYSIWYG (what you see is what you get) editing environments that make it easier to preview posts before going live.

**design customization** Simpler blog software solutions limit design options to a few standard templates, while more robust applications allow both sophisticated third-party templates and the ability to fully personalize a blog's look-and-feel using mechanisms like CSS stylesheets.

**newsfeeds** Options for generating newsfeeds will ideally include various RSS and Atom formats (see "Syndicating Blogs" later in this chapter), as well as allowing authors to choose whether to syndicate full text, excerpts, or summaries of their posts. In the best cases, blog authoring software facilitates autodetection of the resulting feeds by subscribers' news aggregators.

**search** Visitors should be able to search your blog content. Some blog software restricts searches to blog posts only; some include searches of static pages, such as those containing biographies and reference pages.

**categories/tags** Blog software that allows you to label individual entries with descriptive tags makes it that much easier for visitors to find entries of greatest interest. Plus, potential visitors using search engines that track tags will be more likely to find your posts.

**domain names** Blog software on hosting services should allow you to use your own domain name (*yourblogname.com*), rather than forcing a hosted domain (*yourblogname.blogservice.com*, for instance). This is important for establishing an identity, but it also ensures portability should you decide to change hosting environments in the future.

**multiple authors** For blogs with more than one author, the administration interface should make it simple to assign various levels of permissions and to include the author's name with each post.

**privacy** Blog software may provide a variety of privacy options for setting permissions for authors, readers, and those who comment.

**multimedia** If you plan to showcase media files like photos, video files, or audio podcasts, the software should provide a simple interface for uploading, displaying, and managing the files.

**moblogging** Some blog software allows authors to post text entries, photos, and audio files from cell phones and other mobile devices.

**blogroll** Many bloggers provide a list of links to other blogs they believe will be of interest to their own readers. Blog software should make these lists easy to maintain.

**static pages** It can valuable to create static web pages for biographies, contact information, and reference texts, but not all blog software solutions accommodate this.

**support** Responsive technical support by phone and email should be part of any paid blog software solution. Free solutions generally don't provide official support, but the best boast very active community forums in which fellow bloggers gladly answer questions and provide solutions.

**localization** Some blog software options facilitate publishing in more than one language, an imperative if you plan to present content in multiple languages.

**extensibility** No matter how full-bodied the feature set of a blog solution, those that are open source and that attract third-party developers will ensure ongoing access to useful plugins, templates, and other add-ons as blogging evolves.

**referral logs** Server logs record facts such as the number of visitors, which browsers they used, as well as the search terms and links they used to find your blog. These can be part of your blog software solution or your web server software package.

# mapping blog authoring tools

Once you have a checklist with the features most important to you, you're ready to begin assessing the blog software field. Two main questions will help to focus your attention. One, do you want a solution that lives on a blog host's server, or would you prefer a standalone software package that you install on a server of your own choosing? Two, are you willing to pay modest monthly fees, or do you prefer one of the many free solutions?

## hosted blogs v. standalone applications

Hosted blogs are the easiest way to jump into bloggish waters. All the necessary software and all your posts and reader comments reside on centralized blog servers controlled by the hosting service. After a simple browser-based setup sequence, you log in to your blog authoring web page, start typing, hit the Submit button, and your blog is live. The advantage of hosted blogs is largely ease of launch and general maintenance—tasks like backup and upgrades are handled by the hosting service. For those with little time or little prior technical experience, these can be a godsend.

The alternate solution is not unlike that used by anyone launching a traditional website. You install the blog software on either your own server or on a commercial web host's server. (Many web hosts now offer pre-installed blog software.) Installing it yourself is generally fairly simple. The main advantage in hosting your own blog is greater access to customization tools, plugins, and other third-party add-ons that extend functionality.

## free tools vs. for-a-fee blogging

Next up, a new blogger needs to decide whether to lay down a bit of hard cash or go with one of the free solutions. It's great that there are free options, since this dramatically reduces barrier to entry, and some of the free solutions are as full-bodied as any of their costlier competitors. It's good to remember that in general, free options don't come with official technical support (so check out their user forums), and some freebies generate revenue for themselves by placing ads—some more discreet than others—on your blog.

Also, if you plan to go with a free, host-your-own solution, you may have to factor in monthly web host costs, just as you would for a new website. Finally, it's good to keep in mind that just because a product is free today, this doesn't mean that it is certain to remain free forever.

## selecting blog authoring tools

The business models driving blog-related tool companies vary, but none promise any staggering profits in the near term. Many popular blog tools and services are, in fact, free for the downloading or signing in. Tools for purchase are generally very reasonably priced, with the bulk of the fee going toward future development. This is good for your pocketbook, but these kinds of ventures can sometimes leave us in a software or database backwater, without support or ongoing development. It pays to know a bit about the rationale and potential stability of the companies (or in many cases, individuals) providing the tools and services we invest the most time and effort using.

A few blog environments are owned by giants, like Blogger, from Google, and MySpace (myspace.com), from News Corp., but for the most part, blog software is written and distributed by aficionados, programmers, and designers who develop tools to suit their own individual needs and whims. Even Six Apart, Ltd. (sixapart.com), the San Francisco company that distributes several of the more notable commercial blog software solutions, began in 2001 when Ben Trott wrote Movable Type to help his wife, Mena, publish her weblog. Some popular blog software options, such as WordPress.org and WordPress.com, are the outgrowth of an open software movement that attracts thousands of developers all willing to improve the tool, offer support, and craft custom solutions.

What follows are a few recommendations based on various real-life criteria. Keep in mind that blog software is evolving at a rapid pace. I'll provide occasional updates on dispatchesfromblogistan.com, but it's always a good idea to do a few web searches on any new products you're thinking of trying. Read reviews of the newest versions. Visit the discussion forums that grow up around some of the more popular solutions. You can learn a lot about a product's best and worst points by lurking and reading through recent topics on these forums.

## free, hosted solutions

**Blogger** (blogger.com) The granddaddy of free, hosted blog solutions, Blogger's been part of the Google family since 2003. It is an obvious choice for those who just want to get online fast, at no cost, and who are not fanatical about customized design or niceties like built-in, categorical tags. The blogs do come with a few text ads on blog pages and spammers have tainted the brand somewhat, but Blogger remains a popular choice for those wishing to launch a blog with the least effort and expense. URLs for Blogger sites generally look something like http://www.yourdomainname. blogspot.com, although there are workarounds for pointing to your own domain name.

**WordPress.com** (wordpress.com) Launched late 2005 as a hosted version of the venerable standalone solution at Wordpress.org (see below), WordPress.com boasts many of the features of its popular open source cousin, but bear in mind that in this hosted version design customization is currently limited. It's possible that a fuller-featured version will be available for a fee at some point in the future.

**Blogsome** (blogsome.com) Blogsome has been offering a free hosted service for WordPress.org software for some time and has a faithful community of users. Advertising appears on the hosted blog pages, but the terms of service (TOS) say that you may remove them. An active user community provides useful technical support.

**LiveJournal and MySpace** (livejournal.com) (myspace.com) San Francisco-based Six Apart purchased LiveJournal at the beginning of 2005 and by summer, Rupert Murdoch's News Corp. had snapped up MySpace. Both provide free, hosted blogging within established networks of users. In keeping with the overt community feel, both offer robust privacy options for those wishing to restrict access to their blog content. Both skew toward younger participants, with girls making up the majority of LiveJournal users. Interestingly, many Russian blogs reside on LiveJournal servers, as well. MySpace is the largest of the social networking sites, with more than 50 million users counted in early 2006.

**MSN Spaces and Yahoo 360** (spaces.msn.com) (360.yahoo.com) Both of these solutions offer free blog tools that are integrated within larger toolsets, including mail, instant messaging, address books, and shared photo collections. Some fault Yahoo 360 for pushing related Yahoo services too hard within the blog environment. Others point out that MSN Spaces' terms of service claim the right to use and republish any content you post to your blogs there and that the company censors blog names (those seven dirty words). Still, both are reliable options that aren't likely to go away.

## free, standalone solutions

**WordPress.org** (wordpress.org) WordPress boasts hundreds of thousands of downloads. Installation is a snap, the default tools are robust, and there are thousands of free design templates, called themes. It is this freedom to customize and to add third-party plugins that draws so many to the open-source solution. The large and active user base keeps user forums lively with advice and critiques. Spam controls are among the best in blog-dom. Dispatchesfromblogistan.com runs on WordPress.org software.

**Movable Type** (sixapart.com/movabletype) Movable Type from Six Apart offers an entry-level product that is free. Installation is a little trickier than with WordPress, and updating blog pages requires rebuild-ing the files on the server, which can slow your blog down a bit, but the product inherits many rich features from its pricier cousin (see below) and an avid user base makes up for the lack of official technical support for the free version.

**Textpattern** (textpattern.com) Textpattern is another well-designed free application that powers some elegant blog designs. The product special-izes in—surprise—controlling the formatting and display of text.

## for-a-fee, hosted solutions

**Typepad** (sixapart.com/typepad) Another Six Apart offering, Typepad owns the market for blog-specific solutions that are hosted for a modest fee. It comes in three versions, ranging in price from $5 to $15 dollars a month, each with most of the features deemed mission critical. At the time of this writing, blog search is still lacking, as are the abilities to cre-ate non-blog pages or require registration for comments. The top level, TypePad Pro, allows for multiple authors and individual user levels. Design customization is somewhat limited, but there are some handsome templates among those available. One of the best features is the ability to paste Rich Text content into the blog editor fields and have it translate to clean HTML that preserves links. There's a 30-day free trial period for those wishing to take a test run. Overall, Typepad is a solid product that's continually updating its feature set.

**LiveJournal** (sixapart.com/livejournal) LiveJournal offers a premium ser-vice that allows users to upload a gigabyte of photo files to a ScrapBook, post from your phone, customize the design, and exchange text messages, as well as allowing you to search for users by geography, age, and other "friends." Paying users also get a livejournal.com email address and are allowed to point their LiveJournal content to their own domain name. Hosting fees range from three dollars for one month to twenty dollars for a year.

## for-a-fee, standalone solutions

**MovableType** (sixapart.com/movabletype) The original product offered by Six Apart, Movable Type is a trusted brand used by many bloggers willing to pay from $70 for software that allows an unlimited number of blogs with up to five authors each, to $200 for a full commercial product with a slew of bells and whistles. The purchase price includes technical support. In addition, an active community populates discussion forums, and there are many useful plugins. Not quite as easy to install or use as the free WordPress products, MovableType has a powerful feature set and friendly company support that still make it a contender.

**Expression Engine** (pmachine.com) This higher-end product from pMachine has been around for a while and a good number of users find its $150-200 price point justified, particularly if you plan to manage a large number of bloggers.

# syndicating blogs: creating and subscribing to newsfeeds

One of the decisions that any blog author must make these days is whether or not to enable readers to subscribe to their updated content via syndicated newsfeeds. More and more blogs sport buttons or links labeled *RSS, Atom, XML, newsfeed,* or simply *feed.* Click those links and you'll often find yourself abruptly presented with a web page full of dense, incomprehensible text. What's this all about?

First of all, newsfeeds aren't exactly new. Many of us have been subscribing to them for years, often without knowing it. If you have a personalized web page on Google, My Yahoo, or MySpace, the headlines and stories from the various news organizations you've selected arrive as newsfeeds. So do most podcasts. Additionally, newsfeeds are often used to distribute newsletters and track packages, as well as provide marketing, weather, and stock updates.

Essentially, newsfeeds are syndicated web content delivered to subscribers' news aggregators, sometimes called newsreaders, in real time.

Besides being able to subscribe to the content of blogs, many of the newer search engines allow you to subscribe to updated results of specific search queries. If you wanted to track all the blog posts that include the word "bogosity," for instance, you could conduct a search on Bloglines or Technorati and then subscribe to future search results for the term. Now, each time your newsreader updates your subscriptions, you would receive a list of links to each new blog post containing the term.

Newsfeeds offer a number of advantages over previous content delivery mechanisms. Unlike subscribing to email newsletters, for instance, new content replaces older posts in your newsreader, so you don't have to manually delete content. Remarkably—at least so far— newsfeeds are virtually spam-free. Plus, unlike traditional media syndication, where publishers make their content available for a fee to select distributors, web newsfeed publishers make their text, audio, or video content available to any who choose to subscribe and, for the most part, they charge nothing.

Newsfeeds are one of those things that at first seem mysterious and maybe even superfluous, but after a bit of exposure many readers find them indispensable—addictive, even. With very little effort, you can have the latest information on any topic delivered to your newsreader (more on this below). You can keep up with all your favorite blogs, news sources, and search terms within one easy-to-navigate environment. In a world where there is never enough time and things so often seem scattered and disparate, newsfeeds provide a fast, centralized resource.

## news aggregators on the line

Newsfeeds are generally published in XML format (eXtensible Markup Language), an extension of HTML. The messy page of dense text you see when you click a newsfeed link is raw XML code. To view the content in a more readable form, we subscribe to the feed using software programs called newsreaders or news aggregators. Then, each time new content is added to that blog or news site, the items appear in our newsreaders. In a sense, subscribing to newsfeeds allows you to program your own news and entertainment channels.

HOT LINK:
NEWS AGGREGATORS
AGGREGATED
......................................
**Wikipedia List of News
Aggregators**
http://en.wikipedia.org/
wiki/List_of_news_
aggregators

Just as with blog authoring software, news-readers come in a wide array of web-based and desktop solutions. Wikipedia maintains links to all the known news aggregators and currently lists more than a hundred! Among the variety are sixty solutions for Windows users, nine for Macintosh, and seven for Linux. In addition, most of the newer web browsers integrate news-aggregator capabilities either natively or via extensions. There are even a handful of email-based aggregators that forward subscribed newsfeeds to your usual mailbox.

All these choices are further complicated by the fact that the better news-readers are evolving at a breakneck pace. Still, if you want to take advantage of the ease and timesaving qualities that newsreaders introduce, you just have to jump on the train and ride. We'll take a look at the features distinguishing the more popular news aggregators and offer a few recommendations based on real-world concerns.

## browser-based news aggregators

Among the browser-based options, Bloglines (bloglines.com), owned by Ask.com's IAC Search and Media, and NewsGator (newsgator.com) are two of the more popular aggregators. Bloglines is free, handles audio and video files well, has a full-featured blog search, and provides useful tools for managing and analyzing feeds. You can even use a free Bloglines email address to subscribe to and read traditional email newsletters in your aggregator, rather than your email client. NewsGator offers a free consumer version that provides many of the same capabilities, as well as a paid version that allows posting from mobile phones and PDAs, and integration with Microsoft Outlook. These web-based solutions can sometimes be a bit slow, but it's convenient that you can read updates to your subscriptions using any computer connected to the Internet.

## standalone news aggregators

Some individuals, myself included, prefer news aggregators that reside on the desktop as a separate application. The downside is that you have to access your newsfeeds on the machine on which the application is installed. The advantages vary among newsfeed applications, but most are faster than the browser-based solutions and generally give you more control over organization and layout. The best allow you to combine feeds into folders, assign descriptive tags, view and listen to multimedia files, and search the body of your feeds.

Two of the more popular desktop options are FeedDemon (feeddemon. com) for Windows users and NetNewsWire from Ranchero (ranchero. com/netnewswire) for Macintosh users. FeedDemon requires a $29.95 purchase fee, but it comes pre-populated with dozens of feeds (any of which you can delete, of course), has a clean and intuitive layout with a built-in tabbed browser, and allows you to store items for future reference. NetNewsWire offers a free version and another that costs $29.95. Both are fast, clean, and straightforward. The paid version includes search, the ability to store items, tag subscriptions with descriptive labels, and allows scripting and podcast downloads.

## and yet more news aggregators

Some aggregators aren't obvious at first. For instance, iTunes acts as an aggregator for podcasts. Also, some newer web browsers, such as Mozilla's Firefox and Apple's Safari, automatically detect newsfeeds when visiting websites and have aggregators built in for easy subscribing and reading.

# subscribing made easy

Once you've chosen a news aggregator, you're ready to begin subscribing. In an ideal world, when you click a feed link on a site to which you would like to subscribe, your aggregator would autodetect the correct URL for the feed and, you'd be subscribed, but you may need to coax the subscription process along.

The next time you'd like to subscribe to a newsfeed, find the link on the blog page. It will generally be labeled something like XML or RSS or Feed, although it could say Atom, Subscribe, or even Syndicated Content.

If you click the newsfeed link, it should take you to either that dense page of code or to a customized page on a newsfeed service like FeedBurner (more on this shortly). In either case, what you want is the URL at the top of the browser window. Use your cursor to copy the URL. In your news-reader, choose the menu item that sounds most like "New Subscriptions." In some cases, the copied URL will automatically appear in the subscription address space. If not, paste it into the appropriate box, click Subscribe or OK, and syndicated items should start pouring into your aggregator.

Occasionally, you may want to move a whole set of subscriptions from one aggregator to another. The easiest way to do this is to export the selected newsfeeds as an OPML (Outline Processor Markup Language) file and then import that file into your preferred aggregator.

Newsfeeds are one of those things that you might think sound silly or too much work until you start using them. While working on this book, I'm tracking more than three hundred blogs. Obviously, I can't read every blog every day, but my news aggregator allows me to organize my feeds into categorical folders. Whenever I tell my aggregator to refresh my subscriptions, I can easily click on the feeds and then the individual posts I'd like to read. A simple double-click opens to the actual web page, but I find that I do much of my reading right in the newsreader. I appreciate not having to jump back and forth from my browser bookmarks to the websites I'm tracking. Plus, I don't have to wait for the web page to load unless I actively choose to visit the site. Overall, newsfeeds can be a great boon for those wishing to save time and avoid spam.

## publishing newsfeeds, podcasts, and video feeds

Options for syndicating content will generally include a title for your feed (you can't go wrong with the title of your blog); whether you wish to publish the full text of your blog entries or excerpts; and how many posts you'd like included in your newsfeeds. Once you're satisfied, your blog

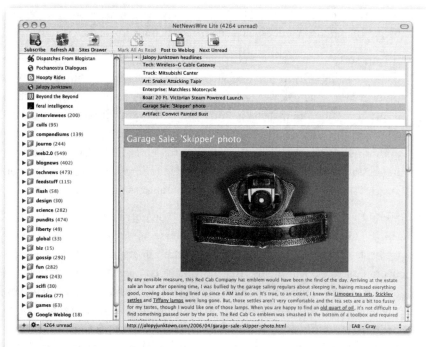

## Newsreader At a Glance

News aggregators like NetNewsWire (pictured here) display newsfeeds in a three-frame window, making it simple to keep up with your syndicated content. As you subscribe to blogs and other XML-enabled services, the names of the newsfeeds appear in the lefthand frame. The most recent headlines for the newsfeed highlighted on the left are listed in the top frame on the right, with images and body text or excerpt of the newsfeed (the choice is up to the author) filling the bottom frame below it. The ability to group newsfeeds in folders makes navigating large numbers of newsfeeds much simpler. Double-clicking the subscription title in the left column opens the front page of the blog or news service in your preferred browser, while double-clicking a live link in the upper right window takes you to the permalinked page for that item. Clicking a live link within an excerpt or full text opens the designated web page.

software will generate the URL for your newsfeed, usually something like http://dispatchesfromblogistan.com/feed. That's it. You're a syndicator.

If your software doesn't support newsfeeds, or even it if does, you might consider using a third-party service like FeedBurner (feedburner.com) to publish your feeds. The reason FeedBurner is currently managing more than a quarter million newsfeeds is fairly straightforward: It provides accurate counts of the number of subscribers, something difficult to do in most blog authoring environments. There are always tradeoffs. In this case you balance better statistics against the fact that a newsfeed address based on feedburner. com or the like can be confusing to some potential subscribers.

Should you publish the full text of your blog entries or a truncated version? This is a hotly debated point. Those in favor of summaries or excerpts often want subscribers to view their posts in the context of their overall blog environment, trusting that their newsfeed headlines and teasers will convince subscribers to click through and read the full text on the blog itself. They also hope to foil unscrupulous sorts who subscribe to newsfeeds and then republish the content on their own sites, sometimes called *splogs*, collecting advertising revenues from contextual ads placed against the purloined content.

**HOT LINKS: PODCASTING TIPS**

**Podcasting Tips from Engadget**
http://engadget.com/2004/10/05/engadget-podcast-001-10-05-2004-how-to-podcasting-get

**Podcasting—The Basics**
http://performancing.com/node/1236

Those in favor of publishing full-text newsfeeds argue that what matters most is what you have to say, not how pretty your pages look, and that any distribution is good distribution. They also point out that with more and more people using news aggregators to keep up with blogs, publishing full text is much friendlier. Even more convincing, a number of the most popular blog search engines index the content of newsfeeds rather than a blog's pages, so if you want your entire posts to be included in their searches, you must publish full-text feeds.

For those wishing to up the ante and begin syndicating audio podcasts or video newsfeeds, it's good to know that most blog authoring software makes it fairly easy. For podcasts, within the blog administration interface, you select an .mp3 file, upload it to your blog server, name it, and tell your blog software to include a bit of code in your blog file to enable the link. The technology is always changing, but luckily there are helpful folks willing to offer a hand-up to those behind them.

Video bloggers, sometimes called *vloggers*, often use either Windows MovieMaker, which comes free with Windows, or Apple iMovie, which is part of the $79 Macintosh iLife package, to prepare their files. Some choose to upload their videos to special server environments like Vimeo (vimeo.com), vSocial (vsocial.com), or the phenomenally popular YouTube (youtube.com). The servers are optimized for video display and individuals can apply descriptive labels, commonly called *tags*, to their videos, making finding visual content much easier.

### What Does RSS Stand For?

Web veterans with the longest memories say RSS stands for RDF Site Summaries. RDF, in turn, stands for Resource Description Framework, a geeky Web specification published in 1997 that allows bits of descriptive text called metadata to accompany files sent over the Internet. RDF metadata can include elements such as headline, author name, and excerpts or full texts. One might call these—you guessed it—Site Summaries. Hence, the RDF Site Summaries.

Most bloggers, however, will assure you that RSS stands for Rich Site Summary. Or, perhaps, Really Simple Syndication. Or sometimes even, Rich Site Syndication. Given the confusion surrounding the acronym, it perhaps won't come as a surprise that there are seven—count them, seven—versions of RSS in use today. The first was released by Netscape in 1999, some of the middle versions were subsequently released by Userland Software, and a quasi-final version 2.0 is currently distributed under a Creative Commons license by the Berkman Center for Internet and Society at Harvard Law School. There are no official plans to update RSS 2.0, and so we are beginning to see alternate protocols for distributing newsfeeds, the most prominent being Atom, which is based on a specification authored by the Atompub Working Group within the Internet Engineering Task Force (IETF), the same body that oversees protocols for the World Wide Web. It's hard to tell which protocol will survive, but for most subscribers the differences are transparent since the aggregators generally recognize all the most popular versions. The protocol may continue to fork and evolve, but syndication remains one of the best tools in a blogger's kit.

# searching blogs: old and new search engines compared

From a technical standpoint, one of the main differences between a traditional website and a blog is that blog software is configured to send *pings*—bits of identifying code—to blog-specific servers each time an author posts new content. Several new search engines monitor these pings, allowing them to index blog content in close to real time. This timeliness is critical to the millions of spontaneous conversations taking place across blogs.

In general, traditional search engines like Google (google.com), Yahoo (yahoo.com), MSN (msn.com), and Ask (ask.com) gather their information by sending out small software programs, sometimes called *spiders* or *bots*. These spiders make regular rounds of the millions of pages on the web, collecting new URLs and changes to older pages, and then beaming the information back to the search engines' servers for indexing and ranking. The truth is, most bloggers find these engines to be downright laggardly; most web pages don't change very often, and it is sometimes weeks or even months before a spider revisits a website.

Traditional search engines do poll a handful of sites more often. Major web pages that display news, weather, stocks, and sports are sometimes visited every fifteen minutes, for instance. But these are exceptions, and bloggers who post daily or even hourly are understandably unhappy with the lag between when an entry appears on their blog and when a link to the entry appears on the big search engines' results pages.

Compare this to the blog search engines. Just as Google and Yahoo began as small, innovative ventures that successfully filled a void, new engines like Technorati (technorati.com), BlogPulse (blogpulse.com), Feedster (feedster.com), PubSub (pubsub.com), and IceRocket (icerocket.com) are quickly gaining momentum. Ari Paparo maintains a constantly updated list that includes links to several dozen contenders.

None of these new search engines are as good at calculating relevance as the big boys, but they can compete because they greatly reduce the time lag between when an article is posted and when it shows up in their blog search results. Some, like Technorati and BlogPulse, take advantage of the pings that your blog software sends every time you post a new article. Others, like Feedster, PubSub, and Blog Search (blogsearch.google.com) index and search the content of your newsfeeds, rather than the content on your blog pages.

> **HOT LINK: BLOG SEARCH ENGINE RESOURCE**
>
> **Ari Paparo's Big List of Blog Search Engines**
> http://aripaparo.com/archive/000632.html

Blog search engines begin to solve the timeliness problem, but not without running into a few speed bumps of their own. Some of the new search engines are proving so popular that they often exceed their server and bandwidth capacities, slowing down indexing and search and yielding erratic results. In addition, spam blogs, or *splogs*, sometimes clog the system. And increasingly, bloggers complain that the results pages generated by the blog search engines favor blogs and news resources that are already well known, decreasing opportunities for newcomers to be noticed.

## search engine ranking explored

How search engines rank results has always been a sore point. Traditional search engines like Google and Yahoo use sophisticated equations, called *ranking algorithms*, to determine the order for results. The algorithms are closely kept secrets, but by analyzing search results and carefully reading patents, web analysts have learned a bit about how they weigh results. They tell us that traditional search engines gauge the relevance of a web page by calculating the frequency with which content is updated and the placement of keywords (see Chapter 9 and 11 for specifics on keyword placement). In addition, they value older websites over newer ones. They penalize websites that engage in bad practices (more on this in a bit). And last, but far from least, they count *inbound links*—the number of other websites linking to a page.

The newer blog-specific search engines use less refined ranking tools. Technorati, for example, calculates its Top 100 solely on the basis of a count of inbound links. Critics complain that the resulting lists of Top 100 or even

Top 500 blogs published by the larger blog search sites skew heavily toward general interest blogs because they attract the greatest number of inbound links. (See Chapter 11, "Promoting Your Blog" for more insight on this problem.) More and more bloggers are asking when search results will better address the interests of less mainstream bloggers. Some forward thinkers suggest incorporating the ability to calculate the number of comments, topic frequency within a blog, and indirect mentions on other blogs.

All this said, keeping track of the lively conversations taking place within and across blogs would be impossible without the timeliness introduced by these new search engines. Some, like Technorati, PubSub, and Bloglines even let you subscribe to ongoing results for specific search terms. BlogPulse distinguishes itself by providing graphing tools for tracking trends and a Conversation Tracker that gathers related posts into threaded conversations. The new blog search engines are in mad competition as they add new features and tools, continually improving our chances of finding relevant blog entries.

Useful as these blog-specific search engines are, their results vary widely, so when conducting important searches, you may want to use more than one. In Chapter 11, "Promoting Your Blog," we'll take a closer look at what steps bloggers can take to raise their ranking on search engines, along with other tips and tricks for attracting visitors to your blog. Chapter 13, "Social Networks on the Rise," discusses innovative new services, sometimes called *memetrackers*, that rank entries according to readers' votes.

# tagging blogs: folksonomies aid discovery

Technorati currently reports that nearly 50,000 new blog entries are being published every *hour*. How do we hope to find the gems amidst all that glut? How can we hope that our own pages will ever be found? Search engines optimized for the real-time nature of blogging are critical to a sense of engagement, but finding blog entries of personal interest is still ridiculously hard.

Search engines often feel like slot machines. We plug in a word or three, cross our fingers, and hope that a relevant link pops to the top of the results page. If none does, we may turn to hierarchical listings like the Yahoo Directory (dir.yahoo.com), or more blog-specific catalogues like Blogwise (blogwise.com) or Bloghub (bloghub.com). Hunting for blogs listed under logically organized, topical headings definitely facilitates discovery, but the truth is that human editors can review and categorize only so many pages, and with petabytes of content coming online, these kinds of top-down directories can never hope to be all-inclusive.

Enter *folksonomies*, bottom-up categorization strategies that rely on individuals like you and me, rather than trained professionals like librarians, to decide which descriptors, commonly called *tags*, to apply to any given blog entry, uploaded photo, or webpage bookmark.

Tagging began in 2001 when Joshua Schachter took a few moments from his day job as a programmer at a large Wall Street firm to write an application that would help him keep track of his browser bookmarks. The idea was simple. He could assign descriptive labels, as many as he liked, to any webpage, greatly easing subsequent retrieval. Not long after, he began allowing others to share their own tags and "social bookmarking" was born. He called the resulting service del.icio.us. Yes, that's the entire URL (http://del.icio.us).

Not long after, the photo-sharing website Flickr (flickr.com) introduced tagging to its own service, greatly enhancing the ability of its users to categorize and find not only labeled images, but communities of like-minded others. By the time the blog search engine Technorati (technorati.com) began tracking tags for individual blog posts in early 2005, tagging as a peer classification system was well on its way to giving hierarchical taxonomies like the Dewey Decimal System and the Yellow Pages a run for their money.

We'll talk more about the good and bad points of hierarchical and free-form classification systems in Chapter 13, "Social Networks on the Rise," but the bottom line is that even with its inevitable inconsistencies, blog tagging has proven immensely successful. Technorati currently tracks more than six million tags, encompassing everything from "art" to "zoos" and "earthday" to "punkrock."

# tagging made practical

As a tool in a blogger's kit, more and more bloggers are finding tagging indispensable. With just a few keystrokes, you can assign as many descriptors to your new blog post as you like, making it much easier for your visitors to find entries of interest. Plus, assigning the labels allows those searching tags on Technorati, del.icio.us, and the numerous other tag-tracking services to find your pages more easily. You could even make a new friend or become part of an affinity group as a consequence of common naming schemes.

Many blog authoring solutions—Movable Type, WordPress, and TypePad, among them—include tags in their basic feature sets, sometimes calling them "categories." Even if you use a product like Blogger that doesn't currently support tags, you can add the following bit of code to the body of your posts and when your software pings search services or syndicates your feed, your tags will be counted:

```
< a href="http://technorati.com/tag/tagname"
rel="tag">tagname</a>
```

Technically, tags are a "reltag microformat," but don't let the jargon scare you. In truth, you wouldn't need to link to Technorati in the above example. To have your tags tracked, you could link to any website, even your own blog, as long as the code includes the rel="tag" bit, but most blog software is already configured to ping Technorati's servers, and so the code above is a safe bet for getting counted if your blog software doesn't natively include tagging capabilities.

For those doing searches on tags, it's worth noting that blog search engines like Technorati and IceRocket, along with the new tag-specific search engine Wink (wink.com), not only let you explore all the posts tagged with a given label, they once again allow you to subscribe to a newsfeed that includes all future posts containing the tag. This can be a real boon when trying to keep up on a hot topic of interest.

One other tag trick is sometimes called *meblogging*. If you post to several blogs, but would sometimes like to see all of your posts on a single page, create a unique tag and apply it to all your posts—xyzzz, for instance. Then you can search for posts using the unique tag on Technorati or IceRocket, or even have a newsfeed with the new posts sent to your newsreader.

We'll discuss some tactics for choosing the best tag terms in Chapter 10, "Writing that Engages," and look at tricks for using tags to help let others know about your blog entries in Chapter 11, "Promoting Your Blog."

# monetizing blogs: making them pay

There are occasional stories that claim some bloggers are making millions of dollars by allowing contextual ads to appear on their pages. Your probable first instinct—that this is bunk—is, for the most part, correct.

Certainly there are a few blogs that claim to be generating that kind of income, but these are pages that can count millions of regular visitors and that require entire staffs working to keep the pages popular. Still, there are bloggers managing to find ways to at least support their blogging habits. How do they do it?

## contextual advertising programs

The most common money-maker for bloggers is contextual advertising. If you come across a boxed advertisement, often text-only, at the top or side of a blog page that interests you and you click on that ad, the blogger receives payment from whomever is serving the ad. If you sign your own blog up with one of the enabling services, it's possible that you might find at least nickels entering your coffers.

Once again, Google rules the roost, this time with its AdSense program (google.com/adsense). AdSense complements the Google AdWords program in which potential advertisers place bids on search keywords, with highest bidders' ads appearing on search results pages for the keywords. (See Chapter 11, "Promoting Your Blog" for more on this topic.)

**HOT LINKS:
CONTEXTUAL
ADVERTISING
RESOURCES**

**Blog Advertising
Directory**
http://www.econsultant.
com/lists/top-10-
advertising-networks

**39 Google AdSense
Alternatives**
http://www.google.com/
support/adsense/bin/
answer.py?answer=20957

**AdYack Online Ad
Networks Discussions**
http://www.adyack.com/
index.php

**Google AdSense
Tutorials**
https://www.google.
com/support/adsense/bin/
answer.py?answer=20957

**Yahoo's View Bids Tool**
http://uv.bidtool.overture.
com/d/search/tools/
bidtool/index.jhtml?
Keywords=blogging+
book&mkt=us&lang=en_
US&Partner=userbidtool

Signing up for the AdSense program is simple. You fill out a form with contact and login information, as well as your blog's URL. You choose whether or not to include a Google search box on the pages, and you agree to basic terms of service (among the terms, no clicking on your own ads, no incentives for clicking, and no porn or illegal content on the pages). Click Submit and you are presented with a bit of code that you insert in the HTML of your pages. Ads that Google's engines determine are related to your content begin appearing on your pages.

It's difficult to gauge how much you might earn in advance, partly because it depends on how much an advertiser is willing to pay to appear on pages like yours. Also, there is, once again, a great deal of imposed secrecy surrounding contextual ads. AdSense's constantly evolving terms of service consistently state that publishers may disclose gross revenues, but no other statistics or specifics. (It's your responsibility to keep up with the changes.)

AdSense is the gorilla in the contextual advertising jungle but not your only choice. Yahoo and MSN are both conducting closed beta trials for competing services and there are several dozen other contenders, among them AddBrite (adbrite.com), Chitika (chitika.com), and Burst Media (burstmedia.com). Most work on a cost-per-click (CPC) model, but some, like Amazon, calculate revenues based on a cost-per-acquisition (CPA) basis, while still others rely on a cost-per-thousand (CPM) model (M being the Roman numeral for 1000).

## contextual advertising caveats

Contextual ads may well be in keeping with the tone of your blog, and some of your readers may even be grateful for pointers to products and services related to the topic of the blog; but not all blog audiences take kindly to seeing ads on blog pages, and some curtail their visits if the ads conflict with the perceived intent of the blog. To test the temper of their audience, some bloggers poll their readers before or after including ads.

Just as advertisers in magazines and newspapers adopt a look-and-feel that sets them apart, contextual ads stand out on a page. This is good for potential clicks, bad for overall aesthetic. Most ad programs do allow at least some customization of color scheme, aspect ratio of the ads, and their placement on the page.

And then there's click fraud. One variety sees bloggers clicking on the ads placed on their own websites in order to up the click-through rate and their revenues. Google and the other ad programs police this activity carefully and will ban anyone it catches from the program, as well as their search results. Another type of click fraud involves clicking repeatedly on competitor's ads, decreasing the chance that actual potential customers see the ads, since the advertisers are paying by the click and generally have set monthly budgets.

# private ad networks

Blogs with stable audiences in viable niches sometimes court their own stable of advertisers. This can be lucrative in the right categories, but the number of blogs doing well selling their own ads is small and the upkeep required makes it a chore most would rather avoid.

# affiliate programs

Again, if you're in the right narrow category, you may be able to contract to sell the products or services of others. The Amazon Associates program boasts more than a million members world-wide, each of whom displays specially formatted links to specific products that allow Amazon to track sales and kick back up to 8.5 percent in quarterly referral fees. If there are businesses in your sector that sell products or services you believe your readers would appreciate, you can sometimes broker private deals that accomplish much the same purpose.

## shopping carts

If you offer a product or services that you'd like to be able to sell directly to your audience, you might want to provide purchase opportunities on your blog pages. Options for shopping carts are always evolving, but most of the more commonly used blog authoring software solutions have links to extensions or plug-ins that provide fairly simple and secure shopping carts.

A few blogs, primarily the best-known ones, offer branded products—t-shirts, mugs, bumper stickers, and the like. As more musicians, artists, and published authors begin blogging, the opportunities for these kinds of sales are expanding.

## influence

A blog doesn't have to generate cash directly to help fatten your pocketbook. If you are an expert in a field, your blog posts may result in professional contracts, speaking engagements, book sales, and, perhaps, job offers. A compelling bio on your blog can go a long way toward furthering these goals.

## revenue realities

The truth is that few bloggers make much if any money blogging. That's not what's fueling the millions of individuals launching and maintaining blogs around the world. This is not to say that wise implementation and exact targeting won't earn you a little cash, but it makes sense to approach blog revenue models with realistic expectations.

# keeping the toolkit tidy and up-to-date

Phew. If you've made it this far, you're well on your way to packing a blogger's toolkit that suits your needs and is full of useful and well-coordinated tools. This chapter will serve as a reference for current and future tool choices, but keep in mind that the blogosphere is a constantly changing environment. Watch dispatchesfromblogistan.com for updates on the newest advances in blogging technology. Occasionally check in with the support forums for the tools you choose and for any you might consider switching to. Fellow bloggers provide invaluable feedback and commentary on the newest trends in blogging. If you're still undecided about which tools and features you believe will suit you best, the next chapter steps through a typical blog page and shows how each of the features mentioned in this chapter fit together. Armed with the information in these two chapters, you'll be ready to launch a blog that makes you proud.

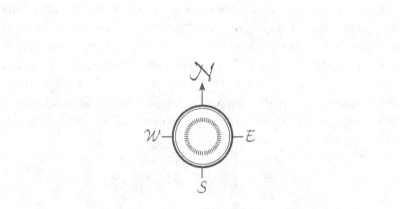

# anatomy of a blog page

The earliest blog pages were simple. Barely formatted entries were presented in reverse chronological order and may or may not have included a date stamp. Over time, blogs have evolved to reflect the complexities of their authors, incorporating any number of page elements, some of them downright mysterious to newcomers. Today, a typical blog entry generally includes a headline; date and time stamps; the author's name if it's a group blog; links to reader comments; a permalink; and a trackback URL. Photos, video, and audio elements are common, as well.

In addition to individual posts with any or all of the above elements, blogs often sport search boxes, links to newsfeeds, collections of past posts in weekly or monthly archives, categorical archives, blogrolls, links to recent or featured discussions about a post, blog statistics, polls, a calendar, a shopping cart, and even ads. Increasingly, blogs also include links to static pages containing biographical or reference information.

In this chapter, we'll look at various potential page items and provide explanations, tips, and pointers that will help you create pages that suit your purposes, attract readers, and are relatively simple to maintain. (See "Blog Page Dissected" at the end of this chapter, which illustrates the elements on a typical blog page.)

# craft a clear identity

First impressions still matter. Many excellent blogs fail to find readerships because the title of the blog is vague, tedious, cutesy, or even misleading. The title of your blog—the text that appears in the top bar of the browser window—is essentially your brand and can help to set your blog apart and attract readers. Choosing a name that tells potential readers what they might expect to find does more than increase the chance that they will click when they come across your blog in web searches or links from other blogs; a title with recognizable keywords will convince search engines to place your blog higher on their ranking pages. "Joe's Daily News" may help your grandmother find your blog among her bookmarks, but "The Drunken Poet's Blog" is more likely to win readers among both oenophile and aspiring bard circles.

## own your own domain name

Domain names cost less than a good hamburger these days. The two best arguments for purchasing one for your blog are credibility and stability. If you house your blog in a subdirectory of a traditional website, your address might be something like http://www.yourmainwebsite.com/blog, which can be cumbersome and not that memorable.

Even more importantly, if you start out using a blog hosting service (more on this in the previous chapter), your default web address might be something like http://yourblogname.typepad.com. If, at a later date, you change blog hosts or decide to house the blog on your own server, all your associated blog web addresses (main domain, permalinks, and newsfeed, for instance) will break.

By starting out with a unique web address for your blog, you ensure that faithful readers continue to find you no matter where the blog is housed and that your links remain valid. This doesn't mean you can't use blog hosts like Typepad or Blogger, of course, since almost all hosting services allow you to point your blog at your own domain name.

# tell your readers who you are

Blogs inevitably reveal a great deal about their authors—their tastes, opinions, and spelling quirks, for instance. It might seem superfluous to specifically point to biographies or other "about" files, and many bloggers choose not to, but a bio can be a useful way to offer readers a window onto your background and intent. Without face-to-face contact (often written as *f2f* in blogs and other online environments), we are deprived of the gestures, intonations, and subtleties that help us to gauge honesty and humor. A bio not only helps to build trust, the simple act of writing a bio can help an author to refine his or her purpose and set the tone for the rest of the blog.

If you do post a bio, it's probably best to write something specifically for the blog. Bios ported over from work resumes may seem stilted. A hastily updated bio originally written a decade or more ago might seem out of date. The best online biographies speak in the voice of the author, mixing personal notes with professional information. A dash of humor never hurts. As in all blog writing, brevity increases the chance that your readers stick with you to the end.

## photos for those who dare

Some bloggers can't wait to post a photo of themselves. Others dread even the thought. Providing a visual image can make your blog more personal. The fact that you are not a kid or that you have bright blue hair may provide context for some of your commentary. This is purely an individual choice. One option photo-phobes may want to consider is a line drawing or a caricature. If you decide to put up an image, don't forget to compress the file so that it doesn't slow the display of your page.

## aim for a graceful look and feel

Page display matters! When deciding on a look and feel for your blog, it's good to keep simplicity in mind. No matter how brilliant your writing, a page with too many colors, jarring font mashups, a noisy background image, or (shudder) blinking elements can cause first-time visitors to flee without reading a word. Some blog authoring environments allow more design customization than others, but when choosing a template or crafting your own page layout, you'll do yourself and your visitors a favor if you hold to the old maxim, "Less is more." It's no accident that Google's main search page, with its stark but utterly useful page elements, is one of the most popular web pages ever. Decide which elements you really want on your blog and discard the others. Choose a color scheme that's easy on the eye, and keep your font sizes readable. It's important to aim for a distinctive page that reflects your persona, but let the design elements whisper rather than scream.

# provide proper infrastructure for posts

Each time you post an entry to your blog, you're refining the blog's shape and momentum. We'll look at a variety of writing tips in the next chapter, but the section below discusses potential page elements that frame and support the actual entries. For the most part, these options are included in the more popular blog software solutions and can be turned on and off or tweaked to suit your needs.

## date and time stamps

Letting readers know when you posted an entry not only tells them that you were awake and madly typing at 3 AM, it provides a temporal context for entries that readers discover later via *permalinks* or *trackbacks* (more on these in a bit).

## author names for group blogs

If only one author posts to a blog, this field is unnecessary, but if two or more individuals post, providing the author's name for each entry helps readers to become familiar with the interests and idiosyncrasies of each. It also helps to ensure accountability. This is useful in building and maintaining community interest and is highly recommended.

## headlines that tell the story

Some bloggers choose not to top their entries with headlines, but there are compelling reasons to do so. If you syndicate your content via newsfeeds, the headline may be all that your readers see. Plus, search engines grant extra weight to keywords in entry titles. We'll talk more about keyword strategies in the next two chapters.

## excerpts lure the reader

If you plan to syndicate your blog content and wish to provide excerpts of your blog entries, rather than the full text, it's particularly useful to hone your *lede*-writing abilities. A lede is the first sentence or three of an article and should summarize the main points of your post, as well as provide an intriguing teaser.

## outbound links knit you into the blogosphere

Within the body text of an entry, be generous in linking to sources for your writings and imagery. In the early days of the web, it wasn't unusual for web authors to be stingy with their links. Popular knowledge had it that you wanted to keep readers on your own site for as long as possible. Today, the more links you provide to valuable outside sources, the more often your visitors are likely to return. Plus, authors on other websites and blogs often watch their trackback and referrer logs to see who is linking to them, and many will return the favor. Links are sometimes called the currency of the blog world, and that isn't really an exaggeration. Most blog software packages make the task of embedding the necessary HTML code fairly simple. The most common mistake seems to be user error—embedding an incorrect address!

## rich media deepens the experience

It is becoming increasingly popular for bloggers to include photos, drawings, video, and animations within their blog entries. It's true that many popular blogs are text-only, but we live in a media world that's rife with visuals, all competing for attention. A photo of the individual about whom you're writing or an animation or video clip illustrating the phenomenon you're discussing can help to convince your visitors to read more deeply. If you are posting your own images, do remember to compress them for quick download. If "borrowing" images from other websites, you will ideally request permission from the image's originator. At the least, you should acknowledge the creator and provide a link to the source. (See Chapter 12, "Keeping It Legal," for a discussion of copyright and fair use issues.) All this said, it's perfectly fine to blog without these audio or visual supports.

## give each page element its due

While individual blog entries make up the heart of any blog, a typical blog page contains many individual elements, each of which contributes to the context and value of the blog itself. Not all blogs require all of these elements, but understanding the purpose and potential of each will help you decide which to incorporate into your blog. Below you'll find descriptions of each page element with some suggestions for implementing those you find most valuable.

# encourage dialogue through comments

Blogging has introduced two dynamics that are changing publishing forever: (1) Because the simplest hosted blogging environments are free and remarkably easy to use, the barrier to entry for budding authors is the lowest it's ever been; (2) the fact that it is equally simple for any reader to post a comment means that practically overnight publishing has become two-way and global.

This potential for dialogue, like so many things in life, is both good and bad. On the one hand, open discussions often result in a richer, broader understanding of a given topic. Also, authors sometimes improve their writing and presentation skills once they find their readers hold them accountable. On the other hand, angry or ill-informed comments, and even off-topic rants, can derail perfectly valid conversations.

Another very real dilemma introduced by commenting is, once again, spam. An increasing number of unscrupulous marketers have taken advantage of the open nature of comment fields, using them to display teasers for questionable implants, Nigerian investment opportunities, or simply lists of links designed to enhance the marketer's own search engine ranking. Nearly all of the blog software packages have introduced anti-spam strategies that attempt to contain the ever escalating problem. One relatively successful strategy requires that commenters submit an email address, which is used as an identifier. The first time someone submits a comment from an email address, the comment is held in a queue until the blogger has a chance to either allow it to go live or delete it. Another solution requires commenters to copy a number or word embedded in a graphic, sometimes called a *captcha*, before they can post. Of course, this only stops automated spammers.

Allowing your readers to comment always presents challenges, but there are few mechanisms that contribute as readily to community building. Plus, we inevitably learn from our readers. For some tips on handling the more troublesome aspects of commenting, see "Managing the Commentariat" in Chapter 10, "Writing that Engages."

# provide permanent anchors with permalinks

Among the more mysterious blog elements is the *permalink*, a clickable term often found at the foot of a blog entry. This is a portmanteau term for "permanent link" and, as the phrase implies, permalinks provide unique and persistent web addresses for specific blog entries.

Permalinks are crucial if readers want to link to a specific entry on your blog from their own blog or website. Because content on a blog's home-page constantly updates, with earlier entries migrating to chronological or categorical archives, simply linking to your blog homepage would inevitably prove frustrating; your readers would have to search your blog for the entry they wanted. Allowing your blog software to assign a unique URL, or permalink, to each blog entry solves this problem.

When you click on a permalink beneath a blog entry, you are presented with a page containing only that blog entry along with its associated comments. Those wishing to link to the post simply copy the web address from the top of the browser window and paste it into their own blog posts or emails.

Many blog software applications let you customize your permalinks, and if you hope to be found by search engines, you are strongly advised to tweak the settings so that you generate permalinks that are in plain language, contain keywords, and do away with database gibberish like ampersands and pound symbols.

# allow cross-blog conversations via trackback

Trackback is a little tricky to explain, but because the feature can be so handy, it's worth taking a moment to understand its purpose and mecha-nisms. In a nutshell, a trackback link beneath a blog entry is similar to a permalink, but with an additional trick up its sleeve; it provides a unique URL that others can use to notify you and your readers that they've responded to your entry on their own blog.

The main reason that others might choose to respond on their own blog, rather than simply posting a comment beneath your entry, is that they'd like their own blog visitors to read what they've written and perhaps spark a discussion tailored to the interests of their own readers. Also, they have more control over their commentary on their own sites and can correct typos and errors, or otherwise edit texts after posting.

Besides facilitating conversations across blogs, the rank of your blog page is enhanced each time others use trackback notification for one of your posts, since search and aggregation sites like Technorati and Bloglines regularly poll registered blogs for new links, and their algorithms will reward you for the trackback link.

What's the bad news? What else? Spam. This is the dark side of both trackback and comments. There are anti-spam plugins for all the major blog applications, some purporting to work against spam in both comment and trackback fields, but it is likely that you will occasionally have to manually remove spam links when particularly virulent specimens make it past your safeguards.

OK, there's one more bad thing. Because only the blognoscenti understand trackback, not many people use it yet. Nevertheless, as automation and standard practices improve, this ability to converse across blogs promises to be among the most powerful features in blogging. For those wishing to learn more about how trackback actually works today, "Trackback Demystified," steps through a trackback scenario.

## trackback demystified

Responding to someone else's blog post on your own blog is simple. Letting other bloggers know that you've continued the conversation on your own blog is a little more complicated and involves using the trackback mechanism provided by many blog authoring environments. We'll step through a trackback scenario to illustrate that while the process is a bit tricky until you get the hang of it, the extra effort often pays off.

Let's say your Aunt Magda really likes your latest blog entry about frog butter and wants to share it with her own readers. On her blog, she starts a new entry, telling her friends why she thinks they'll like what you posted, along with a short excerpt from your blog. She'd like her readers to be able to click a link in the body of her entry to go to your blog and read the full text, so she clicks the permalink beneath your entry. A window opens containing only that post, and the web address in the browser is the unique URL for that entry, its permalink. Magda copies the URL and pastes it into the body of her own entry. So far, so good. Her readers can now happily read her commentary and the short excerpt from your site. They can even click the link to read the full text on your blog.

But you and your readers still don't know that Aunt Magda started a side conversation about frog butter on her blog, so she next clicks the trackback link under the entry on your blog. A window opens with a brand new URL at the top of the browser, that entry's unique trackback address. Magda pastes this new address into a special trackback field in her own blog. The field may be called something cryptic like "Trackback an URL" (in WordPress) or "URLs to Ping" (in Movable Type). In addition to pasting the unique trackback address, she probably also types in a short trackback headline, copies an excerpt from the entry on her own blog, adds the permalink for her entry and she clicks to submit.

On your blog, you see that in the parentheses after the trackback link for your frog butter entry, the zero has updated to the number one. If you click on the trackback link, the window that opens now includes a live link to Magda's blog, along with her excerpt. (On some blogs, the trackback content appears automatically after an entry.) Subsequent trackback links by other bloggers wishing to comment remotely will update the trackback number on your blog, allowing you to know how many other sites are commenting about the entry on their blogs.

# broaden reach with syndicated newsfeeds

You already know about newsfeeds from the previous chapter and why syndication is an excellent addition to your blog distribution plan. I'll admit that I was a little nonplussed by the whole concept at first. Until, that is, I began subscribing to feeds from my favorite blogs and websites. Now, rather than having to jump back and forth from my bookmarks to individual websites, waiting for some of the bulkier ones to load, and then clicking around looking for the newest content, all the new items from all my subscriptions collect in one, easy-to-navigate interface. No spam. No watching the hourglass fill or the beachball spin. I scan my daily round of RSS-enabled sites in mere minutes, choosing which to read in my news-reader, which to let scroll by, and which to read on the blog's own pages.

Syndicated feeds facilitate a wide array of tasks. They deliver news, publish newsletters, collect email, track packages, provide marketing and stock updates, provide communications within organizations, allow content to be posted and viewed from mobile phones and other portable devices, and even enhance search engine ranking.

Setting up a feed is fairly simple in most blog applications. Once your feed is up and running, don't be shy about letting your readers know that they can subscribe. Place the link high on the page. You might even want to provide a link to an informational how-to file.

Finally, you'll want to let various search engines know that your content is syndicated. For some tips on registering with various RSS-specific search engines and aggregators, along with other promotion techniques, see Chapter 11, "Promoting Your Blog."

# blogrolls provide context

A *blogroll* is a list of links to other blogs that an author regularly reads or thinks her readers will enjoy. Including a well-curated list on your blog is a good idea. It provides a bit of context, telling the world whom you admire or at least feel the need to regularly read. Plus, if readers come to your blog because they appreciate your finely tuned sense of humor or your grasp of paleobiology, they may be grateful for the links to similar sites, thereby enhancing reader loyalty. If those on your blogroll include a link to your site on their own blogs, it increases your traffic and ranking. In some cases, blogrolls acquire enough value that they are themselves syndicated.

## provide search and they shall find

If your blog software allows you to offer your readers the ability to search your blog, don't hesitate to include the feature. Even if you tag your entries with categorical labels, as content accrues in your archives, it can become increasingly difficult to find isolated factoids or barely remembered tidbits.

## categorical tags aid discovery

Blog entries generally appear in reverse chronological order. The construction lends a sense of timeliness to blogging, allowing us to watch trends unfold and to participate in conversations. But this same construction—newest entries at the top with older ones shunted to archives as they make room on the front page—makes it difficult to follow threads of thought, particularly if the blog addresses more than one topic. A reader with a penchant for physics who regularly visits a blog to read posts about qubit theory might be put off by interspersed musings about a cat. Or vice versa, of course.

One solution that's quickly gaining momentum is *tagging*. In Chapter 8, "Packing Your Toolkit," we introduced tags and discussed some of the mechanisms for appending them to your posts. When thinking through the design of your blog page, it pays to carefully consider how you present tags to your readers.

Generally readers access blog posts marked with categorical tags in one of two ways: by choosing from a list of categories in a sidebar on your main page, or by clicking the name of a category appended to an entry. If you've dutifully tagged your posts, fans of qubits can click the "physics" link in either location to read all your entries on the topic. Feline lovers can do the same by clicking "cat." An entry that discusses Schrödinger's cat might sport links to both categories.

Assigning categorical tags to individual entries can also help you promote your blog, both because some software packages map categories against existing tagging systems, and because some of the search engines that specialize in blogs look for tags when attempting to gauge search relevance. You can read more about these techniques in Chapter 11, "Promoting Your Blog."

Not all blog applications support tagging. At the time of this writing, the ever-popular Blogger does not, for instance, although as we saw in the last chapter, there are workarounds. And, not all blogs are improved by categorization, but if you believe that your blog will benefit from the organization that tags allow, this could influence your choice of software.

## chronological archives provide context

With categorical archives becoming more popular, chronological archives of entries that have scrolled off the main page are less of an imperative. You can, of course, include both tag categories and chronological archives.

## links to lively posts on your blog

Real estate on any blog page quickly becomes limited, but it can be useful to include links to your best archived posts or to ongoing conversations taking place in response to older entries.

## email addresses open the door

Providing an email address for readers wishing to contact you directly makes sense. It provides a useful channel for feedback and for carrying on conversations that might not be of interest to your readership as a whole. Who knows? You might open your mailbox one day to find that dream job offer or a mash note from your favorite high school sweetheart.

Keep in mind that unscrupulous marketers have grown quite savvy when culling email addresses for their lists. One way to subvert the spammers is to spell out your email address: suzanne (at) dispatchesfromblogistan (dot) com.

## clickable calendars facilitate retrieval

Some blogging tools allow you to place a graphic calendar on a sidebar. Clicking on a date retrieves posts from that day. It can be a nice touch, but if your page is starting to feel crowded, you could drop this feature without losing much of the interest or functionality of the page.

## today's soundtrack/weather/ moon phase ...

Bloggers often use custom fields to provide a bit of personal context for each of their entries. They might call out the music they're listening to, whether it's sunny or raining, or what the cat is doing at the moment. This is a whim that annoys some readers while others find it endearing. (In the spirit of full disclosure, I post the name of the song I'm listening to when I post to dispatchesfromblogistan.com.) Online environments lack physical and social cues and these tidbits can help to build trust and a sense of camaraderie.

## shopping carts and affiliate links

Obviously, blogs with immediate online sales as their main objective will want to feature a shopping cart on their main pages, but even if yours isn't an overtly commercial enterprise, you may discover opportunities for selling items of interest to your readers. The most popular blogs often sell t-shirts and mugs or bumper stickers celebrating their brand. Bloggers who cater to special interests may find that their readers welcome the chance to buy those old Bakelite knobs or download an mp3 of your band's newest tune.

Whether you install a full shopping cart equipped with the ability to accept credit cards, enable a simple link to Paypal, or sign up as an Amazon sales affiliate, you'll want to position the sales pitch carefully on the page. If it screams too loudly, your readers may find it crass. But if you believe your readers will genuinely be happy with the opportunity and the graphic presentation fits with the rest of your blog design, by all means place the offer "above the fold," a newspaper term that here means "viewable without scrolling." Provide a bit of information about what is for sale on your top page, but consider leaving the hardcore sales pitch for a linked page. Once again, don't be afraid of the personal touch or a little humor. This is a blog and not a formal marketing environment, after all.

## contextual ads generate revenue

You've no doubt noticed the fairly discreet text advertisements on the sides of some blog pages. Many of these contain links to websites or other blogs that contain commercial information related to the content of the blog. The mechanics of these ads are discussed in the previous chapter. In terms of design, it's good to know that you have at least a little control over the color scheme and aspect ratio of the ads, but these ads are their own creatures and you don't want visitors confusing them with your content. If you choose to integrate contextual ads, it's best to let them stand honestly at the top of the page or in a sidebar.

## copyright and licensing notices

You own your own words, but not every one respects this fact. It's generally a good idea to place either a copyright notice or license notice like those supported by the Creative Commons group (creativecommons.org) at the bottom of each blog page. A copyright notice should include the term "Copyright," the copyright symbol, the year of copyright, the name of the copyright holder, and the phrase, "All Rights Reserved." For more information about copyright and licenses, see Chapter 12, "Keeping It Legal."

# 10 practical tips for great blog design

Some blogs are a pleasure to read and navigate. Others are a pain. No matter how brilliant your commentary, if the look and feel of your page is forgettable, plug ugly, or difficult to navigate, your visitors are less likely to return. There are no absolutes in the world of blogs, but a familiarity with the general rules of good online design makes it easier to break a few of those rules and still attract new readers. Whether you plan to use default design templates or employ formidable CSS (Cascading Style Sheet) skills to tweak your blog to your exact specifications, here are some useful things to keep in mind.

## look around

Visit your favorite blogs. While the editorial content of the blogs will probably be the greatest unifying aspect, spend some time analyzing how each presents its content and organizes navigation. Take notes on unique or particularly graceful linking solutions or informational blurbs. Note color combinations that you find pleasing (or horrific). The smart grasshoppers learn from those who have gone (and stumbled) before them.

## have a plan

Before you touch the templates or tweak a line of code, draw up a clear set of goals. Is this a business-related blog or a personal diary? Do you want traffic or a committed and active community? Will you mainly be passing along links to other blogs and websites? Posting a diary? Writing for fellow politicos or niche enthusiasts? Clowning? Selling? How knowledgeable can you assume your readers will be about the mechanics and terminology of blogs? How much time do you want to spend maintaining the blog? The more honestly you answer these questions, the more successful you are likely to be. Use the answers to determine overall design and content decisions. You probably don't want to launch with an edgy, controversial design if you're trying to win over a stodgy local electorate. By the same token, the default template that comes with your blog software could make you look naive to a tech-savvy crowd. Research, come up with a plan, and then try to stick with it.

## broadcast your identity

The best bloggers let you know right away who they are. Earlier in this chapter, we emphasized how important your blog title can be to your online identity. Integrating these into the graphic logo that sits atop your page is worth a bit of effort but doesn't have to be that difficult or expensive. Your logo can consist of a simple font treatment; that's essentially what dispatchesfromblogistan.com uses, after all. You can integrate your own graphics or photos or do a web search on free or inexpensive stock photos or clip art. You could even submit your design needs to a service like Elance (elance.com), where you browse portfolios and then invite designers to bid on your logo or blog design.

## arrange links logically

Let the design of each page tell its own story. At the top, your banner and logo establish the mood and signal your intent. The arrangement of the other page elements fills out the storyline. Your blog entries are the heart of your page. Choose a typeface that reads well on any system; sans serif fonts like Verdana and Arial reside on most computers, display well onscreen, and scale well for visitors who prefer to boost the font size. Cap your entries with complementary, well-defined headline treatments; you can choose another font for these, or just embold your body type. Beneath each entry, your links to categories, comments, trackback, permalinks, and the like should be uniform, explicit, and understated. Logic is the best guide when arranging links and information in side columns. On dispatchesfromblogistan.com, for instance, the lefthand column houses blog links to categorical archives and the blogroll, while the links on the right lead to pages related directly to this book. There are always stray links to biographical information, email, syndicated feeds, search, and whatever else you feel necessary to your goals. Think carefully about how often people will use them and what actions you want most to encourage. Keep your most important elements "above the fold." Your page should feel like a short story, not a circus poster.

## keep it clean

Even blogs devoted to naughty topics are well advised to keep their design crisp and clean. Visitors who find what they're looking for are much more likely to become regular visitors. The tricks are simple. As in any good digital design, ensure that all your navigation links are obvious and easy to read. Limit the number of fonts. Choose a coordinated color scheme and stick to it. Avoid blinking icons or frenetic animated gifs. Of course include photos or even video in your entries when they contribute to the overall understanding and enjoyment of the topic, but don't force them into service when the story can be told just as well without. Be cautious in including sound files. Many people find them annoying, particularly if they log onto your site at work or just after the baby falls asleep. Include a button for turning sounds off. Make sure that any graphic or sound element is compressed within a nanometer of its life. Who has time to wait? In a nutshell, include elements you honestly believe contribute your blog. Kill the rest.

## be consistent

Consistency inspires trust. Long experience on the Web has taught us that even a little onscreen confusion can send a viewer scuttling off to the next website. Once you've chosen your fonts and colors and graphic elements, be police-like in deploying them. Throughout your pages, assign uniform styles to links, headlines, column headers, and side links. Keep terminology uniform. For instance, some call the chunks of text that you regularly publish to a blog "posts" and others call them "articles." For the purposes of this book and its blog, I've chosen to refer to them as "posts" or "entries." It's not that the others are wrong, but particularly in a realm as murky as blogging, consistency makes it more likely that I'll be understood.

## design for interaction

Not all bloggers look forward to interacting with their readers; some choose to not allow comments or encourage cross-linking. But unless you're already a celebrity, you'll probably benefit from the increased reader involvement, as well as the search engine pings that come with these interactions. In addition, the phrasing, design, and placement of your links to interactive elements all contribute to the activity level of your blog. If the link to your comment page fades into the background or your trackback link is poorly implemented, you lose. Accept that many, if not most, people will not be landing on your homepage but will arrive via links to individual entries. Ensure that those pages display comments attractively and make it easy to add a new comment or discover your trackback or pingback links.

## provide clues

In general, websites no longer require much explanation. Four-year-olds happily mouse their way through mazes, and Uncle Nick sends ever more photos of his grandkids. Blogs, on the other hand, still contain enough arcane lingo and Rube Goldberg-like mechanisms that they intimidate some would-be blog regulars. You can boost the confidence of these readers by incorporating discreet explanations into your design. The permalink window could open with, "You will always be able to link to this entry using this permalink address." If you plan to moderate your comments by requesting an email address as identification before allowing a post to be viewed, write a friendly explanation that assures your new correspondent that the address will never be made public and that you will never use it for any purpose other than comment identification. These tips could win you fans for life. Well, at least the life of your blog.

## permalinked pages matter

Remember that most visitors may well enter your site via a permalink address rather than your main homepage. Links from other blogs or your syndicated feed lead directly to these subpages. Make sure that the display of the various page elements—the original entry, the trackback address, prior comments, the ability to comment—have a coordinated feel and that links are clear and obvious. Don't forget links to your categories, if you use them, as well as to your blogroll and any other elements on your home page that you don't want your readers to miss.

## test, test, test

Once you have your design in place, test it. Test it yourself, making sure all the links work and that you've made everything as clear as you can. Look at it in as many browsers as you have available and make whatever changes necessary. Next, ask a few friends to use the blog, preferably with you watching over their shoulder. Try to pick individuals who represent various experience levels. You might learn more from a neophyte than from a jaded blog regular. Resist the urge to tell them what to do or yelp when they press the wrong button. You will learn a great deal from this casual user testing. Finally, let the blog loose into the world and encourage feedback from your readers about the design. Be open-minded. Design critiques can be frustrating because they so often revolve largely around taste, but don't react if you can help it. Listen. You will often learn. Implement. Revise. Refine. Lather. Rinse. Repeat.

# wrapping things up

We've covered a lot of territory. Don't let all the details slow you down. You now know what all those page elements can or can't do for you. Do some exploring. Find some blog templates that suit your temperament and toy with them. You can always freshen up the design and add or delete sections later. The important thing is to launch. If you can feel a blush of pride because your blog is well-organized and handsome, all the better.

For an overview of a typical blog page, see the following figure.

Blog Title/Logo   Newsfeed   Search

Tags   About Pages   Email   Time Stamp   Static Pages

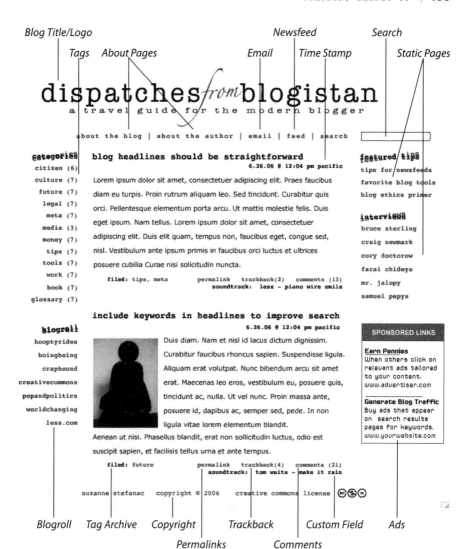

# dispatches *from* blogistan
### a travel guide for the modern blogger

about the blog | about the author | email | feed | search

**categories**
citizen (6)
culture (7)
future (7)
legal (7)
meta (7)
media (3)
money (7)
tips (7)
tools (7)
work (7)
book (7)
glossary (7)

**blog headlines should be straightforward**
6.26.06 @ 12:04 pm pacific

Lorem ipsum dolor sit amet, consectetuer adipiscing elit. Praes faucibus diam eu turpis. Proin rutrum aliquam leo. Sed tincidunt. Curabitur quis orci. Pellentesque elementum porta arcu. Ut mattis molestie felis. Duis eget ipsum. Nam tellus. Lorem ipsum dolor sit amet, consectetuer adipiscing elit. Duis elit quam, tempus non, faucibus eget, congue sed, nisl. Vestibulum ante ipsum primis in faucibus orci luctus et ultrices posuere cubilia Curae nisi solicitudin nuncta.

filed: tips, meta    permalink   trackback(2)   comments (13)
soundtrack:  less - piano wire smile

**featured tips**
tips for newsfeeds
favorite blog tools
blog ethics primer

**interviews**
bruce sterling
craig newmark
cory doctorow
farai chideya
mr. jalopy
samuel pepys

**blogroll**
hooptyrides
boingboing
craphound
creativecommons
popandpolitics
worldchanging
less.com

**include keywords in headlines to improve search**
6.26.06 @ 12:04 pm pacific

Duis diam. Nam et nisl id lacus dictum dignissim. Curabitur faucibus rhoncus sapien. Suspendisse ligula. Aliquam erat volutpat. Nunc bibendum arcu sit amet erat. Maecenas leo eros, vestibulum eu, posuere quis, tincidunt ac, nulla. Ut vel nunc. Proin massa ante, posuere id, dapibus ac, semper sed, pede. In non ligula vitae lorem elementum blandit. Aenean ut nisi. Phasellus blandit, erat non sollicitudin luctus, odio est suscipit sapien, et facilisis tellus urna et ante tempus.

filed: future    permalink   trackback(4)   comments (21)
soundtrack:  tom waits - make it rain

SPONSORED LINKS

**Earn Pennies**
When others click on relevant ads tailored to your content.
www.advertiser.com

**Generate Blog Traffic**
Buy ads that appear on search results pages for keywords.
www.yourwebsite.com

suzanne stefanac   copyright © 2006   creative commons license

Blogroll   Tag Archive   Copyright   Trackback   Custom Field   Ads

Permalinks   Comments

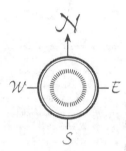

# writing that engages

We all write all the time. Lists. Emails. Obligatory thank-you notes. Maybe even the occasional letter to an editor. But none of these really prepare us for blogging.

We open a web browser to our blog authoring pages and start typing. We click the upload button and our words are instantly on view all around the globe. Grandma, the boss, and that cute new kid in the mailroom can all read whatever we've written. Not only that, they might respond. And not all of them politely.

Blog writing has its own logic. It's easy to be seduced by the spontaneous informality that distinguishes the tone of the best blogs. We wonder why our own first scribblings feel so stilted and shot through with clichés. We steam after our first encounters with interloping provocateurs, perhaps not really mad as much as embarrassed by our reactions.

But with practice, blogging gets easier. Even professional writers are sometimes surprised by the voices that blogging releases. Getting the hang of it involves consistency and a kind of fearlessness.

Ernest Hemingway once wrote, "There is nothing to writing. All you do is sit down at a typewriter and bleed." With all due respect to Hemingway, the act of writing doesn't have to be that bloody. There are proven strategies for composing blog entries that engage your readers and encourage response. This chapter will address general writing issues, as well as some that are more specific to individual blog elements, such as headlines, body text, comments and descriptive tags. Lively conversations distinguish the best blogs, and "Managing the Commentariat" offers suggestions for both rewarding your best correspondents and taming the troublemakers.

# general writing tips for bloggers

## just do it

The hardest thing for most writers is getting started. Each time we sit down in front of the screen, we can think of a dozen reasons why we should stand back up. It may help to remember that in physics, the laws describing inertia suggest that it's just as hard to stop a body in motion as it is to set one moving. Do whatever it takes to get started.

## embrace the draft

Some authors would like us to believe that they are able to write perfect prose on the first try and that their first draft is their only draft. That may be true in a few rare cases, but the truth is that drafts are generally an integral part of the process. Settle on a topic, think about it for a moment, do a little research if that's called for, and then throw some words at the topic until they start to stick. Don't stop until you have as much down as will come out in one straight push. Once all those words are on the screen, dig up those old editor's spectacles and go over it again, testing for logic and flow, as well as basic grammar and spelling. You might even take another swipe or two if it's an important piece. The draft is your friend.

## be yourself

Certainly there is value in emulating authors you respect, but your own voice is the one that will need to sustain interest over time. Take advantage of the fact that the informal style of most blogs allows you to mimic your conversational tone. If you're in doubt about a post, try reading it aloud. Does it feel natural? Would it hold the attention of a live listener? If not, you may want to recraft the entry.

## be trustworthy

It's not an exaggeration to say that trust is the glue holding blogdom together. Disclose any bias, patronage, or obligations that might influence your content. (See Chapter 6, "Blogs as Newsrooms," for more on this topic.)  Be honest about the differences between opinion and fact. Double-check your facts and provide links to sources. State opinions boldly, but don't be afraid to change your mind. The trick is to win the confidence of our readers over time.

## be gracious

Be polite, but not wimpy. It's disarming. Certainly a few gossip writers and pundits have made their names being caustic or snarky, but in general a snotty attitude will only undermine whatever point you're trying to make. It can make you look silly—or worse, defensive.

## engage your readers

Gone are the days of one-to-many publishing. Even mainstream media outlets are learning to open their gates. To win the respect of your readers, encourage participation. Respond promptly to comments. Ask questions. Visit their sites and leave comments. (See "Managing the Commentariat" for more on this topic.)

## get to the point

When asked the secret to his enormous popularity as a novelist, Elmore Leonard responded, "I try to leave out the parts that people skip." We would all do well to keep that maxim in mind. No one has enough time these days. If you want to keep readers coming back, stay on topic, make your point, and move on.

## add to the conversation

Typing just to see more of your words online can be the surest way to stop new visitors from returning to your blog. Simply regurgitating what others is saying is not enough. Take a moment to plumb your own depths. Find some vantage point unique to your experience. Your readers will thank you for it.

## know your boundaries

Blogging is, for the most part, a very public venture. It makes sense to decide beforehand how much you're willing to disclose about certain topics. Some are happy to tell all, while others choose to publish more cautiously, perhaps even with a pseudonym. There is no right or wrong in this, only what preserves your own piece of mind. Just remember that it's easier to say something later than to remove the thought from the minds of those who've already read it on your blog or in your newsfeed.

## don't fear the grammar

The basic rules of grammar are rules of logic. They allow sentences to communicate with the least potential for confusion. Our grade school teachers were adamant, "Use the active voice rather than the passive!" This may sound pedantic at first, but it really is much stronger to say, "The man bit the dog," rather than, "The dog was bitten by the man." Likewise, sticking to one verb tense and allowing each paragraph to tell its own story will strengthen whatever point you're trying to make. Try to be specific and succinct. You may not feel as strongly about grammar as Gertrude Stein, who once wrote, "I really do not know that anything has ever been more exciting than diagramming sentences," but if you're feeling a little fuzzy on the subject, consider bookmarking a handful of the reference websites listed in "Online Grammar Resources." All this said, don't agonize over grammar. Blogs break rules all the time. Your aim should be clarity and easy comprehension. Let grammar help when it can in achieving these goals.

---

### HOT LINKS: ONLINE GRAMMAR RESOURCES

**Chicago Manual of Style**
http://www.press.uchicago.edu/Misc/Chicago/cmosfaq/cmosfaq.html

**Strunk and White's "Elements of Style"**
http://www.bartleby.com/141/strunk1.html

**Summary of Strunk and White's Elements of Style**
http://www.journalism.org/resources/tools/writing/lessons/composition.asp

**Grammar Resources on the Web**
http://writing-program.uchicago.edu/resources/grammar.htm

**Dictionary.com**
http://dictionary.reference.com

**Thesaurus.com**
http://thesaurus.reference.com

---

# proof, proof, proof

This can't be stressed strongly enough. Read your post one last time before uploading. It's not that you can't edit a post once it's online, but if some of your subscribers picked up the entry before you edited it, they may never see the correction. Even if that were not the case, we'll all tragically human. One quick read at the end will often reveal that truly embarrassing typo or unfortunate slip.

## writer's block be damned

We all have days when we just can't seem to squeeze a sentence out. You might try tricking yourself into getting started. Sit down with a cup of your favorite brew. Promise yourself a donut when you're done. Type out the lyrics to your favorite song to rev the engines. Whatever it takes, try to get those first few words out and onto the screen. After a bit, inertia will often switch gears and you'll find yourself happily typing once again.

# composing specific blog page elements

At first glance, blog entries seem like such tidy, simple entities. And yet if you analyze the form carefully, you can find several distinct types of writing come into play. Let's look at each in turn.

## the blog post itself

The tips listed in the previous section all apply to actual blog posts, but here are a few structural points to keep in mind. It's smart to fashion your first few sentences to be both summary and teaser. (More on this in the section on *ledes* below.) If your readers subscribe to newsfeeds of your posts, this may be all they see unless they click. Even visitors reading posts on your own page may be skimming. Your readers are more likely to stick with you if you compose your posts with intrigue at the top, details and arguments in the middle, and summaries that provide logical counterpoints to your opening.

## headlines sell your story

Many blogs, venerable ones among them, don't bother with headlines, but there are excellent arguments for including them. Blog search engines reward meaty headlines with higher ranking scores. Readers who subscribe to your newsfeeds will decide whether to click to your blog based on the headline and perhaps an excerpt. Those who write about your entries on their own blogs find it much easier to reference your post if the headline is descriptive. Here are some tips for titling your entries that will take advantage of these opportunities.

## plain and simple wins the day

Save your cleverest verbal gambits for the body of your entry. Unlike a newspaper, where the main text follows directly beneath the headline and so can afford wordplay or irony, blog content is often previewed as headlines, and some search engines see only the entries' titles. When crafting your headlines, imagine the title orphaned on a newsfeed list or embedded as a link on another blog. Let it tell the story plainly and succinctly.

## shorter almost always better

All online writing rewards brevity. Shorter headlines will scan better in newsreaders, and you can use the headline as part of the naming scheme for your permalinks—something else that search engines reward.

## keywords rule

Those same search and ranking engines will be even friendlier if your headline contains *keywords*. We discuss keywords in greater detail in the next chapter, but suffice it to say here that the idea is to include words you think potential readers might use as search terms to find your post.

## test-ride your headline

If you're feeling really ambitious, copy your headline into the search engines you think are most relevant to your audience and see what related entries or websites are listed on the results pages. In Google, check to see if sponsored ads appear on the right hand side of the page. If you like the company your headline attracts, you have a keeper.

# ledes have never been more important

The word *lede* may be familiar only to journalists and their stalkers, but the concept has never been more important. A lede is the first few sentences in an article—the ones that tell the reader who, what, where, when, and maybe even a little bit about how. As mentioned in Chapter 2, "A Brief History of Open Discourse," ledes first rose to prominence during the American Civil War. Reporters in the field never knew if the telegraph line would stay open long enough to send an entire story, and so they wrote in an "inverted pyramid" style, with the most important information at the top.

A good lede reassures the reader that there is a point to the story; it doesn't have to give away the punchline. The trick lies in providing enough information to act as a summary while still acting as a teaser for the details in the full text of the story. Many journalists have made their careers on the basis of their ability to craft engaging story openers. It's true that for a few decades the lede lost its luster as journalists spent more words telling readers about the cab ride to the interview than they did about the supposed subject of the article. Rest assured that today the lede is back with a vengeance.

For one thing, our reading habits are changing. Print editors complain that the attention span of today's reader is as short as Cartman's temper. Online, the problem is exacerbated by the medium itself. Readers forage through their links, glancing at a headline here, reading the first few sentences there, quickly bouncing away as the next shiny thing presents itself. Or promises to present itself.

Ledes are as important for blogs as they were for American Civil War journalists. Craft them with care. Let them tell their own story while teasing the full post. You may not want to go so far as answering each of the classic who, what, when, where, and how questions, but it doesn't hurt to at least consider each of these as you decide what to include in the lede.

# letting links knit you into the web

Links are the threads that knit your blog into the larger online world. They allow your readers to benefit from your own research and provide context for your own entries. Use care in choosing the words in your text that serve as the link anchors. If you're quoting what someone else has written and providing a link to the full text, you can simply link phrases like, "as Ben Franklin writes" or "in today's column." Sometimes you'll want the link text to be more explicit, perhaps linking phrases such as "recently released statistics" or "a compendium of Thomas Jefferson quotations." Avoid using empty phrases like "click here." Link text that provides context and tells its own story will allow readers to click with confidence, plus it will improve the link rank for those to whom you are linking.

# categorical tags to the rescue

Blogs are a perfect medium for recording the moment, for identifying, tracking, and feeding trends. What they haven't done as well is serve as repositories for consecutive thought. The reverse chronological order that places newest entries at the top and forces older posts into weekly or monthly archives can make it difficult to follow a train of thought or to find entries about a specific topic after they've scrolled off the front page.

The previous two chapters touched on tagging, the surprisingly successful solution to this retrieval problem. Tagging, sometimes referred to as *folksonomy*, is also notable for the speed with which it's being adopted and the seeming randomness of the mechanisms involved.

Tags are sometimes confused with keywords, but the distinction is simple. Keywords are words or phrases integrated into blog headlines and entries that authors believe a potential reader might use to search for content like their own. (Learn more about keywords and search optimization techniques in the next chapter.) Tags are freely chosen descriptive labels that authors type into special tag fields. An author may assign as many tags, sometimes called *categories*, to a single entry as they like. Blog visitors can then click on a category name to view all the entries marked with that tag on a single blog, or they can search across blogs for entries marked with the tag using tag search engines like Technorati, IceRocket, or Wink.

Technorati introduced tag search across blogs at the beginning of 2005, and by the end of the year the service was tracking more than six million tags. The key to the success of this tagging strategy is the ease with which bloggers may choose and assign labels. The descriptive tags can be any word the author chooses, quite the opposite of strict taxonomies with cascading levels of hierarchical logic like, say, the Dewey Decimal System.

It's almost uncanny the way folksonomy's scattershot approach is providing a useful map of the blogosphere. *Tag clouds* provide visual representations that are almost like topographical maps in that they show the tag terms used most often in larger, bolder type and those used less often in smaller, paler type (see "Tag Clouds Make It All Clear"). As popular as tag tools are turning out to be, an inevitable question arises: Why do busy individuals bother taking the time to invent and assign these freeform labels? Certainly thousands of bloggers bother to tag because the labels are so useful, but perhaps even more importantly, they do it because it's so easy. The effort-to-benefit ratio makes it worthwhile. This ease in assigning tags is an imperative if tagging is to continue to grow as a grassroots classification system.

## choosing the best tags

It helps to think of tagging as a probability engine. Visit some of the services that track tags—Technorati, del.icio.us, Wink, IceRocket, and Flickr, for instance—and view their tag clouds. Because terms that are used most often are in bolder, larger type, we can begin to gauge the probability that potential visitors will search on those terms. If we assign the most popular tags to our blog entries, they might get lost in a sea of other sites using the term. If we choose ones that are too obscure, the chances that anyone will search on them become increasingly unlikely. Using the tag "games" will find you lagging behind more popular blogs in search results, but "cribbage" may win you readers who share your enthusiasm for all things muggins.

Experiment. Check your web logs to see which search terms visitors used to find your site. Try new terms. Don't be afraid of overlap, but likewise, don't be afraid to use more than one tag when it seems too confusing to decide between them. Watching tag evolution over time suggests that singular terms are often more successful than plurals.

In the end, what's important is to get started tagging and then keep tagging. Don't agonize too much over your choices or you may lose the will to tag. Just as tagging itself is evolving to better reflect the temper of online discourse, we learn to adopt the labels that best suit our blogging over time. Who knows? We might even learn something about ourselves in the process.

---

All time most popular tags

05 amsterdam animal animals architecture art august australia autumn baby barcelona beach berlin birthday black blackandwhite blue boston building bw california cameraphone camping canada canon car cat cats chicago china christmas church city clouds color concert day dc december dog dogs england europe fall family festival florida flower flowers food france friends fun garden geotagged germany girl graffiti green halloween hawaii hiking holiday home honeymoon hongkong house india ireland italy january japan july kids lake landscape light london losangeles macro me mexico moblog mountain mountains museum music nature new newyork newyorkcity newzealand night november nyc ocean october paris park party people photo portrait red river roadtrip rock rome san sanfrancisco school scotland sea seattle sky snow spain street summer sunset sydney taiwan texas thailand thanksgiving tokyo toronto travel tree trees trip uk urban usa vacation vancouver washington water wedding white winter xmas yellow york zoo

---

**Tag Clouds Make It All Clear**   Most services that track descriptive tags allow users to view tag clouds that display more frequently used tag terms in larger, bolder type and less frequent terms in smaller, lighter type. This tag cloud provides a window onto the top 100 tags created by users on the photo-sharing site, Flickr. Clicking on any of the terms provides links to images tagged with the descriptors.

# wrapping it all up

The truth, of course, is that all of us skip one or more of these steps when we're harried or not in the mood, but the small amount of extra time spent thinking a bit about the topic, jotting down your first thoughts, and then juggling them into a coherent whole is almost always worth the time. It will become second nature after a bit, and your readers will thank you for

## managing the commentariat

Allowing comments on blogs can be a lot like setting up a microphone in a mall. Anyone can respond, and not all responses are equal or even welcome. But blogs are part of an ongoing global communications revolution, and a healthy dialogue between authors and audience is responsible for a great deal of blogging's growing popularity. Certainly there are blogs that don't benefit from comments. The ultra-famous may be hounded by fans who just want to see their logins on the same page. The painfully shy may find just the act of publishing a blog as much exposure as they're willing to bear. In general, however, comments breathe life into a blog and are to be courted. What follows are a few tips for making the dialogue worth-while for all concerned.

▶  encourage comments

Whether out of fear or pomposity, some bloggers seem to actively discourage their readers from commenting. If you bother to allow comments on your blog, be proactive. Encourage dialogue. In both your main posts and in responses to comments, ask questions. Invite specific individuals to share their thoughts. We might all learn something new along the way.

▶  respond to threads

For the most part, it's best to respond to comments quickly and graciously. Some tactics for dealing with trolls (annoying commenters) are described below, but in general, you want to keep the conversation lively and informa-tive. The ideal is to spark dialogue without dominating the flow.

▶  admit when you're wrong

We all make mistakes. If you make a bad call factually, or even temperamentally, be prompt in admitting the false step to your readers. They will often have already noticed anyway. It's best to not quibble, and defensiveness is an ugly posture. A gracious mea culpa will allow you to move on without losing much, if any, face. As long as you don't repeat the mistake right away, of course.

▶  establish rules of engagement

It's much easier to maintain standards of conduct if you provide your readers with guidelines in advance. Your blog is your living room, and you're entitled to make a few rules. Most blog software solutions allow you to screen comments before they go live. If you just can't bear to read another thing about Britney Spears, make it clear that you will delete any comments about her. At the same time, recognize that if you set too many rules, ban too many commenters, or shut down too many topics, you will sacrifice some of the vitality of your blog.

▶ delete or ban with care

Blog software allows us to delete comments and ban certain visitors from commenting (on our own blogs, at least), but it's best to use these tools with great discretion. Some individuals may make you a little uncomfortable, but you'll gain the respect of your readers if you consistently deal with these incidents with grace and fairness. A thick skin can be most becoming online. Spam comments are an obvious exception and may be deleted with abandon.

▶ reward the best

If all goes well, some among your readers will begin to stand out. Identify the best and publicly applaud their finest efforts. This will not only encourage them to continue contributing in a useful and entertaining manner, it will provide examples for others reading and responding to your posts. In a best-case scenario, readers will begin nominating each other for such call-outs.

▶ don't feed the trolls

Trolls, individuals who willfully and maliciously work to derail online conversations, are as old as the Internet itself. Years of experience teach that the best way to deal with trolls is to ignore them. Many are remarkably tenacious, and you're unlikely to enlighten them. If you must respond, do so to your entire readership and solicit their help in keeping the conversation going by joining you in ignoring the troll. If the troll persists, ban him or her from comments, but once again, this should be a last resort. Very often, trolls will move on of their own accord if they're not fed.

▶ never post mad or drunk

This sounds obvious, but we've all done it. Someone writes something about us or a topic dear to our hearts and we hammer out a response and hit Submit without taking a breath. Regret is almost always the result. If your heartbeat is up, it's perhaps a good signal to step away from the keyboard for a bit.

▶ heated exchanges attract readers

Posting angry should be avoided, but heated exchanges based on strong feelings, well-reasoned arguments, and a dash of humor can be an excellent recipe for attracting and involving readers. It's up to you to decide how much heat you're willing to allow, but don't be afraid of a good debate.

▶ if all else fails, take a break

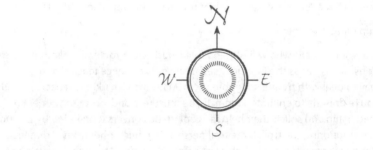

# promoting your blog

Launching a blog is bracing. Waiting for visitors can be, well, awkward. You may have polished and tweaked your debut to a Pulitzer gleam, but if no one visits your pages, it's easy to lose heart. There are strategies that can help raise the profile of just about any blog. There are no silver bullets, and most of the techniques require a bit of work and testing, but an honest desire to be discovered and a basic understanding about how blogs are interconnected will go a long way toward earning you a viable spot on the Blogistani map.

# emulating the giants

While most of us can never hope to match the popularity of the top-ranked blogs, there is still much we can learn from the giants. BoingBoing (boingboing.net) is consistently at or near the top of any Top 10 blog listing, with hundreds of thousands of visitors flocking to see which web pages the site's five editors are highlighting each day. Engadget (engadget.com) attracts similar numbers of visitors by providing dependable and entertaining reviews of the latest electronic tools and toys. Daily Kos (dailykos.com), with its highly charged political commentary, follows close behind.

What do these blogs and others at the top of the heap have in common? First and foremost, the quality of the content is consistently top-notch. Secondly, all three publish with great frequency. At the time of this writing, Blogpulse (blogpulse.com) reports that BoingBoing updates its pages 73 times a week, Engadget 114 times, and Daily Koz 89 times. Third—and here's where it starts to get tricky—all three attract thousands of links from other blogs and websites. Technorati shows 66,219 links to BoingBoing, 64,307 links to Engadget, and 46,072 links to Daily Kos.

This third point, the *inbound link count*, is important. Links are, in a sense, votes. They tell readers that this is a site or blog worth visiting. Little wonder then that search engines rely heavily on counts of inbound links from other sites when gauging a blog's popularity and awarding rank on search results pages.

We can all aspire to quality content and frequent posting schedules, but how can the rest of us hope to compete with the giants on the inbound link front? Quite simply, we probably can't. And the beauty of the blogosphere is that we don't have to. A blog doesn't have to appear on any Top 100 or even Top 1000 list to be successful. There will, in all likelihood, always be a handful of ultrapopular sites drawing huge crowds, but we are watching as millions of other blogs are finding their places, and their fans, along blogdom's Long Tail.

# what is this "long tail" anyway?

Discussions about "long tail" distribution patterns among blogs are popping up everywhere. The concept, sometimes referred to as "power law distribution," grew out of research in economics and linguistics. The economist Vilfredo Paredo showed that wealth in most populations follows an 80/20 rule in which 20 percent of the population controls 80 percent of the wealth. Similarly, linguist George Zipf showed that word frequency within texts follows a similar Power Law curve with a few words like "the" and "a" occurring with enormous frequency, while instances of other words occur with decreasing frequency. Graphing a Power Law distribution results in an L-shaped curve with the few, high-volume instances forming the "head" of the curve and the many, lower-volume instances trailing off along a "long tail." (See "The Long Tail of Blog Search Results" for an illustration.)

Clay Shirky, a professor of new media at NYU, first applied the concept to blogging in an early 2003 post to the "Network, Economics, and Culture" mailing list. At the time, bloggers were beginning to voice disgruntlement because a few "A-list" blogs consistently dominated any listing of popular blogs. Shirky pointed out that the phenomenon fit Power Law distribution patterns and that the concentration of links and resulting popularity wasn't a case of ill will or collusion, but rather a consequence of scale. He wrote, "What matters is this: Diversity plus freedom of choice creates inequality, and the greater the diversity, the more extreme the inequality."

Chris Anderson, *Wired* magazine's editor-in-chief, took the concept a step further. First in a magazine article titled "The Long Tail," and then in a book of the same name and a website (longtail.com), he applied Power Law theory to the distribution of cultural artifacts like books and movies. Traditionally, book sales were limited to the number of titles the largest bookstores could fit on their shelves. Similarly, movie rental options were constrained by the shelf space available to brick-and-mortar outlets. This dynamic forced a hit-driven economy that essentially limited distribution to products populating the head of the curve.

The introduction of services like Amazon (amazon.com) and Netflix (netflix.com) altered the dynamic dramatically. Because they take advantage of centralized warehouses and online ordering, they require no physical outlets and can afford to carry more niche products. The surprising result, as reported by Anderson, is that Amazon now cumulatively sells more niche products along the tail than the more popular books and movies still populating the head of the curve. Sales for any individual item along the tail may be low, but the overall dynamics of the system now justify distribution. "When consumers are offered infinite choice," Anderson writes, "the true shape of demand is revealed."

# focus is the secret

The good and bad news for bloggers is that the distribution curve for blogs results in an almost impossibly long tail. It's great that anyone can publish a blog on any topic, but getting noticed when you're one among tens of millions of blogs is a definite challenge.

As Shirky noted, there are always a few blogs that attract the greatest number of inbound links and, therefore, dominate search results. If our interests run to less mainstream topics, how can we hope to solve this problem of discovery—finding and being found along an ever-lengthening tail?

The trick is focus. The most successful mid-tier blogs don't try to be all things to all readers. Their intent is well-defined and intelligently supported throughout the site. A new blog that attempts to write about the full spectrum of electronic doodads, for instance, will find it difficult to compete with Engadget. If, however, you have a passion for robotic vacuum cleaners and you focus your blog on that niche, you stand a much better chance of attracting an avid community of similarly inclined eccentrics, I mean, individuals. If you pull focus too tightly—say, launching a blog about nothing but furry bug costumes for Roombas—you may own the category, but once again find yourself twiddling thumbs as you wait for like-minded visitors.

So this is the bottom line: Well-chosen focus will aid your discovery. For those producing content along blogdom's long tail, some readers will find you by following links from related blogs in the same niche. Those links, in turn, will raise your rank on search engine results pages. Yet more readers will then find you as a result of doing keyword searches related to the niche. The mechanisms aren't perfect, but we are entering a new distribution era in which non-mainstream content is starting to find an audience that is like-minded, appreciative, and responsive.

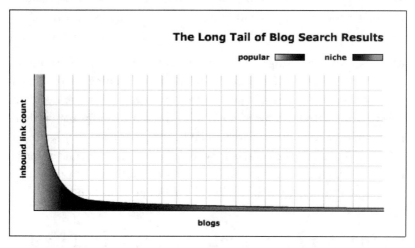

Most blog search engines rely on a raw count of inbound links when ranking sites on their search results pages. A few blogs consistently attract the greatest number of inbound links and so rank highest on the results pages, while the bulk of the remaining blogs are stretched out along the "long tail."

# search engines act as gatekeepers

I sometimes joke that search algorithms are second only to plumbing when ranking advances in civilization. Still, useful as search engines have turned out to be, they often feel more like ogres than superheroes when you're trying to coax them into displaying links to your web pages more prominently on their results pages.

Whole industries have grown up around search engine optimization, known in the trade as SEO. Major websites have been hiring SEO firms to advise them for years, and that's still a prudent path for commercial ventures, but there's a great deal that you and I can do without hiring their services to enhance the ranking of our own blogs.

Be forewarned. Search optimization is sometimes murky, and what was true last year or even three months ago is often untrue today. Dozens of search engines, old and brand new, are in frantic competition—not only with one another, but also with unscrupulous scammers who are relentless in their attempts to artificially raise the rank of their own properties.

Also, it's worth repeating that search engine ranking is only one criterion by which a blog's success should be gauged. Depending on your community of interest, there are always other avenues for discovery. Actively commenting on related blogs, continually presenting information that's fresh and of value to others with similar interests, and non-blog strategies like embedding the web address for your blog in newsletters and advertising are all viable mechanisms for raising your visibility within your target community. Still, it never hurts to take a peek under the hood.

## traditional search engines still rule

As we read in Chapter 8, "Packing Your Toolkit," new search engines, particularly ones built to address the unique needs of bloggers, are popping up everywhere, but the traditional stalwarts—Google, Yahoo, and MSN—still rule the roost. It's easy to take these giants for granted. Type in a word or phrase, and within seconds, or even split seconds, link after link appears, each pointing to a webpage containing the search terms. Not only that, the search results are ranked. We may not always agree that the links at the top are the ones most relevant to our current needs, but that doesn't stop us from wanting to see our own blog pages listed high on the list.

If it seems that most discussions about search and website ranking focus on Google and its PageRank algorithms, that's because for years Google stood alone, feeding results to most other search engines. At its height, Google facilitated 80 percent of all search activity. Google still dominates, but the recent introduction of proprietary search schemes by Yahoo and

MSN have somewhat leveled the field. In addition to providing competitive search capabilities, all of the major players now actively vie for user loyalty, providing services like free email, sizable free storage, syndicated newsfeeds, localized maps, and personalized news and entertainment pages. The March 2006 Nielsen NetRatings for search share in the United States showed Google providing 48 percent of the total search returns, with Yahoo at 22 percent and MSN at 11 percent. So, while it's true that Google's PageRank algorithms are no longer the single golden standard against which to measure all searches, Google is still a gorilla that any blog publisher would do well to please. If you rank well on Google's pages, you're very likely to do so on competitors' pages, as well.

There are literally dozens of factors that influence search ranking, some of which might at first seem contradictory. A website that has been around longer is ranked higher than a newcomer, but a recently updated page gets more points than a stale one. The careful use of keywords that are in keeping with the general theme of your site can up your ranking; used too often on a page, these same keywords may set off spam sensors, resulting in a penalty or even banning the site from the search engine's results.

While no one outside the search engine companies' war rooms knows exactly how each of these factors is weighted at any given moment in time, we do know that two of the most important factors are the frequency with which content is updated and the number and quality of inbound links from other websites and blogs—the more often others link to the pages that link to yours, the higher your own ranking. Because many bloggers post new content with great regularity and link obsessively to each other, blogs are, by nature, well-positioned for ranking by the venerable search engines.

# blog search engines introduce timeliness

Also in Chapter 8, we noted that the newer blog-specific search engines like Technorati, BlogPulse, Feedster, and IceRocket take advantage of blog pings and constantly updated newsfeeds to offer more timely results than those offered by traditional search engines, which must wait for their spider bots to scour the Web for new content. As mentioned, the downside of the new search engines is that they largely rely on a single ranking criterion—a raw count of a blog's inbound links or number of subscriptions to newsfeeds.

There are subtle differences in how these engines do their counts, of course. Technorati emphasizes ongoing discussions by only counting links on a blog's front page, while Bloglines uses a total link count. Bloglines even counts links within your own blog, which most others don't. Among the other variables are whether links in blog rolls are counted, how far back data is mined, and whether multiple links on a webpage are each counted or reported only once. Blog search engines are constantly being tweaked to address spam concerns and to leapfrog competitors as they offer more refined search and additional services.

It is heartening to see these engines evolving and responding to user needs. Ideally, they will gradually become better at gauging and telegraphing relevant spheres of influence. Raw counts of inbound links will always favor blogs that address more popular topics. Tools that raise the visibility of niche topics and that gauge the vitality of attending communities will go a long way toward solving this problem.

In the end, it pays to experiment with a number of the blog search engines, testing them to see how your own pages fare, as well as gauging how relevant they are for your own searches. Some of the things you might want to look for are: how well does the engine filter spam; how relevant are the results to your query; how fast is the response rate; how complete are the listings in comparison; how consistent are the results over time.

# keywords unlock search potential

As we've noted, blogs are by nature better optimized for search than most websites. We update them frequently, and interlinking among blogs is commonplace. Plus, many blogs stick to a specific topic. This focus greatly improves a blog's chances of incorporating keywords that potential readers might use when conducting web searches.

There are no hard-and-fast rules for choosing the most effective keywords, and there is no substitute for testing potential search terms and phrases. If a keyword or phrase is too general—simply "dogs," for instance—your blog may appear on search results pages, but buried deep behind websites and blogs with more inbound links and history. If a keyword is too specific—say, "boxerdoodle"—few readers will think to try it. Visit related websites and blogs and cull them for useful phrases. The trick lies in finding unique terms that are specific to interests you share with your ideal readers.

When you have a healthy handful of possible keywords and phrases, give them a test run in a few search engines—Google, Yahoo, Technorati, BlogPulse, and PubSub, for instance. In addition, you might check out how the terms fare as tags on Technorati, Wink, and del.icio.us. (We discuss tags in greater detail in Chapter 8, "Packing Your Toolkit.") As you're analyzing the results of your searches and associated tag clouds, keep your eyes open for related terms that might prove useful and test those, as well.

While looking over the resulting pages of links, ask yourself a few questions. Do you like the company your pages would keep using those keywords as primary search terms? Would you honestly stand a chance at making your way onto the top pages for searches on these keywords? What word or phrases would more appropriately define your content? Which terms do others in your field of interest use most often or most profitably?

---

**HOT LINKS: KEYWORD RESOURCES**

**Thesaurus.com**
http://www.thesaurus.reference.com

**Ontology Finder**
http://gorank.com/seotools/ontology

**Google AdWords Research Tool**
http://adwords.google.com/select

**Overture's Keyword Tool**
http://inventory.overture.com/d/searchinventory/suggestion

**Spannerworks' Link Popularity Checker/ Keyword Density Analyser**
http://spannerworks.com/seotoolkit.0.html

**WordTracker**
http://www.wordtracker.com

# where to feature keywords

Once you've tested and settled on a few primary and secondary keywords or phrases, you'll need to decide how to best integrate them on your blog pages. Do keep in mind that overusing keywords can set off spam filters, not to mention alienate those whom you hope will become regular visitors. We described blog page elements in Chapter 9, "Anatomy of a Blog Page." Here, we'll analyze how individual page elements might benefit most from the judicious inclusion of keywords and phrases.

## domain name

Choosing a domain name that contains one or more of your keywords can go a long way toward ensuring placement on traditional web search engine results pages. The closer the keyword is to the beginning of the domain name, the better. One or two hyphens are fine, but more than that may set off spam sensors. Speaking of spam, Google and PubSub are among the engines that rank domain names higher if they are purchased for more than one year since spammers tend to launch and abandon domains within short timeframes.

## title bar

When you view a web page, the words at the top of the browser window make up the title bar. If the title bar contains keywords, again preferably at the beginning, you get Google points for searches on those terms.

## headlines for posts

Not all bloggers choose to provide headlines for their entries, and not all blogs are improved by headlines, but for those wishing to make it more likely that others will find their content via search engines, omitting them is a missed opportunity for several reasons. Headlines highlight the content of an entry and serve as friendly gestures to your busy readers, alerting them to entries of greatest interest, particularly if they read your syndicated blog content in a newsreader. Furthermore, you can often configure your blog authoring software to use the text in your headlines to generate search-engine-friendly permalink URLs for individual posts. The URL http://dispatchesfromblogistan.com/tips/trackback-demystified includes not only the headline for the post, but the tag category as well. Odd as it may seem, search engines prefer human-readable URLs over ones that contain database symbols such as ampersands, equal signs, and question marks.

## body text of a post

In classic search engine optimization for commercial websites, you would generally want 5 to 20 percent of the total words on a page to be keywords. This can be a bit heavy-handed when talking about blog entries that are more conversational and, ideally, don't read like market-speak, but gracefully incorporating a keyword or three that reflect the general tenor of the blog and that call out the specific topic of the entry will make it easier for potential readers to find the page in their search results. Placing these keywords near the beginning of the body text influences weighting, as does formatting keywords in bold.

## anchor text for outbound links

Too many outbound links (many dozens, say) can trigger search engine scrutiny since they often suggest *link farms*. That said, a judicious number of well-chosen links to other websites will please your readers and those to whom you link. It's good to remember that when you link to others from your blog, knitting keywords into the anchor text you use to signal the link can contribute to the ranking of that site.

---

### bombs away!

You may have heard of Google "bombs." This trick takes advantage of the search engine's penchant for ranking links higher if they use consistent anchor text. To launch a bomb, a cabal of site developers all agree to use the same phrasing as anchor text for a link and, voilà! higher ranking for the linked page. The first major instance of a bomb occurred in 1999 when the search phrase "more evil than Satan" returned Microsoft's homepage. While perhaps amusing for temporary practical jokes or political actions, it's generally a bad practice for blogs since the engines are always on the lookout for those attempting the scam.

## image alt attributes

Alt attributes, often referred to as alt tags, are the text labels that a browser displays if graphic elements cannot be viewed. Embedding keywords in the alt attributes' HTML code can provide search engines with a bit of extra grist, but the tactic has been so abused by spammers that you should probably be fairly restrained in the use of keywords in these tags.

## site navigation

If you use graphic files for your navigation links without appending text versions, spiders won't be able to read them. It's never a bad idea to include navigation, perhaps in the footer, that is text-based, explicit, and, where practical, includes keywords.

## meta tags

There are two types of HTML meta tags. *Description meta tags*, as the name implies, are short site summaries of 200 characters or fewer that appear on some search engine results pages. *Keyword meta tags* are much shorter, generally ten keywords or fewer, and merely call out the keywords you want the search engines to notice. Both sets of tags are contained in the source code for your HTML pages and can be read by spiders. Meta tags have been greatly abused by spammers and so are of much less importance than they were a few years ago, particularly on Google. Definitely avoid using any keyword more than once in either type of tag since this sets off the spam watchdogs. You can also be penalized for placing keywords in the meta tags that don't appear in the main blog content.

## categorical tags

Assigning categorical tags to your posts—as well as to your blog as a whole—can go a long way toward making blog content more findable. It's true that you can search the full text of any post, using both traditional and blog-specific search engines, but searches narrowed to tags greatly increase the likelihood of finding relevant content. We've talked about assigning descriptive tags to your posts in previous chapters. Potential visitors to your blog use services like Technorati and Ice Rocket to search for blog posts tagged with specific descriptors. Technorati even lets you assign tags to your blog as a whole. Once they've found your pages, visitors might assign their own tags using a social bookmarking site like del.icio.us. (Don't forget to assign tags to your own posts on del.icio.us!) Sweetening the tag pot a bit further, there are new tag search tools that seek tagged content across a spectrum of tag-enabled services—Technorati, Ice Rocket, and del.icio.us, of course, but also Flickr, Craigslist, and the social news aggregator Digg. See Hot Links: Cross-Service Tag Search.

**HOT LINKS: CROSS-SERVICE TAG SEARCH**

**Wink**
http://www.wink.com

**Tag Central**
http://tagcentral.net

**rel8r**
http://www.rel8r.com

**keotag**
http://www.keotag.com

# some common search optimization mistakes

Search engine algorithms are, for the most part, as secret as the parentage of Donald Duck's three nephews, but endless tests (and mistakes) by search engine optimization consultants, along with a careful reading of Google's patents, provide a few clues.

In general, search engines are always on the lookout for spam and other attempts to game the system. Too many links, particularly if they are unrelated, will set off spam alerts since these may signal a "link farm." It may seem innocent enough to try and increase your inbound link count by submitting your blog or even paying a modest price to have your links listed on these pages, but search engines often dub these sites "bad neighborhoods" and can be quick to impose penalties on both the offending servers and those being served. Penalties can range from merely placing you lower on the results pages to banning offending pages from the search index.

One way to gauge if Google has penalized a site is to visit the potential link farm's page using a browser that is enabled with Google's Toolbar

(toolbar.google.com). Once installed, the PageRank tool lets you see a small green sliding bar supposedly indicating Google's rank on a scale of one to ten. The actual PageRank listed is not very dependable, but if there is no green showing, the site may be in the doghouse—and you will be, too, if you associate with the page. A sliver of green is fine; it just means that the site hasn't yet accrued many links.

A related strategy involves consensual cross-linking among a networked suite of blogs. This can be completely valid, much like a web-ring, helping individuals with similar interests find relevant content. The participating blogs may enjoy higher search rank as a result of the links, but the bigger search engines do try to discern which of these cooperative efforts are purely venal. It's tricky, and you can get caught in a penalty net if the interlinking is too aggressive, particularly if all or most of the participating blogs reside on the same server or if there is little similarity among the participating sites. Duplicate content on multiple domains definitely sets off the spam sensors.

Among the other devices quick to garner a penalty is *cloaking*. Offending websites present one webpage to search engines and another to everyone else. Another bad tactic is sometimes called "keyword stuffing" and, as the phrase implies, involves using dozens or even hundreds of keywords in body text and meta tags on a single page. Links that are hidden (keywords hidden behind a <div> layer or white type against a white background, for instance) are likely to result in a penalty. Plagiarism is always a bad idea, but if a content author reports stolen images or other content, the search engines may ban the offending domain's pages from future searches.

For the search engines, combating spam and other dirty deeds is really a lot like the old carnival game, whack-a-mole. The better the search engines get at blocking spam, the more cunning the spamsters inevitably become. Needless to say, trying to trick the search engines is not for the timid. And really, it's not necessary.

# register with search engines and directories

One step that bloggers often forget is to register their blog and feeds with the many search engines and hierarchical directories to ensure that they index your content. Robin Good's list of search engines mentioned at the beginning of Chapter 8 includes links to most of the specific submission pages. (A list of updated resource links mentioned in the book can always be found at dispatchesfromblogistan.com/hotlinks.) Be prepared to submit a short description of your site. This is the text that will show up on search results pages and should be clear, compelling, and include a call to action.

Bear in mind that Google often imposes a probationary period before listing a website in its searches. Sometimes called the "sandbox," this waiting room was invented to thwart spammers, but it can be discouraging for new bloggers since the probation period can last several months. One solution open to those willing to lay down a bit of hard cash involves placing targeted ads using Google's AdWords program, but in general, it's at least comforting to know that most of us spend a bit of time in the sandbox.

Directories are hierarchical listings that generally resemble the organization of the Yellow Pages. With the many improvements in basic search capabilities over the years, these pages have become somewhat less useful, but it still makes sense to submit your blog to the major directories. Once again, be prepared to submit a brief description of your blog that will spur action.

Technorati allows you to "claim" your blog on its service, which adds links to your profile, a photo, and associated tags to search results. Don't forget to tag your blog as a whole on the service, since this will help raise your visibility in Technorati's directory, called Blog Finder (technorati.com/blogs).

**HOT LINKS: WEB DIRECTORY SUBMISSION PAGES**

**Yahoo Directory**
http://docs.yahoo.com/info/suggest

**LookSmart**
http://looklistings.looksmart.com

**DMOZ**
http://dmoz.org/add.html

# syndicated feeds broaden a blog's reach

More and more people are choosing to read syndicated blog content in news aggregators, rather than on the blog pages themselves. It's easy to see why. New entries arrive as soon as they're posted. Spam is minimal. The clean interface of most of the newsreaders allows individuals to scan dozens of blogs and news sites, complete with links and images, in a fraction of the time necessary to visit each website in turn. Clearly, syndicating your blog content helps to raise the profile of your blog.

Plus, new visitors are more likely to find you if they're using one of the newer search engines—Feedster and PubSub, among them—that index the content in newsfeeds, rather than the content on blog pages. Once again, if you're hoping to attract new fans via search engines, this is an excellent argument for syndicating the full text of your entries.

There are downsides to newsfeed distribution, of course. Not everyone knows what a newsfeed is or how to subscribe to one. Also, it is difficult to know how many people are subscribing to your feeds unless you run your feeds through a service like FeedBurner, which is useful but can be confusing to potential readers since they must copy a customized FeedBurner URL into their news aggregators rather than one with your blog address as the main domain name. In addition, newsfeeds can burden your web server if your traffic skyrockets, although that's a problem many would like to have.

You can mitigate some of these problems by providing a link to a page that explains exactly how to subscribe to your feeds. Don't forget to place the link for your feeds prominently on your blog. Also, be sure to enable *autodiscovery*, if your blog software includes the feature, since it will eliminate some of the arcane steps currently required when subscribing to many feeds.

Do subscribe to your own feeds on websites like Feedster, Bloglines, and PubSub, as well as news sites like Google, Yahoo, and MSN. Not only will you know for certain how your content looks to others, some of these services require at least one subscription before they begin tracking and indexing a feed.

Finally, you may want to encourage others to display your syndicated content on their own websites and blogs. This can be a win-win in that it increases the distribution for you and provides a source of refreshed content for others. Once again, however, keeping track of the number of feeds viewed remains a problem.

# leverage your own links

Because search engines put so much emphasis on inbound links, we sometimes forget to pay attention to our own outbound links. After uploading a post, always click on all the links in your posts. Not only will this guarantee that you coded them correctly, it will also cause a link to your blog to show up on that site's referrer logs. Many web authors are religious about checking their logs and will often click the link to see what you've written about them. Similarly, use trackback links whenever you quote or refer to a post on another blog, so readers of that blog know that you've continued the conversation on your own blog. (See Chapter 8, "Packing Your Toolkit," for a refresher on the topic.) Plus, the trackback link will count as an inbound link for you in some search engines. Finally, take the time to tag each of your blog posts on social bookmarking sites like del.icio.us and Furl (furl.net). Others may already be tagging your posts, but who knows better than you what categories potential visitors might consult to find content exactly like yours?

# smart ad buys can drive traffic

If you're intent on reaching specific audiences and you have a modest budget, you may want to investigate placing ads that link to your pages. You can sometimes purchase ad space on websites that cater to specific audiences you're hoping to attract, much as one would purchase an ad in a magazine or on the radio. Another tack involves signing up with Google

Adwords (adwords.google.com) or Yahoo Search Marketing (searchmarketing.yahoo.com), programs in which you bid on potential keywords that you believe others might use to find content like your own. If your bid wins, your ad, usually consisting of a few lines of text, appears with other sponsored links on results pages for those keyword searches.

These ads can be effective, but knowing in advance how much they will cost is tricky because the price fluctuates as others bid on the same keywords. You can set a monthly limit on how much you are willing to pay, but if bidding becomes heated and you've set your budget fairly low, your ad may only run a few days out of the month. Just as with all strategies that rely on keyword searches, it pays to do a little testing before placing your bids. Do normal searches on Google or Yahoo using the keywords you're considering and see which ads appear in the sponsored areas of the page. If the ads are for major products or services, the bidding may be too rich for your budget. Choose a slightly less common keyword and try again. Ultimately, you won't know whether these ads result in actual traffic until you try it, but you can experiment by joining the services for limited periods of time and with set monthly budgets. (See Chapter 8, "Packing Your Toolkit," for a list of contextual advertising resources.)

# and then there are stunts

All the world may not exactly be a stage, but a blog can mimic one. If you decide to stage a stunt, keep in mind the caveats listed earlier in the chapter since search engines are quick to penalize sites they believe are trying to game the system. That said, why not? Make up weekly horoscopes based on astrological signs of your own devising and post links from within comments on astrology blogs. Unveil a series of photos that slowly tell a story and offer a prize to whomever submits the best text to accompany it. Announce a jingle contest using high-traffic keywords. Invite fans of Lego blocks to submit photos of their most daring sculptures. It's worth noting that almost any Top 10 (or Top Any Number) list will attract readers, which is why so many magazines and TV shows exploit lists on their covers and in their promos. Or simply post polls. There's no explaining it, people love to participate in polls.

# evangelize your blog

Don't be embarrassed to tell the world about your blog. Mention it to friends and associates. Include the web address in your bios and email signature, as well as on business cards—job gods allowing, of course. Link to your blog from any other websites that you control. Engage in conversations on your own blog and in comments on related blogs. Many bloggers allow you to include your own URL as a link when you comment. Hubris is unbecoming, but honest enthusiasm for your own works will help to attract like-minded fans.

# engage in conversations

It's important to remember that what distinguishes many of the most popular blogs is their sense of community. They engage their readers and facilitate lively dialogue. Blogs are a little like gardening. They require constant planting and weeding to remain vital. Visit related blogs and post comments that contribute to the conversations going on there. On your own blog, be generous in reaching out to your readers. Link to their pages when appropriate. Ask questions. Encourage comments. Respond promptly to comments. Weed out the troublemakers. (See "Managing the Commentariat" in Chapter 10, "Writing that Engages.")

All this talk about search engine optimization and blog rank are well and good, but in the end, most blogs are judged on their ability to nurture community. It's good to understand a bit about search engine optimization strategies, but don't let your quest for rank undermine the quality of the dialogue taking place on your blog.

# best/worst-case scenario

The best-case scenario would seem to be getting mentioned on one of the top blogs or news filter sites. This will almost certainly result in an enormous number of people visiting your pages. The results of this kind of attention can be both bad and good. If your servers can't withstand the traffic, visitors greeted with a 404 notice are unlikely to return. If they manage to see your content and like it, there is pressure to continue presenting material that is on a par with whatever attracted them in the first place. To alleviate these problems, it's best to plan and implement as though you might attract that kind of traffic at any time. Bigger bandwidth doesn't cost that much these days and best quality content should be our goal every day.

# bringing it all home

All this talk about search engine rank, keyword choices, and overall self-promotion can be discouraging for some, but it's important to remember that not every blog requires thousands of visitors to be successful. The tips and tricks in this chapter can just as easily be used to identify and court a small number of ideal readers who appreciate your efforts and who enjoy entering into ongoing conversations with you.

As the number of blogs competing for eyes and hearts continues to grow, it behooves all bloggers to at least be aware of the promotion options open to them. The blog landscape is continually shaping and reshaping itself. You can be part of this dynamic evolution. Consider the tips and tricks in this chapter to be a starting point. We're watching as a variety of products and services scramble to provide better tools for tracking and promoting our blogs. The best of these are learning from their users and becoming more relevant in the process.

The bottom line is that no matter how successful you are in getting people to visit you that first time, the real trick is in getting them to return and participate. Put your main effort into building quality and a sense of community and your blog will stand out among its peers.

# keeping it legal

Blogs make publishing so simple, it's easy to forget that legal responsibilities and liabilities are part of the package. Most problems can generally be avoided by keeping common sense and common decency in mind, but a familiarity with the basic laws governing *intellectual property, defamation, privacy, obscenity,* and *journalistic privilege* will go a long way toward ensuring that your blogging days are tort-free.

One of the realities complicating any discussion of blogs and legal issues is that laws differ from one state or province to another, and from country to country. This chapter will focus primarily on laws in the United States, but the larger legal issues discussed will be of concern to bloggers everywhere. Another reality is the fact that the laws being applied to blogging were, for the most part, written to address print or broadcast media, forcing blogging and other online media into legal molds that aren't always a perfect fit.

All this said, ignorance of the law is not a permissible excuse, so it makes sense to have at least a passing familiarity with pertinent legal issues. Throughout this chapter, you will find pointers to organizations that provide deeper and more specific information about individual topics. In particular, any blogger would do well to peruse the *Legal Guide for Bloggers* posted by the Electronic Frontier Foundation (EFF), a grassroots legal advocacy non-profit. Links to web pages mentioned in this chapter appear in the Hot Links list titled "A Blogger's Legal Resources" and are listed on the Dispatches from Blogistan blog (dispatchesfromblogistan.com/hotlinks).

The information in this chapter is not meant to substitute for professional legal advice. If you should find yourself facing a libel or copyright suit, or a letter advising you to remove content or cease and desist publishing, it's best to consult a lawyer familiar with the laws in your jurisdiction.

The most important thing is to not let all this legal talk dissuade you from publishing. Many of the laws discussed below were instituted specifically to protect the rights of citizens to speak their minds. Certainly there will always be individuals, corporations, and even governments that wish to intimidate or otherwise impose a "chilling effect" on the speech of those who would critique them, but it is in the thoughtful exercise of our rights and freedoms that we strengthen the ability of our societies to withstand these assaults.

# intellectual property laws and blogs

When you publish a thought or image on your blog, you have a reasonable expectation that others may not legally appropriate your work for their own benefit. Reciprocally, you may not plagiarize the works of others. Intellectual property laws have grown up in an attempt to provide incentives for the creation of new content, but as with all real-world issues, there are complications. Chief among the forces blurring intellectual property discussions are differing societal norms, fuzzy and inconsistent application of prior law to digital media, and a general disinterest on the part of the consumer. Copyright has never been a static concept, and as constant headlines about copy protection schemes and their detractors attest, it's unlikely to be settled soon.

# copyright evolves over time

During the latter half of the fifteenth century, Europe's first printing presses churned out more than 10,000 unique titles, a great many of them without the permission of their authors. Laws governing copyright were spotty and clearly hadn't yet caught up with the new technology.

In 1491, the Republic of Venice granted author Peter of Ravenna the exclusive right to print and sell copies of his work, *Phoenix*, arguably the first true copyright. In 1501, the dramas of Hroswitha of Gandersheim were the first German publications to enjoy exclusive publishing privilege. In 1518, Richard Pynson, official printer to the British King, was allowed to publish copies of a speech with the first *regium impressorem*, or royal seal. Like similar exclusive grants for salt, coal, and beer, this printer's privilege was officially referred to as a "monopoly."

> In 1511 Albrecht Dürer attached this formidable warning to his prints: Hold! You crafty ones, strangers to work, and pilferers of other men's brains. Think not rashly to lay your thievish hands upon my works. Beware! Know you not that I have a grant from the most glorious Emperor Maximillian, that not one throughout the imperial dominion shall be allowed to print or sell fictitious imitations of these engravings? Listen! And bear in mind that if you do so, through spite or through covetousness, not only will your goods be confiscated, but your bodies also placed in mortal danger.

By 1623, the Statute of Monopolies dictated that these grants be referred to as "patents." Whether called monopolies or patents, the British system still denied authors any rights. They were forced to submit to government censorship, and they received no royalties after selling their works to the few designated printers.

Perhaps recognizing that this was a distinct disincentive to the creation of new works, the British Parliament passed the Statute of Anne in 1710. The statute did away with ad hoc monopolies, replacing them with individual copyright guarantees for new works. In addition, the ruling imposed a time limit on the copyrights—fourteen years after publication, with the possibility of one fourteen-year extension. After this period, works would enter the public domain and might be copied at will.

In United States, the Copyright Act of 1790 was modeled on the Statute of Anne. It bore a telling subtitle: *An Act for the Encouragement of Learning, by Securing the Copies of Maps, Charts, and Books to the Authors and Proprietors of Such Copies.* Like their British counterparts, American authors, artists, and scientists now controlled the copyrights for each of their works.

The Berne Convention of 1887 extended reciprocal copyright protections among cooperating nations. An innovation introduced by the agreement is the automatic assignment of copyright, which persists today, meaning that creators do not have to actively register a work for it to be copyright protected. Once a work is "fixed" (recorded on some physical medium), the author enjoys full and exclusive rights to the work and its derivatives until he or she gives up the copyright or until the copyright term expires.

By 1909, the United States felt the need to revise its own Copyright Act in order to address growing concerns about the balance between a creator's rights and the right of the public to have access to such works. The new bill stated, ". . . [I]t has been a serious and difficult task to combine the protection of the composer with the protection of the public, and to so frame an act that would accomplish the double purpose of securing an adequate return for all use made of his composition and at the same time prevent the formation of oppressive monopolies . . ." *(H.R. Rep. No. 2222, 60th Cong., 2nd Sess., p.7).*

A further revision to U.S. Copyright law, 1976, attempted to take into consideration new technologies, as well as put the United States in better accord with other nations participating in the Berne Convention. As was already true in Europe, it extended copyright for the lifetime of the author plus 50 years (works for hire were protected for 75 years). Fair use doctrines were codified (see below), and protections were extended to even unpublished works. The Sonny Bono Copyright Term Extension Act of 1998 extended U.S. copyright to 70 years after an author's death.

Also in 1998, the Digital Millennium Copyright Act (DMCA) established safe harbors for online service providers and included amendments addressing Internet broadcasting. The most controversial measure in the bill is Section 1201, which criminalizes circumvention of technological copy-protection measures. Many complain that these mechanisms undermine the "protection of the public" and promote monopolies rather than encouraging innovation and creativity, the original argument for providing creators with copyright protections.

For those wishing to study the history of copyright in more detail, the Association of Research Libraries and Wikipedia both provide useful overviews. (See "A Blogger's Legal Resources.")

# keeping within the bounds of fair use

Some content is free to use without fear of copyright violation—government publications, older works that have passed into the public domain, and content that is published under the least restrictive Creative Commons licenses (see below). Most text and images on the Web, however, are copyright-protected and, other than for fair use or other statutory exemptions, may not be copied without the express permission of the copyright holder.

If a copyright holder believes that you have violated fair use, you may find yourself the recipient of a takedown notice demanding that you remove the offending content. You could even face a civil suit and, if found guilty of copyright violation, be required to pay the copyright holder substantial damages.

According to United States copyright law, fair use includes the right to quote short statements from copyrighted content for the purpose of "criticism, comment, news reporting, teaching, scholarship, or research." When copying content from another source, here are four tests that the courts apply to determine whether a copyright has been violated.

## transformative uses

A straight copy-and-paste of copyrighted material will almost always be dealt with more severely than a "transformative" use. In a practical sense what this means is that if you provide context for an excerpted quote—criticism, parody, or extenuating comments, for instance—you are less likely to be found in violation of copyright.

## non-commercial uses

If you're making money from your blog content, you're more likely to be considered liable for copyright infringement. The courts treat non-commercial uses more liberally.

## portion used

Fair use guidelines often use the word "short" to describe the length of a selection that may be legal to use. However, if the original work is already short, you may be accused of publishing a "substantial" portion of the work. Other than common sense, there is no formula for determining what portion constitutes fair use.

## market potential

Even if the work as a whole is fairly lengthy, if you publish the "heart" of a work—a surprise ending, say—you may be violating copyright. The test is whether the republished work undermines the market potential of the original material. This applies even if the original work is offered for free.

# "creative commons" licenses clarify rights

Although a creator of texts or images doesn't have to include a copyright notice for a work to enjoy copyright guarantees (thanks to the Berne Convention), many creators include the copyright mark (©) and the words "All rights reserved." This explicit gesture is good if you want your audience to know for a fact that you don't permit any reproductions or redistribution, but what if you would like to allow at least some copying and redistribution?

Creative Commons is a non-profit organization that offers a consistent mechanism for letting audiences know exactly which kinds of uses an author allows. Creative Commons licenses don't replace copyrights, they supplement them. The types of Creative Commons licenses are described below. Choose the one that best suits your interests and publish notice of the license with a link back to the Creative Commons website. (See "A Blogger's Legal Resources.") Some websites, like the photo-sharing service, Flickr, allow users to choose Creative Commons licenses while uploading content.

Creative Commons licenses, in descending order of restrictiveness, are:

## attribution, non-commercial, no derivatives

This license allows others to copy and distribute copyrighted content as long as they link to the author, there is no financial gain for the copier, and no changes are made to the content. This is sometimes referred to as the "free advertising" license.

## attribution, non-commercial, share-alike

Once again, the copier must link to the author and the work must be distributed for free, but the content may be altered, remixed, or otherwise integrated into the works of others—as long as the new work is distributed under this same license.

## attribution, non-commercial

This license is the same as the one above, but without the requirement that the copier distribute the derivative work with the same license.

## attribution, no derivatives

Others may copy works with this license as long as they link to the author and make no changes, even if the derivative work is commercial.

### attribution, share-alike

The copyrighted content may be altered and included in a commercial package as long as it is distributed with a link to the creator and with this same license.

### attribution

The copyrighted work may be distributed, tweaked, and even offered for sale as long as there is a clear link to the original creator.

### other licenses

In addition to the six licenses listed above, Creative Commons also provides more specialized licenses for things like file sampling, music sharing, and software distribution, as well as a Public Domain Dedication that allows you to remove all copyright restrictions.

## parody as a special case

Parodies that use recognizable elements from the thing being ridiculed can sometimes result in civil lawsuits. In the United States, the courts are inclined to protect parody, perhaps agreeing with the English poet and playwright Ben Jonson, who wrote in 1598, "A Parodie, a parodie! to make it absurder than it was." Parody does not imply a blanket protection, however, and authors of satirical texts and cartoons are advised to keep fair use guidelines and the general constraints surrounding defamation in mind. (More on defamation below.)

A defining parody case pitted *Hustler* magazine founder Larry Flynt against religious broadcaster Jerry Falwell. An issue of the magazine published in 1983 contained a parody of an ad for an alcoholic drink, titled "Jerry Falwell Talks About His First Time." A photo of a thoughtful-looking Falwell accompanied the text, which purported to be Falwell detailing a drunken bout of incest with his mother in an outhouse. "Mom looked better than a Baptist whore with a $100 donation," the ad read.

Falwell sued Flynt, claiming libel and intentional infliction of emotional distress. The case made it to the Supreme Court, which decided that a public figure may not recover damages for intentional infliction of emotional distress based on a satire, since this would tend to "chill" critiques of public figures. A public figure may recover damages if there is a "false statement of fact" and the satirist can be shown to have acted with "actual malice," meaning there was reckless disregard for the truth. The Court ruled that no reasonable person would believe that Falwell had actually made the statements in the parody advertisement.

## acknowledging right of publicity

Individuals who are "public figures" sometimes sue publishers or commercial ventures if they believe that their likeness has been used to commercial advantage without their consent. Free speech guarantees allow the use of another's name or likeness as long as whatever is being said is truthful and no false endorsements are implied.

## avoiding trademark violations

Trademark law clearly forbids using anyone else's trademark to deceptively market your own products, but you may use trademarked names and logos to identify companies, products, or services, as long as you don't imply any endorsement. This applies even if you are criticizing the trademark owner. You may, for instance, sell a product as "HP-compatible," or a hotel room as "convenient for Disneyland visits." There is some gray area, however, if your blog offers products for sale or contains advertising, since the courts may then view your website as "commercial," which results in fewer protections.

## keeping trade secrets secret

Bloggers who write about their jobs and place of employment must take special care not to disclose trade secrets. Trade secrets include any information that provides a business with a competitive advantage, and the laws governing this area provide protections for information about physical devices, processes, software, formulas, patterns, plans, designs, and even "know-how." Obviously, if you've signed a non-disclosure agreement or other contract forbidding you to discuss certain matters, you may not talk about them on your blog, but the law regarding trade secrets can sometimes be interpreted to include even implicit understandings about what constitutes "competitive advantage." The Chilling Effects Clearinghouse is a joint effort between the EFF and several universities, including Harvard, Stanford, and The University of California at Berkeley. Among the many excellent resources on its website is a relevant *Trade Secrets FAQ*. (See "A Blogger's Legal Resources.")

# balancing privacy against the right to know

Aristotle drew a line between *polis*, or political activity, and *oikos*, domestic activity. Seventeenth-century social contract theorist John Locke equated the right to privacy with the right to private property. In the nineteenth century, philosopher and economist John Stuart Mill argued that the distinction between public and private is explicit. But it wasn't until *The Right to Privacy*, a seminal essay published in the *Harvard Law Review* in 1890 by Samuel Warren and future U.S. Supreme Court Justice Louis Brandeis, that privacy was championed as a unique and inalienable right. "The right to be let alone," they wrote, is the right "most valued by men." (*4 Harvard L.R. 193*)

Legal precedent began defining the right to privacy as control over information about oneself and an expectation that confidential personal information not be publicly disclosed. United States law gradually identified four types of invasion of privacy:

- ▶ "unreasonable intrusion on seclusion" (invasion of privacy)
- ▶ distribution of previously undisclosed private information
- ▶ publicity that places another in a false light
- ▶ appropriation of another's name or likeness

Subsequent privacy-related statutes filled out privacy's legal profile. U.S. laws criminalize surreptitious interception of conversations in a home or hotel room (eavesdropping); interference with first-class mail, telephone service, or "electronic data by wire"; breaching confidentiality of students; publishing video rental histories; accessing someone else's bank records; and in some states, disclosure of library records. Your garbage does not, for the record, enjoy the same privacy protections.

> Besides being the subject of formal laws, privacy codes are also enforced through mechanisms such as professional codes of ethics (see "Ethics Primer for Bloggers" in Chapter 4); confidentiality understandings with doctors, lawyers, and religious representatives; and Terms of Service for many online environments.

In 1965, the Supreme Court extended privacy rights to include an individual's ability to make decisions affecting his or her own life—in the words of Justice William O. Douglas, "a protected zone of privacy." Subsequent privacy-related decisions have guaranteed right to enter into interracial marriage; to view pornography in private; to distribute contraceptives; and in *Roe v. Wade*, to choose abortion.

The right to privacy has gradually gained legal acceptance, but debates on the topic are often heated, and interpretations can vary within jurisdictions and political wings. An ABC News poll in early 2006 found that 30 percent of its viewers felt that the government was intruding on privacy without justification. This number is significant since it's double the percentage just two years earlier.

Globally, privacy advocates argue for more stringent privacy laws, pointing out that individuals, corporations, and governments regularly engage in invasive searches, surveillance, and eavesdropping. One school of opponents argues that "information must be free," and that some expectation of personal privacy must submit to the greater good inherent in efficient and open access to information. Another set of opponents take the socially conservative tack, arguing that public safety comes first, and if some personal privacy rights must be surrendered in the name of greater security, then so be it.

Like intellectual property and defamation law, privacy laws are evolving with the times. The Electronic Privacy Information Center provides useful additional information about libel issues. (See "A Blogger's Legal Resources.") Below is a snapshot of the privacy laws most likely to be of interest to bloggers.

## bloggers and privacy laws

Bloggers write about each other all the time and so are vulnerable to accusations of invasion of privacy. Plus, the spontaneity and informal style of blogging sometimes seduce authors into publishing information that is not well researched, or that exaggerates in a way that might mislead others. Further, it is not unusual for bloggers to publish a bit of speculation or a few barebones facts, trusting their readers to clarify or disprove their contentions.

If what you publish is false (or alleged to be false), then libel law comes into play. If the content in question is true, the subject of your blog post may still attempt to sue you if he or she believes there is proof of "unreasonable intrusion" (trespass, secret surveillance, misrepresentation to obtain consent), false light (an unflattering portrayal of another that misleads the viewer; unlike libel, false light does not require that harm to a reputation be proven, only that the statement or image is "highly offensive"), or appropriation of his or her name or likeness for personal gain.

A judge will attempt to gauge the verifiability of any facts, how harmful the disclosure of the information was to the plaintiff, and whether the information was "newsworthy." In 1964, an Alabama woman sued a local newspaper for publishing a photo of her dress blowing up as she walked past air jets at a country fair. The courts ruled against the newspaper, ruling that the photo had "no legitimate news interest to the public." (*Daily Times Democrat v. Graham)*

California law requires that the plaintiff prove that the disclosure would be considered offensive and objectionable to a reasonable person of ordinary sensibilities. A blog author might argue that the information was newsworthy, meaning that at least some reasonable members of the community entertain a legitimate interest in the disclosure. An item is more likely to be considered newsworthy if the private details involve someone already in the public eye—politicians, entertainers, sports figures, and the like.

Whether writing about the famous or lowly, it makes sense to double-check any facts that you report; confirm that information was gathered legally; gauge the potential "newsworthiness" of the item; and finally, make a conscientious decision about whether or not to expose the private details.

# defamation, libel, and blogging

The best defense against an accusation of defamation is to have published the truth. If you should end up facing defamation charges, even if you are eventually found innocent, defending the suit will likely be very costly, time-consuming, and potentially damaging to your reputation. Defamation laws vary from country to country, and even state to state, but a basic knowledge of defamation law can help bloggers avoid libel charges.

In its narrowest definition, defamation is a false statement of fact that is harmful to another's reputation. The law distinguishes two types of defamation: *slander* and *libel*. Slander is spoken defamation. Libel was traditionally written or printed defamation but now includes a wide variety of media, including television, radio, cartoons, and many online communications, including blogs.

In most jurisdictions, defamation laws require that for a statement to be judged libelous, it must be false; it must have been made available to more than just the publisher and the plaintiff; it must be about the plaintiff; and it tends to harm the reputation of the plaintiff. If the plaintiff is a public figure, he or she may have to prove actual malice on the part of the alleged libeler.

Traditionally, a public figure is someone who has actively sought to influence a matter of public interest. Entertainers, politicians, activists, and policy advocates are all public figures. Defamation laws in the United States, Britain, and many other countries make a distinction between private and public individuals. Your mother, co-worker, or therapist need only prove that your statement was "negligent." A public figure needs to prove that there was "actual malice," meaning that the author knew the statement was false or that the reporting exhibited "reckless disregard" for the truth.

Context can be important in libel cases. A judge might look at how the blog content in question compares with other posts on the same blog, as well as with the comments and trackbacks left by readers. The judge is attempting to gauge the reasonable expectations of the blog's audience, looking in particular for instances of figurative or hyperbolic language.

To illustrate how the courts have defined libel over time, the EFF provides a few examples from California libel law in its *Defamation FAQ*. (See "A Blogger's Legal Resources.") Calling an attorney a "crook" or a woman a "call girl" without specific facts to back up the allegation have resulted in libel convictions. Calling a political foe a "thief" and "liar" in a chance meeting was ruled non-libelous, as were calling a TV show participant "chicken butt" and changing the name of software code from "Carl Sagan" to "Butt Head Astronomer." The EFF points out that there are no hard-and-fast rules, but in general, "non-libelous examples are hyperbole or opinion, while the libelous statements are stating a defamatory fact."

The courts take a number of points into consideration when gauging libel, among them:

## truth

As mentioned above, the best way to avoid or win a defamation lawsuit is to publish only facts that you know to be true. That said, there is a bit of leeway in the law. U.S. case law includes a "substantial truth" clause that states that authors are not to blame for "slight inaccuracies of expression" *(Lathan v. Journal Co. 1966)*. Still, if accused of libel, publishers must prove that the "substance, the gist, the sting, of the matter is true" *(Gomba v. McLaughlin 1972)*. Whether true or not, if the statement in question tends to harm the reputation of another, a publisher may need to prove that wide distribution of the specific information is in the public interest.

## opinion

Opinions are often considered less damaging than statements of fact, and so a defendant might claim that a statement was meant to be viewed as opinion, rather than fact. The courts generally consider the context of the statement when deciding whether a reasonable person would find the statement one of fact or opinion. It can be tricky. A construction may at first glance look like a statement of fact but be judged opinion, as in, "The Beatles suck." Conversely, a statement may be constructed to look like an opinion, but a reasonable person might read it as an implication of fact: "It is my opinion that Reggie stole from the company."

## fair comment

Opinions offered about a matter of public interest can be treated more leniently still. If Reggie is a town mayor facing bribery charges and you state on your blog that you believe he did it, it is unlikely that a court would uphold Reggie's contention that you libeled him.

## false names

Changing the name of the person you are writing about will not necessarily protect you from defamation charges. This is particularly true if the person being discussed is reasonably identifiable within the context of your remarks.

## republication

Republishing content that already appears on another source does not absolve you of responsibility for the truthfulness and accuracy of the content.

## statute of limitation

If someone wants to sue for defamation, he or she generally must do so within a prescribed timeframe, the *statute of limitation*. California, for instance, only allows libel cases to be brought within one year of publication. If sued, it makes sense to check locally applicable statutes of limitation.

## retractions

If you are requested to print a retraction, be courteous. In general, errors should be corrected promptly and with the same level of prominence on your site as the offending material. In some states, a retraction will lessen your financial liability if the suit goes before a judge. That said, retractions can be considered an admission of guilt in court. If you have any questions about whether and how to respond, it's not a bad idea to consult a lawyer before publishing the retraction.

## insurance

If you're really worried about defamation lawsuits, there are liability insurance policies available, but many bloggers will find annual premiums averaging $3000 for a $1 million policy with a $5000 deductible to be a steep price.

## bottom line

In the end, most defamation cases can be avoided by using common sense. If your statements are clearly opinion and make no factual assertions that you can't back up, you are less likely to be accused of defamation and more likely to win if you are. Don't let fear of lawsuits hinder your style too much. Defamation laws are meant to protect individuals (and even corporations) from spurious and damaging statements and are not evil in themselves. You may find yourself protected by the same laws at some point.

For more information about defamation law in the United States and Britain, the Independent Press Association and the BBC both offer useful web pages. (See "A Blogger's Legal Resources.")

# journalistic privilege and blogging

In many jurisdictions, journalists enjoy certain privileges that allow them to research and report information that benefits the public. Originally these laws applied only to professional journalists in the employ of some established publisher. Over time, the guarantees have stretched to include individuals like book publishers and documentary filmmakers. Gradually, the courts are beginning to grant journalistic privileges to other authors who can prove they were disseminating legitimate information to the public.

Whether or not bloggers are included in these special protections is still being sorted out on a case-by-case basis. Overall, bloggers who exhibit a knowledge of journalistic ethics and the rules governing traditional newsgathering will be much more likely to be protected. Some of the journalistic issues that relate to bloggers are:

# reporters' privilege

In the United States, members of the press enjoy certain privileges designed to help them report fairly and with reduced fear of retribution. Most notably, journalists are allowed to keep the names of confidential sources private. Courts will sometimes subpoena journalists if information is unavailable from any other source. Journalists who do not comply may be held in contempt of court, and some reporters have gone to prison rather than disclose their sources.

In addition, many U.S. states provide additional protections to at least some journalists. As an example, voters in California approved a reporters' *shield initiative* that provides "absolute protection to nonparty journalists in civil litigation from being compelled to disclose unpublished information," as long as it isn't "overcome by a countervailing federal constitutional right." How bloggers will be considered under such laws is yet to be determined, since the law specifically protects persons "connected with . . . a newspaper, magazine, or other periodical publication." The Reporter's Committee for Freedom of the Press website contains a round-up of the reporters' privilege laws as they apply to various U.S. state jurisdictions. (See "A Blogger's Legal Resources.")

# public proceedings

Bloggers are allowed to report on public proceedings, although here again, the exact wording of statutes varies from state to state. In general, it pays to adhere to the "fair and true report" rule. Your reporting of a public proceeding doesn't have to be verbatim, but it should capture the substance of the proceeding and refrain from misleading the reader about the gist of what occurred.

## press credentials

Journalists apply for press passes that allow them access to certain events and individuals. Government agencies cannot arbitrarily decide to whom they will issue press credentials; they must publish the standards used to evaluate submissions. Bloggers may request credentials, and those who follow the guidelines are increasingly being granted passes. In particular, government agencies may not deny access based on "arbitrary and unnecessary regulations with a view to excluding from news sources representative of publications whose ownership or ideas they consider objectionable."

## public records

Thanks to the Freedom of Information Act (FOIA), United States citizens may request access to public records held by federal agencies. Bloggers may be able to receive the fee waiver given to the news media. Once again the Reporters' Committee for Freedom of the Press provides a useful guide titled "How to Use the Federal FOI Act." The American Society of Newspaper Editors provides examples of stories printed because of FOIA. (See "A Blogger's Legal Resources.")

## anti-SLAPP laws

One strategy for silencing protected speech about an issue of public concern is for an individual, organization, or even a governmental body to file a suit that claims defamation, conspiracy, nuisance, malicious prosecution (if a countersuit), or even "interference with economic advantage."

These cases usually lose in court but often win in the larger world. The accusers generally have deeper pockets than those whom they are attempting to silence, and often just the threat of a long and drawn-out court case is enough to cause a would-be critic to self-censor. Collectively, these attempts to intimidate citizens and "chill" free speech are called Strategic Lawsuits Against Public Participation (SLAPP).

Half of all U.S. states have passed specific anti-SLAPP laws that allow a defendant to file a special motion at the outset of a lawsuit, striking complaints if the conduct mentioned in the suit is protected by First Amendment guarantees. Among other legal advantages, defendants who have filed an anti-SLAPP motion and who subsequently win their cases are entitled to a mandatory award of reasonable attorney's fees. The First Amendment Project and California Anti-SLAPP Project both have additional information about the topic. (See "A Blogger's Legal Resources.")

## podcasting

Whether a professional journalist or a blogger, you are allowed to record your interviews and provide downloadable or streaming versions for the public. You must obtain permission from everyone recorded, however. One way to document this is to ask interviewees as you begin recording to first state their name and confirm that you have their permission.

# jobs and blogging

The media likes to cover stories about people fired for blogging. When Delta Air Lines fired Ellen Simonetti for posting a photo on her blog showing a sliver of bra while wearing her stewardess uniform, news outlets from gossip columns to staid business pages all pointed to the blog. A few months later when Google fired Mark Jen, an associate product manager, the press immediately began pointing to Jen's blog, on which he speculated quite openly about his employer's strategies and even its finances.

While this attention was good for upping the number of page views for the terminated bloggers, it didn't get them their jobs back. Some of the less-informed news articles invoked free speech protections, but the truth is that while the First Amendment protects Americans from government censorship, it places no such constraints on private companies. Basically, a company may fire its employees at-will, for any reasons that aren't themselves prohibited by law.

Five U.S. states—California, New York, Colorado, North Dakota, and Montana—have passed laws that limit an employer's right to fire individuals for activities unrelated to work, such as political activism or lifestyle choices. In addition, union employees enjoy some extra protections, since federal law specifically allows union members to organize and to exchange information about the workplace. And government employees do have at least some recourse to First Amendment protections.

Whistleblowing comes with its own protections and constraints. There are legal protections in place for individuals who expose illegal or harmful activities for the public good, but in order to be eligible for these protections, an employee is required to first report any violations to the overseeing governmental or law enforcement bodies before disclosing the information publicly.

The truth is, compared to the tens of millions of individuals now blogging, the number of terminations related to blogging is still quite small. San Francisco writer Curt Hopkins keeps a running tally of fired bloggers at his *Statistics on Fired Bloggers* page. (See "A Blogger's Legal Resources.")

## employee guidelines for blogging

Increasingly, companies are coming around to the idea that employee blogging may be good for a company. Blogs that are company-centered can test marketing messages, solicit customer feedback, and harvest new ideas. Employees' private blogs might mention the company only occasionally, but this casual connection can help to put a human face on a company and allows employees to learn more directly from customers and partners.

If employees know ahead of time which topics will be considered off-limits or even illegal, they can approach their blogs with greater confidence and avoid putting themselves or the company in jeopardy.

One of the best ways to keep the number of blog-terminations low is through education. Unions and trade organizations are beginning to provide their members with guidelines for blogging. Bloggers all over the world are sharing job-related tips and war stories. Perhaps most importantly, many companies are formulating blog policies and actively communicating them to their staffs, just as they do guidelines for guarding against sexual harassment suits and maintaining trade secrets.

A policy that builds trust between employer and employees will grant employees explicit permission to blog, as long as certain guidelines are followed. These guidelines will vary by industry and company whim but will probably forbid blog content that violates the privacy or publicity rights of others; that insults customers, partners, or other employees; that discloses trade secrets or other confidential information; or that in general condones illegal activity.

Whether employers can forbid topics like political activity or sexy content depends on state laws. A company that forbids its employees from writing about chicken because they work at a pork-processing plant would be silly but within legal rights. *A Guide to Workplace Blogging* from c|Net is a good resource for deeper reading this topic, as is author Biz Stone's *How Not to Get Fired Because of Your Blog.* (See "A Blogger's Legal Resources.")

### tips for bloggers with jobs

▶ Acknowledge that if you don't put your blog content behind a password, anyone, including your boss and fellow employees, might someday come across it.

▶ If your company has an explicit blog policy, study it and request written answers to any questions you think may relate to your particular blog.

▶ Avoid using company computers, servers, or software for personal blogs. Just as companies in general have the right to read any email that travels across their servers, they will have more direct access to your blog content and patterns.

▶ If you do blog from work, be careful about when you post entries. Each entry is date- and time-stamped, and your argument that you blog only during breaks will fall apart if you're blogging on the hour.

▶ Be clear in your own mind about which company-related facts are confidential or considered trade secrets, and never write about them.

▶ If you plan to engage in whistle-blowing, a foot-fetish blog circle, or political activism, you may want to consider blogging anonymously.

# adult material and blogging

The laws governing adult content in the United States can understandably seem confusing. On the one hand, the Supreme Court has ruled that the First Amendment guarantees citizens the right to communicate legal adult content to the public. On the other, obscenity is considered unprotected speech and is, in some cases, criminal to express publicly.

What is obscene? The courts have spent the past fifty years trying to define obscenity. In 1964, Supreme Court Justice Potter Stewart famously said, "I know it when I see it." This is a fine distinction if you're deciding what your twelve-year-old should see or not, but it's not a good gauge if you're posting photos or steamy stories to your blog and want to know whether or not you are in compliance with the law.

The definitive case is *Miller v. California*. The Supreme Court heard Marvin Miller's case in 1973 and found the direct-mail purveyor of adult material guilty of violating California Penal Code 311.2—knowingly distributing obscene material. Acknowledging the "inherent dangers in undertaking to regulate any form of expression," the Court devised three criteria for gauging obscenity:

- an average person, applying contemporary community standards, must find that the work, taken as a whole, appeals to the prurient interest,

- the work depicts or describes, in a patently offensive way, sexual conduct specifically defined by applicable state law, and

- the work, taken as a whole, lacks serious literary, artistic, political, or scientific value.

The Miller ruling lies at the heart of all subsequent obscenity cases but raises as many questions as it answers. Which community standard? What, exactly, is considered "prurient" and "patently offensive"? Who gets to decide what constitutes "serious literary, artistic, political, or scientific value"?

And then there are the larger questions. Justices Warren Burger and William J. Brennan, Jr., were among those who questioned whether obscenity should be excluded from First Amendment protections at all. Many, like musician Frank Zappa, who was called to testify before the Senate during hearings about the content of song lyrics, ask whether we really want a society in which only content deemed fit for children is allowed.

The community standards question looms large. The Child Online Protection Act (COPA), passed by Congress in 1998, criminalized any communication for commercial purposes that is "harmful to minors." Whether or not the content was considered harmful would be gauged by community standards, but because Web-based content is available in every community, there was fear that all content would be judged by the most stringent standard. Challenges to the law have delayed its enforcement but the arguments continue.

So how do bloggers gauge their vulnerability when posting adult materials? One thing is absolutely clear. Possession or transmission of pornography that depicts children is absolutely illegal. If someone attaches an image depicting child pornography to a comment on your site, reporting the violation to a law enforcement agency will provide you with a defense to the claim of knowing transmission.

Providing a mechanism that requires visitors to your blog to affirm that they are 18 years old or older before viewing questionable content provides some protection. Providing the content for free will invite less legal scrutiny than a site that requires a fee. A recent federal law forbids the use of any domain name for adult material that might mislead a minor into viewing, such as names resembling cartoon figures or television or literary figures appealing primarily to children. (*18 U.S.C. section 2252B*)

For those wishing to learn more about the topic, the First Amendment Center has an excellent overview of the topic titled Indecency Online. (See "A Blogger's Legal Resources.")

# blogging anonymously

Anonymous blogs are legal in the United States. In 1995, the Supreme Court ruled: "The decision in favor of anonymity may be motivated by fear of economic or official retaliation, by concern about social ostracism, or merely by a desire to preserve as much of one's privacy as possible. Whatever the motivation may be…the interest in having anonymous works enter the marketplace of ideas unquestionably outweighs any public interest in requiring disclosure as a condition of entry." *(McIntyre v. Ohio Elections Comm.)*

The Electronic Frontiers Foundation cautions that simply posting under a pseudonym may not be enough to keep others from identifying you. Check out the EFF's *How to Blog Safely (About Work or Anything Else)* webpage for tips, guidelines, and links to more information about anonymity online. Reporters Without Borders also provides a thorough online guide titled *How to Blog Anonymously*. (See "A Blogger's Legal Resources.")

Complying with all the technical recommendations for maintaining anonymity is one thing; refraining from disclosing details that might give away your identity is another. Anonymity requires a rigor that not everyone is willing to impose, but if you choose to go that route, it's best to avoid disclosing telling details—the area in which you live, your exact profession, your birthday, children's or pets' names, or a previously used pseudonym. Even an anagram of your name might be discovered by a particularly tenacious researcher.

Obviously, the right to publish anonymously does not include the right to publish defamatory information or to invade the privacy of another. And be aware that your Internet Service Provider (ISP) or blog service provider could be subpoenaed to disclose your identity. Should you find yourself in this situation, the EFF recommends immediately contacting an attorney and filing a motion to quash (kill) the subpoena.

# have no fear

Don't let all this talk about legal issues intimidate you. If you publish with some degree of forethought and at least a basic understanding of the types of laws governing online communications, you're unlikely to ever encounter the types of problems outlined in this chapter.

If there are issues above that deeply concern you, consider supporting an organization that is actively working toward the end you favor. After all, most of these laws are the result of courts attempting to accommodate the will of the people.

## a blogger's legal resources

(listed in the order they appear in the chapter)

**EFF/Legal Guide for Bloggers**
http://www.eff.org/bloggers/lg

**Association of Research Libraries/U.S. Copyright Timeline**
http://www.arl.org/info/frn/copy/timeline.html

**Wikipedia/History of Copyright Law**
http://en.wikipedia.org/wiki/History_of_copyright

**Creative Commons/Choosing a License**
http://creativecommons.org/about/licenses

**Chilling Effects Clearinghouse/Trade Secrets FAQ**
http://www.chillingeffects.org/tradesecret/faq.cgi

**Electronic Privacy Information Center**
http://www.epic.org/privacy/privacy_resources_faq.html

**EFF/Defamation FAQ**
http://www.eff.org/bloggers/lg/faq-defamation.php

**Independent Press Association/Surviving Libel Lawsuits**
http://www.indypress.org/site/toolbox/Libel.html

**BBC: How to Avoid Libel and Defamation**
http://www.bbc.co.uk/dna/actionnetwork/A1183394

**Reporters Committee for Freedom of the Press/Reporters' Privilege**
http://www.rcfp.org/privilege/index.html

**Reporters Committee for Freedom of the Press/How To Use the Federal FOI Act**
http://www.rcfp.org/foiact/index.html

**American Society of Newspaper Editors/Examples of Stories Printed because of FOIA**
http://www.asne.org/ideas/rtk/rtkstrategies_examples.htm

**The First Amendment Project/Anti-Slapp Resource Center**
http://www.thefirstamendment.org/antislappresourcecenter.html

**California Anti-SLAPP Project/Survival Guide for SLAPP Victims**
http://www.casp.net/survival.html

*(continues on next page)*

**a blogger's legal resources** (continued)

(listed in the order they appear in the chapter)

**Statistics on Fired Bloggers**
http://morphemetales.blogspot.com/2004/12/statistics-on-fired-bloggers.html

**C|Net's Guide to Workplace Blogging**
http://news.com.com/FAQ+Blogging+on+the+job/2100-1030_3-5597010.
html?tag=nefd.ac

**Biz Stone/How Not to Get Fired Because of Your Blog**
http://help.blogger.com/bin/answer.py?answer=661&query=blogthis&topic=&type=f

**First Amendment Center/Indecency Online**
http://www.firstamendmentcenter.org/speech/internet/topic.aspx?topic=
indecency_online

**How to Blog Safely (About Work or Anything Else)**
http://www.eff.org/Privacy/Anonymity/blog-anonymously.php

**Reporters without Borders/How to Blog Anonymously**
http://www.rsf.org/article.php3?id_article=1501

# social networks on the rise

Blogs constitute a distinct online phenomenon, but hardly an isolated one. In truth, blogs are inextricably knit into a much larger fabric of new web-based services and data repositories, all of which are sometimes lumped under the rubric *Web 2.0*.

It's a clumsy coinage, one redolent of market-speak and hewing perhaps a bit too closely to an era of shrink-wrapped software packages and top-down distribution of wares, but, at least so far, the Web 2.0 label is sticking better than most of the other phrasings being thrown at this burgeoning suite of social networking applications.

The services offered are diverse, but they all share key characteristics. The applications reside on the Web rather than on individual computer hard drives and they gain value through an accumulation of content voluntarily contributed by users, content that is then aggregated and parsed for the benefit of the user group as a whole.

All around the globe, individuals are flocking to these innovative new web-based social networks. The examples proving most popular are those that are built on open standards; that feature simple, elegant interfaces; that can be personalized; that easily exchange information with other applications and services; that continually evolve, largely in response to feedback from the user community; that invite unintended uses and iterative hacking (definitely not a bad word in this emerging environment); and that—thanks to the cooperative and distributed nature of these open source solutions—grow more robust and stable the more they are used.

It's a heady mix—and one so recent and so rife with activity that it's difficult to grab even a snapshot of what's going on within the participating developer and user communities. I'm hardly the only one fumbling for words to describe the phenomena in a manner that stands a chance of fostering growth rather than limiting potential. Among the phrasings making the rounds are "architectures of participation," "vehicles for radical decentralization," and "mass amateurization of media." Each of these tells a story, but perhaps the best way to catch a glimpse of this new universe of possibilities is to do a quick survey of a few of the more popular application categories.

# a snapshot of today's social network universe

Because many of these social network applications integrate smoothly with blogs, a number of them have been mentioned earlier in the book. Together, they constitute an intermeshed information landscape that is unprecedented in its breadth and immediacy. See "Hot Links: Social Network Services" for examples of some of the more promising solutions within each of these categories.

## blogs themselves

Blogs lie at the heart of this revolution, not just because bloggers are among those most fervent supporters of these new services, but also because most blog software makes it easy to incorporate features and data generated by the other services on this list.

## real-time search engines

Timeliness is next to godliness in this new world order, and nimble new search engines that tap into the moment are enabling real-time conversations and spurring further innovation. For instance, the ability to subscribe to ongoing search results allows bloggers to stay abreast of developments and discussions for each of their favorite topics.

## tagging services

Almost overnight, freeform tagging solutions have proven invaluable in solving the discovery problem plaguing those seeking specific bits of information amidst the profusion pouring online. This grassroots strategy for categorizing content, often referred to as *folksonomy,* so far stands the best chance of creating topographies of information that highlight and promote niche topics.

## shared photo & video sites

Photo-sharing site Flickr is the grandaddy of these increasingly popular upload sites. Newcomer YouTube is making news with 65,000 videos being uploaded each day. The two entities dominate their individual markets. Music upload sites were the first to hit the scene, but copyright fights put dampers on the medium. Still, sites like MySpace and, in Europe, Bebo are proving popular with bands wishing to promote their efforts by uploading mp3 files. All of these sites make it easy to reference the uploaded content from within blog posts.

## recommendation engines

Computers are best at doing mathematical computations, and that's just what's needed to match your favorites against the favorites of others to generate reliable recommendation lists. On services like music recommendation site Last.fm, individuals build profiles by either uploading personal playlists or by voting for streamed songs. Others, like Pandora, prompt users to submit a song or artist they like and then return a list of recommended artists; listeners then vote yea or nay to further refine the overall engine. All of the existing services are in their infancy, but the genre promises to be quite useful in mining niche topic areas.

> I'm not sure what Truth is these days, but as long as people are honest, we can all use our intuition to ferret out some truth. What we really need are collaborative filtering mechanisms which can utilize the "wisdom of crowds" with controls that help prevent mob behavior.
>
> —**Craig Newmark**, founder of Craigslist
>   (craigslist.com and cnewmark.com)

## user-vetted news filters

Sometimes called "meme trackers" or "news clustering services," these websites invite individuals to submit news stories (from either mainstream media or blogs) which are then voted on by the user community at large; stories with the most votes appear on the top pages and the individuals who submit the most popular stories accrue reputations. The services provide a unique alternative to the editorial elitism of traditional media, but are not without their glitches. The creators of these services are constantly on the lookout for those attempting to game the systems, either to promote stories of personal interest or to raise their own ranking within the reputation engines.

## wikis

Wikis are logically organized, web-based collections of information that allow any registered user to add to or edit any of the wiki's entries, or create altogether new entries. This sounds crazy, but a 2005 study by the editors of *Nature* magazine found that Wikipedia, a wildly popular compendium of populist wisdom, contained no more serious errors than the venerable *Encyclopedia Britannica*, particularly for scientific or technology-related topics. Writing quality is rarely on a par with traditionally edited encyclopedia articles (content is essentially written by committees, after all), but the broad array of topics covered and the fact that, in general, errors are so quickly caught and corrected by the user community means that wikis are proving a welcome alternative resource for savvy web researchers.

## networking services

Exploiting the "six degrees of separation" meme, a variety of web services encourage registered users to make their relationships with other users of the service explicit and public. The potential for networking within both personal and business communities is enormous and the best of these services are among the fastest growing social networks. Each service offers a slightly different set of features and courts a distinct population. Some, like LinkedIn, cater primarily to professionals wishing to make work-related connections, while others, like MySpace and Friendster, are more social in nature. Feel free to join more than one.

## community-based classifieds

Some say that classified advertising websites like craigslist.com in the United States and Kijiji and Gumtree abroad are sounding a death knell for newspapers, since most rely heavily on revenues from their classified sections. The trend is unlikely to change anytime soon. Individuals flock to these online classified services—not only are they free, they foster local communities and are beginning to serve as virtual town squares.

## online phone services

Just as newspapers are quaking at the rise of online classifieds, traditional phone companies are deeply nervous about up-and-coming online phone services, sometimes referred to as VoIP (Voice over Internet Protocol). All you need are a web browser and a headset with a microphone, and you can call just about anywhere in the world. Some services, like Vonage, come with modest monthly fees, while others, like Skype, allow you to make that call to Timbuktu for nothing.

## web-based utility programs

A broad array of clean, fully functional software applications that reside on the web rather than your hard drive are quickly gaining fans. Mail, word processing, spreadsheets, shared calendars, to do lists, and interactive maps are among the many types of services being offered. Building on these applications are an ever growing number of *mash-ups*, user-created solutions that take advantage of the open source nature of most of the social networking apps to combine the data found on one or more services.

## peer-to-peer distribution

Also sometimes counted among the Web 2.0 applications are peer-to-peer (sometimes written *p2p*) distribution services like Bittorrent. Rather than relying on a single server's bandwidth to deliver large multimedia files, peer-to-peer schemes rely on the computer power and bandwidth of their users, sharing the burden of distribution and allowing the systems to scale gracefully, actually growing more robust as more users participate.

# gauging the downsides

There is a great deal of hype surrounding all these new efforts, and while the new applications show enormous promise (and some offer immediate rewards), it's prudent to consider the potential downsides to this new environment before plotting a course.

## disappearing acts

Every day, new Web 2.0-style services and tools are being created and touted by avid fans. Some catch on like wildfire. Others attract small, but rabid, user bases. Some die due to poor conception, lack of exposure, or, surprise, a killing popularity. The potential disappearance of a service we've come to rely on is a point worth considering. It's great that so many of these applications reside solely on the Web and that they store all our volunteered content. Should a trusted service suddenly fold, however, not only do we lose the data stored there, we lose the value inherent in the interconnections between that service and any others that are, in the open spirit of these social networks, borrowing or building on the aggregated data. By all means, take advantage of these useful new services, but if the content stored there is important to you, back it up.

## privacy concerns

Another tension that inevitably surfaces in the wake of these social networks is the one between transparency and privacy. It's great that wikis are self-correcting, that you can look up old high school buddies, and that bloggers fact-check each other's stories and expose otherwise hidden truths. This transparency has the potential to create more open communities and to build trust over time. But with this openness comes an inevitable loss of personal privacy. Our cultures demand laws and mechanisms for protecting our identities, which is excellent, but, as the proliferation of surveillance cameras so aptly illustrates, protections for personal privacy increasingly fall by the wayside. This is a critical issue and one unlikely to be solved in the near term. The only true safeguard is to think first before posting items you may regret seeing broadly discussed at some later point.

> *What's funny and weird when you're fourteen can be really embarrassing when you're going through your Supreme Court nomination hearings when you're 45.*
>
> —**Cory Doctorow**, science fiction novelist and Boing Boing editor (craphound.com and boingboing.net)

## cheating the systems

Yet another problem plaguing these new enterprises is the human tendency to try and tweak or trick systems for personal benefit. Within the deeply intertwined world of social networks, rank and influence are calculated using data such as inbound link counts and vote tallies. Some players can't resist the urge to manipulate the results. The open nature of the applications sometimes makes this simple. Sadly, these manipulations skew the overall results, making them less reliable and undermining that ever-important bedrock of trust that needs to underlie these systems if they are to prove truly useful. Again, this isn't an easy problem to solve, but one that some of the smartest minds in social networking are spending a great deal of time pondering.

## discovery woes

Just as in blogging, within these social networks, discovery remains a perennial problem. Social network pioneers often end up traveling and laboring away in virtual ghettos. We no longer need to be slaves to corporate, hit-driven economies that dictate our tastes, but the search and ranking mechanisms in place for many of these new enterprises still end up rewarding the few while ignoring the many. We need better tools for elevating niche players and for recommending efforts that truly match our interests and needs.

> I'm buying the long tail thing, but I'm not sure the term long tail is exactly right. I think it might just continue to make the head larger. You know, it's like, "Big bloggers get rich! Little bloggers do it for the Revolution!"

—**Bruce Sterling**, science fiction novelist and futurist (blog.wired.com/sterling)

## net neutrality

And, finally, there's the question of net neutrality. So far, this is only an issue of concern for citizens of the United States, but if telecommunications giants have their way, Americans won't be able to access high-bandwidth files like video and audio if the authors don't pay a tariff. This could seriously hamper the growth of open and synergistic systems in the United States.

# tapping into the collective wisdom

Caveats aside, these new social networks seem to be here to stay. Grassroots, bottom-up strategies for collecting and organizing information are winning on too many fronts. Even a few years ago, no one could have predicted the enormous popularity and usefulness of freeform tagging, wikis, and the dozens of other new Web 2.0 applications populating the Web.

We may still be struggling to find the best vocabulary for describing all these disparate tools and services and emerging communities, but the linguistic hiccups clearly aren't slowing development or adoption rates. In aggregate, this new world of social networks is enabling an unprecedented information revolution. Ordinary citizens are finding their voices; cultural topographies are growing up around topics of every stripe and color; synergistic interplays between disparate groups are enriching our world views and helping us to solve both global and personal problems.

History is on the side of these emerging social networks. The urge to share ideas, to foster consensus, and to elicit truths from the mayhem of daily life is ancient. What's new is the ease with which vast numbers of previously unconnected individuals can find empathetic others, exchange knowledge, fuel movements, and satisfy quirky whims. A communal future that is collaborative, adaptable, and personalized doesn't sound that bad.

While we all stand a chance of benefiting from these new developments, it's heartening that even the smartest among us see value in tapping into the wisdom growing up within these social networks. Renowned physicist Stephen Hawking recently asked a question on Yahoo! Answers: How can the human race survive the next hundred years? Within a few hours, more than 10,000 responses poured in! May we all find as many potential answers to our most pressing problems within this new world of information and exchange.

## HOT LINKS: SOCIAL NETWORK SERVICES

..............................................................................................

Below you'll find representative examples of services for each of the categories mentioned in this chapter. Even a quick visit to each will help the adventurous to begin mapping this new universe for themselves. The list is by no means exhaustive and is constantly subject to change. Also, a number of the sites could just as well have been listed in one category as another. (For an updated set of related websites, check out the "Resource Hotlinks" located in the right-hand column of dispatchesfromblogistan.com.)

### REAL-TIME SEARCH ENGINES

**technorati**
http://www.technorati.com

**icerocket**
http://www.icerocket.com

**blogdigger**
http://www.blogdigger.com

**pubsub**
http://www.pubsub.com

**bloglines**
http://www.bloglines.com

**feedster**
http://www.feedster.com

### TAG TRACKERS

**delicious**
http://del.icio.us

**wink**
http://www.wink.com

**dabble**
http://www.dabble.com

**tagworld**
http://www.tagworld.com

### SHARED PHOTO & VIDEO SITES

**flickr**
http://www.flickr.com

**youtube.com**
http://www.youtube.com

**myspace**
http://www.myspace.com

**bebo**
http://www.bebo.com

### RECOMMENDATION ENGINES

**last.fm**
http://www.last.fm

**pandora**
http://www.pandora.com

**last.fm/pandora mashup**
http://pandorafm.real-ity.com

### USER-VETTED NEWS FILTERS

**slashdot**
http://slashdot.org

**metafilter**
http://www.metafilter.com

**digg**
http://www.digg.com

**reddit**
http://www.reddit.com

**tailrank**
http://www.tailrank.com

**rojo**
http://www.rojo.com

**memeorandum**
http://www.memeorandum.com

**techmeme**
http://www.techmeme.com

**findory**
http://www.findory.com

WIKIS

**wikipedia**
http://wikipedia.org

**ebay wiki**
http://pages.ebay.com/help/account/
wiki-ov.html

**wordpress wiki**
http://wiki.wordpress.org

**autism wiki**
http://aspiesforfreedom.com/wiki

**all your ideas**
http://www.allyourideas.com

NETWORKING SERVICES

**myspace**
http://myspace.com

**linkedin**
http://linkedin.com

**ryze**
http://ryze.com

**friendster**
http://friendster.com

**tribe**
http://tribe.net

COMMUNITY-BASED CLASSIFIEDS

**craigslist**
http://craigslist.com

**kijiji**
http://kijiji.com

**gumtree**
http://gumtree.com

ONLINE PHONE SERVICES

**skype**
http://www.skype.com

**vonage**
http://www.vonage.com

WEB-BASED UTILITY PROGRAMS

**gmail**
http://www.gmail.com

**writely**
http://www.writely.com

**backpack**
http://www.backpackit.com

**evdb**
http://www. evdb.org

**43 things**
http://www.43things.com

**google maps mania**
http://googlemapsmania.blogspot.
com

PEER-TO-PEER DISTRIBUTION

**bittorrent**
http://www.bittorrent.com

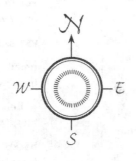

# glossary
# of terms

**Ajax** *Asynchronous JavaScript And XML. n.* Web development technique that combines HTML, CSS, XML, and JavaScript to generate dynamic interactive web-based applications that update page elements incrementally without having to reload the entire page. Examples: Gmail, Google Maps, and Flickr. (Coined in 2005 by Jesse James Garrett.)

**algorithm** *n.* A set of step-by-step operations that accomplish a specific task. Search engines use sophisticated algorithms to determine a web page's rank within search returns. (From Medieval Latin *algorismus*, a poor transliteration of Muhammad ibn-Musa *al-Khwarizmi*, the ninth-century Baghdad mathematician who introduced the concept to the West.)

**anchor text** *n.* A word or phrase on a web page that constitutes a hyperlink. Used by some search engines in the calculation of rank for a web page.

**Atom** *n. Web.* An XML-based format used to generate a newsfeed. Blessed by the IETF, Atom is the most likely successor to the more popular but less flexible and no-longer-updated RSS format.

**bad neighborhoods** *n. Web.* Websites that sell or exchange unrelated links to artificially raise search rank scores. Search engines seek out these sites, sometimes called link farms, and penalize web pages that link to them.

**beta**  *n. Software.* Traditionally, a limited period of time during which a select body of users test commercial software before public launch or the release of major updates. *Web 2.0.* Used to describe browser-based services, generally free of charge, that launch and remain in a development phase, openly soliciting user input and making constant, incremental changes to the infrastructure, feature set, and interface. Sometimes called *perpetual beta* or *live prototyping.* Examples: Flickr, Froogle, and Gmail.

**blog**  *n.* An easy-to-update website characterized by dated entries displayed in reverse chronological order. Originally text-based and written in an informal, conversational style, blogs increasingly feature audio, photo, and video content. Bloggers often link to other blog entries, encourage comments, engage in collaborative tagging schemes, and otherwise contribute to social networks and user-generated databases. (Coined in 1999 by Peter Merholz as a contraction for web log.)

**blogerati**  *n.* Term used to describe better known bloggers. Sometimes called *blognoscenti* or *blogsnobs.*

**blogosphere**  *n.* Commonly used to describe the global network of blogs. Sometimes called *blogistan.*

**blogroll**  *n.* A list of links to other blogs that bloggers regularly visit or with whom they've exchanged links. (Related to the American political term *logrolling,* meaning reciprocal legislative support; also from *Spy* magazine's use of the term to describe reciprocal book reviews by authors.)

**bookmarklet**  *n.* A small web browser extension that allows a user to access a web-based service from a browser bar or tab. Examples: Google Translate, Wikipedia Lookup, and del.icio.us linkbacks. Sometimes called a *favelet.*

**Boolean logic**  *n. Search.* A technique that allows a user to refine search parameters by including operators such as AND, OR, and NOT. Examples: blogosphere OR blogistan; ravens NOT crows. (Named for nineteenth-century mathematician George Boole.)

**bot**  Abbreviation for robot. *n.* Small, artificial intelligence software program that runs automatically and act autonomously. Example: search engine spiders.

**captcha**  *Completely Automated Public Turing test for telling Computers and Humans Apart. n.* A test designed to determine whether a user is human or a spam bot, often consisting of a sequence of obscured graphic letters or numbers that must be typed into a field to continue. Some visually impaired individuals have difficulty reading captchas and spammers are continually developing successful methods of subverting them.

(Coined in 2000 by Luis von Ahn, Manuel Blum, and Nicholas J. Hopper of Carnegie Mellon University and John Langford of IBM.)

**category**   *n. Blogs.* In some blog applications, a feature that allows an author to group similar entries, generally by applying freely chosen descriptors or tags. Past content is easier to retrieve from categorical files than from chronological archives.

**CMS**   *Content Management System. n.* Software that facilitates the storage and retrieval of data. Most blog authoring systems are examples of CMS.

**cookie**   *n. Web.* Code embedded by a website's software on a visitor's computer and used to store preferences or to otherwise monitor activity. Can be benign, useful, or malevolent.

**comment**   *n. Blogs.* A feature that allows readers to publicly respond to blog entries. Commenting can be open to all blog visitors or restricted to designated individuals. Comments are often moderated in an attempt to control comment spam and, on some blogs, unwanted comments. Comments are sometimes threaded, allowing visitors to comment on specific comments.

**comment spam**   *n.* A form of spam that targets blog or wiki comment fields. Generally contains irrelevant links to spam originator websites. Spam filters, captchas, comment moderation, and user registration are techniques used to combat comment spam.

**commentariat**   *n.* The community of readers who leave comments on a blog. May require bloggers to thicken skin.

**CSS**   *Cascading Style Sheets. n.* An HTML extension that allows greater control over web page display by defining style sheets that determine the look of page elements such as body text, headlines, and links. Because multiple style sheets can be used on the same page, they are said to cascade. Most blog authoring software allows CSS personalization of blog pages.

**directory**   *n. Computer science.* A hierarchical index of the files and subdirectories on a hard drive. *Web.* A web server listing links to other web pages organized by topic, sometimes including short descriptions. Generally compiled by human editors using hierarchical taxonomies. If generated automatically and solely for the purpose of inflating search rank, may be penalized as a link farm or bad neighborhood by search engines.

**domain name**   *n. Internet.* The unique text name associated with a numeric IP address. Locates a computer or other device on the Internet. Example: dispatchesfromblogistan.com.

**entry**  *n. Blogs.* Individual blog items. May contain, among other elements, a headline, body text, photos, video, audio files, author name, date and time stamps, permalinks, trackbacks, archives, categorical tags, and reader comments. Sometimes called a *post* or an *article.*

**favicon**  Portmanteau for *favorite* and *icon. n.* A small icon, 16 pixels by 16 pixels, that may appear to the left of a web page's URL at the top of many browser windows.

**feedreader**  See *news aggregator.*

**flame**  *n. Internet.* A hostile or inflammatory comment. *v.* To leave such a comment. A *flame war* is an exchange of such comments.

**folksonomy**  Portmanteau for *folk* and *taxonomy. n.* Describes a dynamic system of user-generated, categorical tags consisting of freely chosen keywords. (Coined in 2004 by Thomas Vander Wal.)

**FTP**  *File Transfer Protocol. n.* A method for uploading and downloading files on the Internet.

**glocal**  Portmanteau for *global* and *local. adj.* Used to denote global solutions adapted to local needs. Example: craigslist.org.

**host**  *n. Web.* A computer or network of computers that provides services to others computers. *v.* To provide computer services to other computers on a network. Examples: Blogger and Typepad are hosted blog services.

**HTML**  *HyperText Markup Language. n.* The authoring language used to create interlinked web pages. (Invented in 1989 by Tim Berners-Lee.)

**hyperlink**  *n.* A reference, or link, within an electronic document that, if clicked, leads to another point in the same document or to another electronic document, or that triggers the download of an electronic file. Generally displayed as highlighted anchor text, an icon, or an image.

**inbound link**  *n.* A link to your website or blog from another. Used by search engines as a primary measure of popularity or rank.

**IP Address**  *Internet Protocol. n.* An IP address is a four-part numerical address in the form 256.256.256.256 that allows one computer to connect to another on the Internet. Related to domain name.

**IETF**  *Internet Engineering Task Force. n.* An open, international community of network designers, operators, vendors, and researchers responsible for defining Internet standards and protocols.

**JavaScript** *n.* A web-based scripting language originally developed by Netscape that can be embedded in the HTML of a web page to extend functionality. Examples: validation of form input and button rollovers.

**keyword** *n.* A relevant word or phrase used in web-based titles, body text, headings, tags, or metatags to facilitate topical searches.

**LAMP** *Linux, Apache, MySQL, and Perl,* (or *Python,* or *PHP). n.* A suite of free programs that serve, respectively, as operating system, web server, database management system, and scripting languages for dynamic websites and servers. Often used in conjunction with discussions of Web 2.0. (Coined in 1998 by Michael Kuntz.)

**link farm** *n.* A website, often automated, containing a long list of links to unrelated web pages created solely for the purpose of increasing the number of inbound links for participating websites. Search engines seek out and penalize link farms and those who link to them. Sometimes called *bad neighborhoods.*

**link rot** *n.* Describes web page links that are no longer valid due to deleted pages or changed URLs.

**long tail** *n.* A colloquial term for an L-shaped diagram illustrating statistical distribution of a small population of high-frequency events along the vertical axis, called the head, and a much greater population of increasingly rare events falling along the horizontal axis, or tail. Examples: distribution of wealth within a culture, frequency of words within a text, or a graph illustrating the popularity of blogs. Sometimes called *Zipf* or *power law distribution* or a *Pareto tail.* (First applied to distribution of digital content by Chris Anderson in 2004.)

**lurk** *v. Blog.* To visit a blog without ever posting a comment. A *lurker* is one who regularly engages in such behavior.

**markup language** *n.* A method for annotating a digital document with embedded tags to determine processing, format, and general display. Examples: HTML and XML.

**meatspace** *n.* An online term for face-to-face encounters with fellow humans.

**meme** *n.* A distinct idea that propagates across networks of individuals. On blogs, often used in combinations such as *meme war* or *meme hack.* (Coined in 1976 by Richard Dawkins in *The Selfish Gene.*)

**metadata** *n.* Information used to describe other information. Examples: meta tag or categorical tag. (From Greek *meta*, beside, and Latin *data*, information.)

**meta tag** *n. HTML.* Several types of information stored in a web page's source code and invisible to the general user. Traditionally used to aid search engine indexing, but abused by spammers who fill the tags with unrelated search terms, an activity sometimes called *keyword stuffing*. Examples: *meta description tags* aid search engines by providing brief summaries of a page's content; *meta keywords tags* display comma-delimited lists of terms relevant to a web page's content, including possible misspellings.

**moderate** *Internet. v.* To screen or otherwise process comments prior to public display to allow deletion of spam or to enforce guidelines. Most blog authoring software features moderation controls.

**moblog** Portmanteau of *mobile* and *blog. n.* A blog that is updated from a phone or personal digital assistant (PDA). Moblog content often contains more photos than text.

**MSM** *MainStream Media. n.* Commonly used acronym on blogs.

**netiquette** Portmanteau of *network* and *etiquette. n.* An unwritten code of online conduct that has grown up over time. Generally dictates respectful, if not always formally polite, behavior.

**news aggregator** *n.* Software that allows a user to subscribe to and read constantly updated newsfeeds. Can reside locally on the desktop or be a web service accessed via a browser. Sometimes called a *newsreader* or *feedreader*.

**newsfeed** *n.* Syndicated web content that is subscription-based. Newsfeed content consists of XML-based RSS or Atom files that may include a title; an excerpt or full text; author name; the date and time the file was uploaded; categorical tags; and a unique URL, or permalink for the entry.

**open source** *adj.* Describes a type of computer program for which the original source code is publicly available, allowing other programmers to contribute to and build upon the core code. Examples: Linux and WordPress.

**permalink** Portmanteau for *permanent* and *link. n.* A unique URL for each blog entry allowing others to link directly to the entry even after it is has been moved from the blog's front page to archives or categorical files.

**ping** *Packet INternet Groper. n.* A utility program that sends a simple message (generally 64 bytes) from one computer to another. *General Internet.* Pings test whether a particular host is operating, returning estimates about round-trip time and how much information (number of packets) may be lost. *Blogs.* Pings notify search engines and news aggregators that new content has just been uploaded or edited. *v.* To use a ping utility.

**plugin** *n.* A small software program that extends the functionality of web browsers, blog authoring software, or other software applications.

**podcast** Portmanteau of *iPod* and *broadcast. n.* A downloadable file, generally audio or video, designed to be played asynchronously on digital players (not just Apple iPods). *v.* To record and make available such a file.

**post** See *entry.*

**protocol** *n. Internet.* A specification, sometimes a standard, that determines how computers will communicate with each other. Examples: HTTP, FTP, and TCP/IP.

**referral log** *n.* A file that records the URLs of web pages that contain links that visitors have used to access your website or blog. If the originating website was a search engine, you can generally view the keyword(s) used in the search.

**relevance ranking** *n. Web.* The most common method used by search engines to determine the order in which search results will be displayed; relies heavily on the number and placement of keywords.

**RSS** *Really Simply Syndication, Rich Site Summary,* or *RDF Site Summary. n.* An XML-based format used to generate a newsfeed. Individuals may subscribe to syndicated RSS content and have it delivered to their news aggregators. It is unlikely that RSS will be updated; Atom is currently thought to be the most likely successor.

**Semantic Web** *n.* Ongoing project of the World Wide Web Consortium (W3C), under the direction of Tim Berners-Lee, which is working on a semantic framework for web content that will allow software to determine the type of HTML page—blog, catalog, or glossary, for instance—promising to improve search relevance ranking.

**SEO** *Search Engine Optimization. n.* Techniques used to improve search engine ranking for websites and blogs. As a discipline, SEO is in constant flux as search engines continually adapt to an ever-changing content and delivery environment.

**slashdotted**  *v.* To be mentioned on slashdot.org, which almost always results in a huge increase in traffic, sometimes slowing or crashing web servers. Now often used to describe any major increase in traffic due to mention on a popular website.

**source code**  *n.* The text, tags, and instructions that make up a web page. Can be viewed by choosing View Source from most browser file menus.

**spam**  *n. Internet.* Unsolicited content, generally commercial in tone, inserted into email, newsgroups, blog and wiki comments, and HTML metatags, often clogging networks and annoying humans. *v.* To create and send spam. (Coined after a Monty Python skit that repeated *ad nauseum* a reference to a canned pork product.)

**spambot**  *n.* An automated software program that generates spam.

**spider**  *n.* A small automated software program sent out by a search engine to discover, download, analyze, and index individual web pages for the purpose of keyword searches and subsequent page ranking. The length of time between visits from traditional search engines like Google or Yahoo can be weeks or even months. Sometimes called a *bot* or *crawler*.

**splog**  *n.* A blog built expressly as a spam vehicle.

**stats**  Abbreviation for *statistics. n.* Web stats applications measure and report the number of pages viewed, number of unique visitors within a given time period, and what search terms or links on other sites readers used to find your blog. Stored in a *referral log*.

**syndicate**  *v. Mainstream media.* To make journalistic content available to other media outlets for simultaneous publication. A fee is often associated with the transaction. *Blogging.* To make XML-format content available to individual subscribers. Syndicated blog content is sometimes republished on other blogs. Blog syndication is almost always free.

**tag**  *n. Computer science.* A type of metadata that acts as a label identifying data in memory. *Markup languages. n.* A sequence of characters contained within angle brackets that denote page elements or formatting. Examples: <head> and <p>. *Blogs and social networks.* A user-generated categorical label that is freely chosen and generally shared across networks. *v.* To assign tags. Sometimes called *folksonomy*.

**tag cloud**  *n.* A semantic visualization illustrating a distribution of user-applied tags with the more commonly used terms represented in a larger font and/or with greater opacity. Sometimes called a *mindmap* or *weighted list*. Example: http://technorati.com/tags.

**template**   *n. Blogging.* A set of rules that determines the look and feel of a blog. The ability to customize a blog differs greatly among blog authoring systems. Sometimes called *themes* or *skins*.

**thread**   *n. Internet.* A series of comments posted in response to a single online entry. Originally used to describe conversations taking place on *bulletin board services* (BBS's), where it is usually displayed in an indented, branching format. Sometimes used to track email or blog conversations.

**trackback**   *n.* A blog feature that allows visitors to notify you and your readers that they've responded to your blog entry on their own blog. Introduced by Six Apart in 2002, a trackback link consists of a unique trackback URL and a mechanism that allows one blog to ping another, providing notification of the cross-linking.

**troll**   *n. Blogging.* One who posts provocative entries or comments with intent to disrupt conversations and/or incite angry responses. *v.* To post such entries or comments.

**ubicomp**   Portmanteau of *ubiquitous* and *computing. n.* Research focusing on networked computers embedded in everyday objects, such as appliances, clothing, cultural artifacts, buildings, and vehicles. Allowing constant connectivity and access. Sometimes called *pervasive computing.* (Coined by Mark Weiser, who claimed to be influenced by science fiction writer Philip K. Dick's novel *Ubik.*)

**URL**   *Uniform Resource Locator. n.* Used to identify the unique address of a web page, generally beginning with a protocol such as http:, ftp:, or mailto:, and ending with the web page's domain name, directory, and specific page name. Although the World Wide Web Consortium (W3C) has deprecated the term in favor of the more accurate URI (Universal Resource Identifier), URL remains the more commonly used term.

**vlog**   Portmanteau of *video* and *blog. n.* A blog that presents video as its primary format, along with some contextual metadata describing the content.

**Web 2.0**   *n.* A label applied to technologies, services, and social networks that build upon the Web as a computing platform rather than merely as a hyperlinked collection of largely static web pages. In practice, services dubbed Web 2.0 reflect open standards, decentralized infrastructure, flexibility, simplicity, and, perhaps most importantly, active user-participation. Examples: blogs, wikis, craigslist.com, del.icio.us, and Flickr. (Coined in 2004 by Dale Dougherty.)

**weblog** Portmanteau for *web* and *log*. *n*. (Coined in 1997 by Jorn Barger on his Robot Wisdom blog to describe the process of "logging the web" as he surfed.)

**wiki** *n*. A type of collaborative, knowledge-based website that allows readers to write and edit content, maintaining a record of all changes. (From Hawaian *wikiwiki,* quick. Sometimes cited as an acronym for "what I know is." Coined in 1995 by Ward Cunningham.)

**WYSIWYG** *What You See Is What You Get. n*. The ability to see content you are writing or editing with the formatting it will have in a browser.

**XHTML** *eXtensible HyperText Markup Language. n*. Similar to HTML, but with a stricter syntax, allowing for automated processing of data and making it easier to deliver the same content across devices.

**XML** *eXtensible Markup Language. n*. File format used to represent data as well as extend and annotate HTML. Examples: RSS and Atom files are formatted as XML files.

# glossary of acronyms

Bloggers often use acronyms and other shortcuts when composing their blog posts or when commenting on other blogs. This is partly to save time and keystrokes, but it also serves as a kind of argot that signals inclusion in a select group.

**AFAIK**   as far as I know

**BMG**   be my guest

**BRB**   be right back

**BTW**   by the way

**FWIW**   for what it's worth

**FYI**   for your information

**F2F**   face-to-face

**IIRC**   if I recall correctly

**IMHO**   in my humble opinion

**IMNSHO**   in my not so humble opinion

**IMO**   in my opinion

**IOW**   in other words

**IRL**   in real life

**JK**   just kidding

**K**   okay

**L8R**   later

**LMAO**   laughing my ass off

**LOL**   laughing out loud

**MOL**   more or less

**NBD**   no big deal

**OT**   off topic

**POV**   point of view

**ROTFL**   rolling on the floor laughing

**SNS**   social network services or software

**SYS**   see you soon

**TBH**   to be honest

**T**   thanks

**TIA**   thanks in advance

**WTG**   way to go

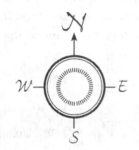

# index

## A

ABC, 32
*Acta Diurna*, 15, 26, 46
activism, online, 100. *See also* advocacy blogs
Adams, John, 78
AddBrite, 130
ads
    affiliate programs, 131–32, 148–49
    blog promotion with, 187–88
    contextual, 129–31, 149
    private, 131
AdSense, 129–30
adult material, 212–13
advocacy blogs, 91–99
    history of, 93–94
    impact of, 91, 93–94, 96–98
    number of, 91
    responsible guidelines for, 95
    sampler of, 98–99
AdWords, 185, 187–88
affiliate links, 131–32, 148–49
al-Ghazali, Abu Hamid, 17
al-Mamun, Caliph, 16–17
alt attributes, 182
Amazon, 131, 174
American Press Institute, 85
American Society of Newspaper Editors, 206
Amrani, Issandr E., 99
anchor text, 165, 181
Anderson, Chris, 173–74
anonymity, 213–14
anti-SLAPP laws, 208–9
The Arabist, 99
archives, 147
*Areopagitica*, 23–24
ARPANET, 33
articles. *See* posts
Ashurbanipal, 12–13
Ask.com, 118, 124
Associated Press, 27, 31
Atom, 123
attention economics, 54
authors
    multiple, 110
    names of, 139
autodiscovery, 186

## B

Bag News Notes, 99
bandwidth, 190
banning, 169
Barger, Jorn, 35
Barrett, Cameron, 93
Basho, Matsuo, 46–47
BBC, 31, 52, 206
Beadle, John, 48
Bebo, 219
Belle de Jour, 52
Bennett, James, Jr., 28, 30
Bennett, James, Sr., 27–28
Berkman Center for Internet and Society, 123
Berne Convention, 194, 196
Berners-Lee, Tim, 33, 36, 37–38, 107
Bernstein, Carl, 83
Beyond Northern Iraq, 52
Beyond the Beyond, 51–52
Bill of Rights, 78. *See also* First Amendment
bios, 137
Bittorrent, 222
blog authoring tools
    features of, 108–11
    free vs. for-a-fee, 112
    history of, 107–8
    hosted vs. standalone, 111–12
    listings of, 105, 106
    newest trends in, 67–68, 133
    number of, 105
    open-source, 43–44, 106
    selecting, 112–16
Blogger (authoring environment), 43, 67, 108, 113, 128
bloggers
    bios of, 137
    characteristics of, 8–9
    goals of, 9
    identity of, 95, 137, 151
    with jobs, 199–200, 209–11
    legal issues for, 191–216
    personality of, 61–62
    photos of, 137
    time spent by, 9

blogging
  democracy and, 44, 55, 88
  ethics and, 85–86, 88
  history of, 35, 36–39
  open nature of, 5–7, 141
  problems with, 7, 54
  reasons for, 8–9, 11
blogjects, 57
Bloglines, 118, 178
blog ping services
  listings of, 105, 106
  number of, 105
  operation of, 124–25
BlogPulse, 125, 126, 172, 177
blogrolls, 110, 145–46
blogs
  adult content on, 212–13
  advocacy, 91–99
  anonymous, 213–14
  as communities, 4–5, 189
  criticisms of, 2, 3
  definition of, 1
  design tips for, 138, 149–54
  as diaries, 45–46, 50–53
  enthusiast, 59–65
  finding, 7
  growth of, 1–2, 11
  hosted vs. standalone, 111–12
  interlinking among, 184
  languages of, 2
  as linkfests, 35–41
  as newsrooms, 71–73, 84–86
  number of, 1
  page elements of, 135, 140–49, 155
  popular, 172, 173
  promoting, 171–90
  social network applications and,
      218–19
  titles of, 136
  writing tips for, 158–64
Blog Search, 125
Blogsome, 114
Boing Boing, 39, 41–42, 69, 172
bots, 124
Branwyn, Gareth, 41
British Library, 33
Buffett, Warren, 71
Burst Media, 130
Bush, Vannevar, 36

**C**

Caesar, Julius, 14–15, 26, 46
calendars, 148
California Anti-SLAPP Project, 209
Campaigns Wikia, 99
captcha, 141
Caruso, Denise, 95
Cascio, Jamais, 98, 100–103
categorical tags, 110, 128, 146–47, 165–67,
      182–83
CBS, 31–32
cheating, 223–24
Chideya, Farai, 86–89, 93
Child Online Protection Act (COPA), 213
Chilling Effects Clearinghouse, 200
Chin Music Press, 99
Chitika, 130
citizen journalism, 55, 72–73, 84–86
classifieds, community-based, 221, 227
cloaking, 184
CNN, 33
comments
  designing for, 152–53
  encouraging, 141, 159
  managing, 168–69
  options for, 109
  spam in, 109, 141
Committee on Conscience, 99
*Common Sense,* 25
consistency, 152
copyright, 89, 149, 193–96. *See also* fair use
Cosby, William, 76
Craigslist, 183, 221
Creative Commons licenses, 89, 149,
      196–98
Cronkite, Walter, 93
cross-linking, 184
Crumlish, Christian, 8

**D**

*The Daily Courant,* 75
Daily Kos, 93, 98, 172
Daschle, Tom, 94
date and time stamps, 138
Davidow, Ari, 65
Dean, Howard, 94
Dedman, Bill, 84
defamation, 203–6
del.icio.us, 127, 183, 187

Delta Air Lines, 209
democracy, 44, 55, 88
description meta tags, 182
design
    blog authoring tools and, 109
    tips, 138, 149–54
diaries, 45–53
Digg, 183
Digital Millennium Copyright Act
    (DMCA), 195
Dillingham, John, 74
directories, 185
DNS (Domain Name Server), 37
Doctorow, Cory, 6, 39, 41–44, 96, 223
domain names
    blog authoring tools and, 110
    keywords in, 180
    purchasing, 136–37
drafts, 158–59

**E**

eBay, 66, 67
Echoplex Park, 53
80/20 rule, 173
Elance, 151
Electronic Frontier Foundation (EFF),
    41, 96, 192, 200, 204, 214
Electronic Privacy Information Center, 202
email addresses, 147
employee blogs, 199–200, 209–11
Engadget, 172, 174
Engelbart, Douglas, 36
enthusiasm, 54
enthusiast blogs, 59–65
entries. See posts
ethics, 81–82, 85–86, 88
Evelyn, John, 49
Evilutionary Virtual Log, 53
excerpts, 139
Expression Engine, 116
extensibility, 111

**F**

fair use, 42, 195–96
false light, 202
false names, 205
Falwell, Jerry, 198–99
Farnsworth, Philo Taylor, 31
FCC, 32

Federated Media, 39
FeedBurner, 122, 186
FeedDemon, 119
feeds. See newsfeeds
Feedster, 125, 177
Finkbuilt, 68
First Amendment, 209–10, 212
First Amendment Center, 213
First Amendment Project, 209
Flame Effects, 65
Flickr, 127, 183, 219
Flynt, Larry, 198–99
focus, importance of, 61, 174–75
folksonomies, 56–57, 126–27, 165–66, 219.
    See also tags
fonts, 151
Fowler, Jerry, 99
Franklin, Benjamin, 24, 25
Freedom of Information Act (FOIA), 208
Friendly, Fred, 32
Friendster, 221
Furl, 187

**G**

Garrett, Jesse James, 107–8
Geens, Stefan, 40
Good, Robin, 105, 185
Google
    AdSense, 129–30
    AdWords, 185, 187–88
    Blogger, 43, 67, 108, 113
    bombs, 181
    Earth, 40
    Mark Jen and, 209
    popularity of, 176–77
    rankings on, 66–67, 125, 177, 180, 182,
        183–84
    registering with, 185
    spiders and, 124
    Toolbar, 183–84
grammar, 160–61
Greeley, Horace, 80
Gumtree, 221
Gutenberg, Johann, 18–20
Gyford, Phil, 48

**H**

*haikai*, 46–47
Hall, Justin, 50–51, 107

Hamilton, Alexander, 78
Hamilton, Andrew, 77
Hamilton, Ed, 52
Harris, Benjamin, 76
Harvard University, 123
Hawking, Stephen, 225
headlines, 139, 162–63, 180–81
Hearst, William Randolph, 80
Henry VIII, King, 22
Hesiod, 13
Homer, 13
Hoopty Rides, 62, 65
Hopkins, Curt, 210
hosted blogs, 111–12
Hotel Chelsea Blog, 52
Hourihan, Meg, 108
HTML, 37, 107
HTTP, 37
Hughes, Stuart, 52
hypertext, 37

**I**

IceRocket, 128, 177, 183
images
    alt attributes for, 182
    posting, 140
iMovie, 123
inbound links
    counts of, 125, 172
    trackback links and, 187
Independent Press Association, 206
Information Aesthetics, 40
Instapundit, 93, 98
insurance, 206
intellectual property laws, 89, 192–200
Internet
    birth of, 32–33
    net neutrality and, 224
    open architecture of, 5–6
    size of, 33
Internet Engineering Task Force (IETF), 123
interviews, 209
iTunes, 119
I Want Media, 85

**J**

Jalopnik, 69
Jalopy, Mr., 9, 61–63, 65–69
Jalopy Junktown, 62, 66

Jefferson, Thomas, 24, 78
Jen, Mark, 209
jobs, bloggers with, 199–200, 209–11
Johnson, Samuel, 75
Jones, George, 80
journalism. *See also* news
    blogging and, 88, 101
    citizen, 55, 72–73, 84–86
    ethics and, 81–82, 88
    history of, 73–83
    investigative, 81, 83
    privileges and, 206–9
Journalist's Toolbox, 85

**K**

Kahle, Brewster, 33
Kamen, Dean, 41
Kawasaki, Guy, 61, 64
keywords
    choosing, 179
    hidden, 184
    importance of, 178
    locations for, 163, 180–83
    meta tags and, 182
    overuse of, 177, 180, 184
    resources for, 179
    tags vs., 165
Kijiji, 221
Klezmer Shack, 65
Kuznetsov, Sergey, 2, 96–97

**L**

Last.fm, 220
ledes, 139, 164
*Legal Guide for Bloggers,* 192
legal issues, 191–216
    adult material, 212–13
    anonymity, 213–14
    copyright, 193–96
    Creative Commons licenses, 196–98
    defamation and libel, 202, 203–6
    for employees, 199–200, 209–11
    importance of, 191–92
    journalistic privilege, 206–9
    parodies, 198–99
    privacy, 200–203, 223
    resources for, 192, 215–16
    trademarks, 199
    trade secrets, 199–200

Lemay, Laura, 4
Leonardo da Vinci, 47
Lessig, Lawrence, 89
libel, 202, 203–6
licensing notices, 149
LinkedIn, 221
link farms, 181, 183
links. *See also* cross-linking; inbound
    links; outbound links
    affiliate, 131–32, 148–49
    arranging, 151
    on blogrolls, 110, 145–46
    blogs as sources of, 35–41
    hidden, 184
    importance of, 101, 139–40, 164–65
    to lively posts, 147
    navigation, 182
    perma-, 109, 142, 153
    trackback, 142–44, 187
Lippman, Walter, 81
LiveJournal, 96–97, 114, 115
Livingstone, David, 27, 28–30
localization, 111
Lodefink, Steve, 68
*London Gazette*, 75
long tail, 44, 173–74, 175
Lott, Trent, 94
Luther, Martin, 21–22

**M**

MacLane, Mary, 49–50
Madison, James, 24, 78
Malda, Rob "CmdrTaco," 38
Marconi, Guglielmo, 30
Maria de Jesus, Carolina, 50
mash-ups, 222
Mazdak, 16
meblogging, 128–29
meme trackers, 39, 220
Merholz, Peter, 35, 108
meta tags, 182
*Miller v. California*, 212
Milton, John, 23–24
moblogging, 110
Moere, Andrew Vande, 40
Mohammed, 16
money, making, 9, 66–67, 129–32
Mother Tongue Annoyances, 64
Moulitsas Zuniga, Markos, 93, 98
Movable Type, 43, 113, 115, 116

MovieMaker, 123
Moyers, Bill, 93
MSN
    contextual advertising and, 130
    popularity of, 176–77
    Spaces, 114
    spiders and, 124
Murdoch, Rupert, 114
Murrow, Ed, 82
music
    recommendation sites, 219–20, 226
    soundtracks, 148, 152
MySpace, 113, 114, 219, 221

**N**

navigation links, 182
NBC, 31–32
Nelson, Ted, 36, 37
Netflix, 174
net neutrality, 224
NetNewsWire, 119, 121
Netscape, 123
networking services, 221, 227
Newmark, Craig, 8, 98, 220
news. *See also* advocacy blogs; journalism
    alternative sources of, 94
    blogs and, 71–73, 84–86, 88
    consolidation of sources for, 83
    future of, 102
news aggregators
    browser-based, 118
    built-in, 119
    example of, 121
    listing of, 118
    number of, 118
    standalone, 119
news clustering services, 220
News Corp., 113, 114
newsfeeds
    advantages of, 117, 145, 186–87
    blog authoring tools and, 110
    definition of, 116
    downsides of, 186
    publishing, 120, 122
    subscribing to, 119–20
    XML and, 117
news filters, user-vetted, 220, 226–27
NewsGator, 118
newspapers
    future of, 71
    history of, 26–28, 71, 74–83

newsreaders. *See* news aggregators
*New York Herald*, 27–28, 31
*New York Times*, 80, 81, 83
*New York Tribune*, 31
Node101 :: Bay Area, 53

**O**

obscenity, 212–13
Ogle Earth, 40
open discourse
    history of, 12–33
    impact of, 11–12
Open the Future, 100
opinions, 204–5
OPML files, 120
outbound links
    anchor text for, 165, 181
    checking, 187
    importance of, 139–40
*Oxford Gazette*, 75

**P**

page elements, 135, 140–49, 155
Paine, Thomas, 24–26
Pandora, 220
Paparo, Ari, 124
Paredo, Vilfredo, 173
*The Parliament Scout*, 74
parodies, 198–99
peer-to-peer (p2p) distribution, 222, 227
Pepys, Samuel, 48–49
permalinks, 109, 142, 153
Phillips, Patrick, 85
phone services, online, 221, 227
photos
    of bloggers, 137
    posting, 140
    sites for sharing, 127, 219, 226
pings, 109, 124–25
Pi Sheng, 17
Pitas, 108
plagiarism, 184. *See also* copyright
pMachine, 116
podcasting, 122–23, 209
politeness, 159
polls, 188
pornography, 212–13
positiveapeindex, 68–69
Posthuman Blues, 64

posts
    author names for, 139
    body text of, 181
    chronology of, 109
    date and time stamps for, 138
    excerpts of, 139
    frequency of, 172
    headlines for, 139, 162–63, 180–81
    keywords in, 180–81
    ledes for, 139, 164
    structure of, 135, 138–40, 162
PostSecret, 53
Power Law distribution, 173–74
PowerReporting, 84
Poynteronline Resource Center, 85
press credentials, 208
printing press, impact of, 17–22
privacy
    blog software and, 110
    as illusion, 89
    laws, 200–203
    loss of, 223
    new definitions of, 55–56, 102–3
product development, 102
Project for Excellence in Journalism, 71
promotion, 171–90
    by ads, 187–88
    focus and, 61, 174–75
    keywords and, 178–83
    long tail and, 173–74, 175
    need for, 190
    nurturing community and, 189
    popularity and, 172, 173
    search engines and, 175–78, 183–85
    self-, 189
    by stunts, 188
    syndicated feeds and, 186–87
proofreading, 161
pseudonyms, 68, 214
public access television, 32
public figures
    defamation of, 203
    definition of, 203
    parodies of, 198–99
    using likenesses of, 199
public proceedings, 207–8
public records, 208
publishing, online, 42–43
PubSub, 125, 180
Pulitzer, Joseph, 80
punditry, 92–94. *See also* advocacy blogs

# R

Rabinowitz, Schlomo, 53
radio, 30, 31, 81–82
Ranchero, 119
Rather, Dan, 94
RDF, 123
recommendation engines, 219–20, 226
referral logs, 111
Reformation, 21–22
reltag microformat, 128
Reporters' Committee for Freedom of the
    Press, 207, 208
republication, 205
reputation economics, 54–55
retractions, 168, 205–6
Reynolds, Glenn, 93, 98
Robot Wisdom, 35
RSS, 123. *See also* newsfeeds
Russia, blogging in, 2, 96–97

# S

The Sartorialist, 64
Schachter, Joshua, 127
Schuman, Scott, 64
search capabilities, 110, 146
search engines. *See also* search
    optimization
    blog-specific, 7, 124–25, 177–78
    as gatekeepers, 175–78
    inbound link content and, 172
    rankings on, 125–26, 176, 177, 178
    real-time, 219, 226
    registering with, 185
    traditional, 124, 176–77
search optimization, 176, 178, 183–84.
    *See also* keywords
Sedition Act, 78
Shaw, Michael, 99
Shikibu, Murasaki, 46
Shirky, Clay, 173, 174
shopping carts, 132, 148–49
Signum sine tinnitu, 64
Simonetti, Ellen, 209
simplicity, importance of, 138
Sinclair, Mark and Carla, 41–42
Six Apart, 97, 113, 114, 115, 116
Sklar, Mikey, 65
Skype, 221
slander, 203

SLAPP (Strategic Lawsuits Against Public
    Participation), 208–9
Slashdot, 38–39
Smales, Andrew, 108
social network applications
    benefits of, 225
    downsides of, 222–24
    examples of, 226–27
    growth of, 217–18, 225
    types of, 218–22
Society of Professional Journalists, 85
Socrates, 13, 14
soundtracks, 148, 152
sources, shielding, 207
Spaltenstein, Ursi, 40
spam
    in comments, 141
    email addresses and, 147
    search engines and, 183–84, 185
    trackbacks and, 143
spiders, 124
*The Spie*, 74
Stamp Act of 1765, 25, 77
Stanley, Henry, 27, 28, 30
Star Chamber, 22–23, 74
static pages, 111
statute of limitations, 205
Steffen, Alex, 98
Sterling, Bruce, 7, 51–52, 54–57, 224
Stone, Biz, 211
stunts, 188
syndication. *See* newsfeeds

# T

tag clouds, 166, 167
tags. *See also* folksonomies
    alt, 182
    categorical, 110, 128, 146–47, 165–67,
        182–83
    choosing, 166–67
    downside of, 89
    history of, 127
    keywords vs., 165
    meblogging and, 128–29
    meta, 182
    need for, 7, 126–27
    search services for, 128, 165–66, 182–
        83, 219, 226
TCP, 37
technical support, 111

Technorati
 number of blogs reported by, 1
 pings and, 125
 rankings on, 125
 registering with, 185
 tag search by, 127, 128, 165–66, 177, 178, 183
telegraph, 27–28
television, 31–32, 82, 83
testing, importance of, 154
Textpattern, 115
Things Magazine, 69
time stamps, 138
title, choosing, 136
title bar, 180
Tocqueville, Alexis de, 79
Tonnies, Mac, 61, 64
Top 10 lists, 188
trackback, 109, 142–44, 187
trademarks, 199
trade secrets, 199–200
traffic, preparing for, 190
trolls, 169
Trott, Ben, 113
trust, importance of, 7–8, 87, 159
truth
 hyperlinks and, 191
 as protection, 203, 204
 quest for, 87
Turner, Ted, 33
Tweed, William Marcy "Boss," 80
typefaces, 151
Typepad, 115

**U**

Ursi's Blog, 40
Userland Software, 43, 123
utility programs, 222, 227

**V**

video
 bloggers, 123
 newsfeeds, 122–23
 sites for sharing, 219, 226
Vietnam War, 32, 83, 93
Vimeo, 123
Vloggercon, 53
vloggers, 123
Voices of New Orleans, 99
VoIP, 221

Vonage, 221
vSocial, 123

**W**

Wales, Jimmy, 99
Wang Chen, 17
Wang Chieh, 17
Warner, Tim, 64
*Washington Post*, 83
weather, 148
Web 2.0, 217
WFMU, 40–41
whistleblowing, 210, 211
Wikipedia, 57, 118, 220–21
wikis, 220–21, 227
Williams, Evan, 108
Wink, 128
Woodward, Bob, 83
WordPress.com, 113, 114
WordPress.org, 113, 114–15
World Changing, 98, 100
World Wide Web
 birth of, 37–38
 size of, 33
writer's block, 162
writing
 style, 157–58, 159
 tips, 158–64
WYSIWYG editors, 38, 109

**X**

XML, 117

**Y**

Yahoo
 Answers, 225
 contextual advertising and, 130
 popularity of, 176–77
 rankings on, 125
 registering with, 176–77
 Search Marketing, 188
 spiders and, 124
 360, 114
YouTube, 123, 219

**Z**

Zenger, John Peter, 76–77
Zipf, George, 173